LORI REID is a professional hand analyst and consulted by people from all over the world. She is perhaps best known in the South West for her many TV and radio broadcasts. Throughout the late 70s she appeared weekly in several series of ZODIAC & Co. on BBC SW, a very popular series of programmes which featured such celebrities as John Cleese, Sue Lawley, Tim Brooke-Taylor, Angela Rippon, Wayne Sleep, etc. In the 80s she had a successful weekly feature on TSW, LAYING IT ON THE LINE, again dealing with well-known personalities in the media. She is regularly featured as an expert in her field both on national radio and television having contributed to such programmes as BODYMATTERS BBC 1, THE TIME . . . THE PLACE . . . ITV, STREET LIFE Cardiff Radio, etc.

On the literary side, Ms Reid has a degree in languages and literature and has written articles for both national and international journals and newspapers. She is a regular contributor of features for women's magazines (these have included PRIMA, MORE!, WOMAN'S WORLD, COMPANY, OVER 21, BEST, FAMILY CIRCLE, FAST FORWARD, MARIE CLAIRE, etc.) In addition, she has published several books: HOW TO READ HANDS (Aquarian Press, 1985), THE FEMALE HAND (Aquarian Press, 1986), HIDDEN KNOWLEDGE (Bossiney Books, 1988), FAMILY MATTERS: PALMISTRY (Ward Lock, 1990). Three more of her books in the FAMILY MATTERS series dealing with Astrology, Numerology and Chinese Astrology are due for publication in 1992.

She is married to a psychologist an̶ ̶ ̶ ̶ ̶ ̶ ̶ ̶ ̶ en in Cornwall.

LORI REID

THE COMPLETE BOOK
OF THE
HAND

A Pan Original
PAN BOOKS
London, Sydney and Auckland

ACKNOWLEDGEMENTS

Thank you to all those who have allowed me to use their
handprints in this book.
My special thanks go to Catherine Cookson, Toyah Wilcox,
John Cleese, Daley Thompson, Robin Hanbury-Tenison,
Sim Harris, Keith Townson, Ken Froggatt, Steve Hill,
and Carole Jenkins.

First published 1991 by Pan Books Ltd,
Cavaye Place, London SW10 9PG

9 8 7 6 5 4 3 2 1

© Lori Reid

ISBN 0 330 31503 X

Photoset by Parker Typesetting Service, Leicester
Printed and bound in Great Britain by
Clays Ltd, St Ives plc

THE HAND

The hand is perhaps the most underrated part of the human anatomy, and yet surely one of the most valuable that man possesses. It can touch, feel, hold, grip; can make and create. It mediates between thought and matter; translates ideas into concrete reality; can become a tool, give comfort, soothe and heal; it can deliver pain and bring pleasure; it becomes eyes for some and, for those who know where to look, it can speak about character and personality: it is an open register of our subconscious, our needs and drives and future impulses.

Lori Reid 1990

For My Children
Sophie and Alasdair
With All My Love

CONTENTS

PART SEVEN

HEALTH IN OUR HANDS 287

PART EIGHT

CHIROLOGICAL COMPARISONS 301

PART NINE

APPENDICES 307

PART ONE

INTRODUCTION

Myths surrounding the art of palmistry abound. To most people hand reading evokes images of fairgrounds, gypsy fortune-tellers and spurious predictions of tall, dark strangers. At best, the subject is considered with mild, humorous interest. At worst, with scepticism and derision. To some who are unacquainted with its modern analytical techniques, it may even be associated with demoniacal practices: a dangerous subject to meddle in, with dire consequences for both practitioner and querant.

It's hardly surprising that palmistry should have earned such a reputation since it has at various times in its history suffered, to use a pun, in the hands of rogues, charlatans and mountebanks alike, all ready to prey on the gullible and those whose peace of mind may be unsettled by doubts and anxieties about themselves, their loved ones or their future.

Today, palmistry is dealt with in a more scientific manner and is generally referred to as hand analysis. Whereas palmistry immediately suggests the interpretation of the lines on the palm, its modern title signifies a more comprehensive approach to the whole of the hand itself, taking into account its shape, the skin markings, nails, measurements and comparison of the digits, gesture, colour and temperature, well before the lines are even considered.

Modern hand analysis also seeks positively to demystify some of the obscure beliefs and principles governing this most valuable method of self-assessment, whilst also debunking many of the superstitions and old wives' tales that have grown up around its forebear.

Essentially, the study of the hand is a useful guide to character evaluation. It registers past experiences and indicates the possible events, influences and opportunities that an individual is likely to encounter. In these days of fast living and uncertainty, more and more people are looking to hand analysis for guidance in their decision-making processes on a wide variety of issues such as career prospects and developments, emotional or relationship worries, financial problems, changes of residence, health, retirement or simply just to try to understand themselves that little bit better.

What is seldom generally understood is that the indicators on the hand can, and do, change according to the individual's nature, conscious decisions, state of health or changes of lifestyle, so that the popular misconception that our 'fate' is irrevocably engraved in our hands is just a myth. In fact, we are not 'stuck with our destinies' at all but we have, to a greater or lesser extent, the power, the free will and the option to choose and make our own destiny for ourselves as we go along.

What a good analysis of the hand can do, then, is not only establish the character of the individual, but also elucidate his or her current personal situation and unravel future possibilities, together with all their ramifying consequences. It lays them on the table, so to speak, thereby enabling the individual to choose and to steer in whichever direction he or she considers best for the future.

That hand analysis is regaining credibility and validation is evidenced by the attention that has been focused on at least one branch of the study by American and European medical research. The area under scrutiny is known as dermatoglyphics (derma = skin, glyph = carving), and incorporates the patterns of ridges and furrows in the skin both on the palm and on the soles of the feet.

These patterns, the most familiar of which are the fingerprints, are formed within the first few months of embryonic development and any chromosomal or congenital hiccups can result in distortion or abnormality in the configuration of the skin ridges. It is being established, then, that certain genetic defects leave their own characteristic signatures on palms and soles, the most widely documented of which is **Down's Syndrome**, although other conditions are also under investigation.

Apart from the skin patterns, it has long been recognized by hand analysts that an individual's predisposition to other clinical conditions may be traced in the hand too – bronchial disorders, heart disease, gastroenteric problems, gynaecological complications, migraine, mineral deficiencies, allergy, anaemia and much more besides. Perhaps, then, it is conceivable that with further research hand analysis and dermatoglyphics could one day be used as a potential aid to medical diagnosis with particular use in genetic counselling.

More research into hand analysis in general is indeed required, for little is yet known as to how, or why, the markings occur on the hand at all; and even more mysterious is the question of their direct representation of the individual's life and events.

Explanations of this correspondence are unclear, although speculation exists about a connection between the body's chemistry and the natural electrical impulses that a person emits which could be responsible for imprinting discrete patterns, not only on the hands but also on other parts of the body. Certainly, the palm contains a vast concentration of nerve endings which render it a fertile and receptive bed on which impressions and recordings could be made.

Unlike Oriental tradition, the Western mind, nursed in scientific method, requires an explanation of the mechanics of a system before it can fully accept its validity. We should beware, however, of falling into the trap of thinking that, because we as yet lack scientific proof of *how* hand analysis works, this disproves or negates the fact that it *does* work and therefore deserves to be rejected or disparaged out of hand.

Another criticism which has been levelled at hand analysis is that it imputes psychological significance into the lines which exist purely and simply as flexure creases.

Logically, then, this argument presupposes that the more the hand is used as in, say, a manual skill, the more lines it should develop. And yet this argument is quite fallacious, as very often it will be found that those whose occupations require greater manual dexterity but few intellectual demands will often possess *fewer* lines than their fellow workers in clerical or cerebral occupations where little use of manual skill is required.

One serious criticism which is as relevant today as it has always been in the past is that hand analysis is a powerful tool. The power of persuasion of the analyst and the receptive capacity for self-fulfilling prophesy of the subject should never be underestimated. A wrong deduction or an unguarded statement by the practitioner could result in untold consequences, even in the case of the most staunchly cynical of subjects, as the seeds of suggestion are sown perhaps to be cultivated at a later, more vulnerable time in their lives.

Yet the merits of this form of personal assessment must surely by far outweigh its shortcomings. Each hand is unique and in it lies a vast wealth of information on all aspects of the person's life, ready to be decoded once the basic principles are understood.

It is a system which is infinitely versatile and able to be used on a variety of levels ranging from identification by fingerprinting, through diagnoses of potential medical conditions, to minute details of the complex psychology of the personality.

Its methodology is a logical and analytical process which may be likened to a fascinating and compelling piece of detective work whereby each clue, gathered from the hand, is put together rather like a photofit picture, until the jigsaw that makes up the human individual is complete.

PART TWO

THE HISTORY OF HANDS

CHAPTER ONE

PALMISTRY THROUGH THE AGES

The earliest evidence of man's interest in his hands may be found in stone-age cave paintings in Spain. These, it is believed, are between twelve to fifteen thousand years old and can be seen in the Altamira caves just outside Santander in northern Spain. That European stone-age man was interested in the portents written in his palms is debatable. Rather, we are more likely to believe that his interest must have lain in purely documenting his environment, recording his experiences, as he perceived them, in primitive pictorial form.

Nothing is known of how, or even of where, the first rudimentary steps were taken towards the development of a body of knowledge that was to become the fascinating study of hand reading. Inevitably, its rise and subsequent spread owed much to the oral tradition through which branches of learning – Astronomy, Mathematics and Medicine, for example – came to be handed down from one generation to another. Whatever its origins, it is believed that its roots lie in the Far East – India perhaps, or more likely China.

That palmistry is mentioned in the Old Testament is often used an an argument for and against its use. Notable references may be found in Job (37.7), Proverbs (3.16), Ezra (7.9), Isaiah (8.11) and Samuel (26.18). But whilst controversy may surround its theological implications and even justification, the fact that it's mentioned at all, and by such diverse authorities, is evidence that it was known about and probably widely used.

One of the earliest documented references to the study as known today may be found in the 'Hast Samudrika Shastra' writings of the second millenium BC, although mention of the art occurs earlier still in ancient Hindu scriptures amongst the Vedic text of sacred knowledge known as 'the laws of Manu'. And in the 'Vasishtha' of Indian literature a similar message to that of the 'Manu' code is repeated in rule twenty-one , an edict which forbids divination by palmistry and astrology in return for money.

The practice must have already been well established in order to necessitate the passing of such laws, and so it is that our journey in search of the beginnings of hand analysis takes us back yet another millenium to the ancient China of three thousand BC. So well recognized at that time was the individuality and uniqueness of the hand that the Emperor was using his thumbprint as a seal on state documents, and thus confirming the use of fingerprints as personal identification marks thousands of years before their recognition in the West.

Evidence would seem to suggest that the art of hand reading was certainly practised throughout the Orient, from whence it spread to central and western Asia – to the Sumerians, Chaldeans, Babylonians, to the Ancient Egyptians, the early Hebrews, and to the Persians.

From Asia Minor palmistry found its way to Ancient Greece. Men of learning – physicians, sages and philosophers alike – valued the principles that lay in the study of the hand and used the knowledge in their work. They believed it was essential to the understanding of human dynamics. Plato, Claudius Galen (the father of medicine), Anaxagoras, Hippocrates, Antemodores of Ephesus and Claudius Ptolemaeus all studied the hand not only as a diagnostic indicator of health but also as a means of character analysis. Homer, it has been said, wrote a treatise on the lines of the hand. Aristotle, too, was well versed in the art and his *Chiromantia* is one of the earliest surviving texts on the study. It was Aristotle, too, who was reputedly commissioned to write a book on hands for Alexander the Great.

Towards the last couple of centuries BC, Roman expansion began to take place and within a hundred years the Empire stretched from Britain to North Africa and from the Atlantic to the Middle East. Undoubtedly, those Romans who had settled in Asia Minor became acquainted with palmistry and brought the knowledge back with them into central Europe.

References in their works by both Plautus (254–184 BC) and Virgil (70–19 BC) suggest they were both well versed in the mysteries of the hand. Julius Caesar, it has been said, knew the subject so well that he felt no one

could deceive him. But even in the first century AD palmistry had its critics. Apparently Juvenal (60–130) was so sceptical that he gave hand reading an altogether bad press. Of the many enlightened men of this period in history Pliny, Albertus Magnus, the Emperor Augustus, Cardamus, Hispanus and Paracelsus are all believed to have respected the science. Soon, palmistry had spread throughout the Roman Empire and, by the Dark Ages, had not only reached northern Europe, but had also found its way on to British shores.

Whether it was felt that palmistry belonged to pagan traditions, or whether it constituted a threat to the newly formed Christian belief system, the practice of hand reading was flatly condemned by the Church. In AD 315 an edict was passed by the Ecclesiastical court declaring that anyone found practising the art would be instantly excommunicated. And thus it was from this point in time that hand analysis gained its dark reputation. The practice went underground, became associated with the occult and with black magic and fell into the hands of rogues and charlatans. It was a stain that was to leave the art tarnished for centuries to come and from which hand analysis has not fully recovered to this day.

Yet despite its censure palmistry has survived, kept alive and carried principally, it is believed, by gypsies from one country to another. Outside the Christian world, the practice flourished and continued unabated. In the Arab world it was valued by physicians and in the eleventh century hand shapes and their meanings were described as part of the principles of medicine in the 'Quanoun fi Ul-Tibb', the equivalent of a modern-day medical text book.

It was the two long centuries of seige and the final sacking of Constantinople in 1453 that was to herald the Renaissance. Fleeing from the might of the Turks, the intelligentsia of the Arabian world scattered and settled in Europe bringing with them their literature, their knowledge and their fields of expertise. Some of that knowledge must have included the principles of hand reading because an upsurge of interest in the subject suddenly occurred during the thirteenth century with several important treatises on hands written by eminent scholars of the time.

And, although banned by the Catholic Church, it was ironic that towards the end of the Middle Ages one of the first books ever to be printed was not only on palmistry but was also written by a monk. Johann Hartlieb was that scribe, a Viennese whose interest in the study resulted in *Die Kunst Ciromantia* which he wrote in Augsburg in 1448, although it was not published until 1474.

Incidentally, *ciromantia*, or **chirology**, better describes the study of hand reading than palmistry which not only suffers somewhat from the stigma of being outlawed by the Church, but also focuses the attention solely on the palm and its lines. Chirology, however – deriving from the Greek *kheir*, meaning hand – refers to the study of the whole hand, with **chirognomy** describing the study of the structure and shape, and **chiromancy** the interpretation and meaning of the lines.

Amongst mainland European intellectuals Hartlieb's book created a new swell of interest. Many Renaissance scholars eagerly took up the study and, with the recently invented method of printing, books on chirology simply rolled off the presses. The brilliant Italian scholar Andreas Corvus wrote his *Ciromantia* in 1497, hotly followed by another book by the influential physician and scholar Alexander Achillinus (1463–1512). Throughout that century, and well into the next, chirology was to flourish in the hands of such eminent greats as Paracelsus (1493–1541), John Indagine (1531), Jerome Cardan (1501–1576), and Robert Fludd (1574–1637).

Meanwhile in Britain, palmistry came into disrepute yet again and was condemned once more, this time by Henry VIII's Parliament which banned palmistry, claiming it was connected with witchcraft and sorcery.

But a good thing won't lie down! In 1595, *Chiromantiae Theorica Practica*, a work on chirology by the German physician John Rothman, became so popular that it was translated into many of the major European languages. Fifty years later it was finally translated into English.

It is interesting to note that despite its seesawing popularity a collection of essays called the *Ludicrum Chiromanticum*, which was printed in 1661, lists a bibliography of well over seventy books on the subject of chirology.

From the middle of the seventeenth century German academics regarded it so highly that they put chirology firmly on the curriculum at some of their universities. It was to prove a controversial move for the rest of that century and into the early part of the next with the pro-lobby maintaining its stand as a subject of scientific value and the anti-lobby insisting upon its occult association, thus branding it as sorcery and witchcraft.

Back in England, the reign of George IV saw a strong backlash with an act of Parliament decreeing that 'any person found practising palmistry is hereby deemed a rogue and a vagabond to be sentenced to one year's imprisonment and to stand in the pillory'.

Amidst the controversy and furore in Europe surrounding chirology, the fascination with the workings of the hand amongst scientists continued apace. In the late seventeenth century Nehemiah Grew, an English physician, investigated the nature of skin patterns found on the palm and fingers of the human hand. In 1684 he presented a paper on his findings to the newly formed Royal Society in which he described in detail the skin ridges with their various patterns and formations.

A century and a half later, Purkenje, a brilliant young Czech doctor, was to research and classify the different types of fingerprints; in his thesis, which he published in 1823, he discussed the genetics of skin patterns and their potential as a tool for diagnosis.

In the field of chirological research two men, Captain Stanislas d'Arpentigny and Adolph Desbarrolles, stand out as giants in the advancement of the subject. Both were nineteenth-century Frenchmen and between them they brought palmistry into the modern age.

A lifetime of observation led d'Arpentigny to classify hands into discrete categories – a classification system which is still used today by many Western practitioners. He published his book *La Chirognomie* in which he described seven fundamental types. The book was an instant success.

Desbarrolles concentrated on the lines. He kept records on hands and noted any differences that occurred over time. The relationship of colour and temperature to particular illnesses was observed, together with symptoms of ill health and disease that were represented in the hand. Between 1860 and 1879 he published many works containing his findings including the popular *Les Mystères de la Main* and *Révélations Complètes*.

Moreover, it was Desbarrolles who was to address the philosophy of will-power and the question of free will in connection with the interpretation of the lines in the hand.

At around the same time, Carl Gustav Carus, personal physician to the King of Saxony – a man with an impressive list of scientific qualifications, a cast-iron reputation and acceptance in all the major international academies – turned his attention to the significance of different hand shapes and their markings. It was his publication *Die Symbolik der Menschlichen Gestalt und Ueber Grund und Bedeutung der Verschiedenen Formen der Hand* in 1848 which pointed out the psychological correlation of personality and hand types.

A few years later, a further study on the psychological implications entitled *Essai sur une Psychologie de la Main* was published by Dr N. Vaschide, director of pathology at a lab-

oratory in France. His emphasis lay in the belief that the lines imprinted in the palm act as a sort of record or memory of muscular movements that are influenced by events in the individual's life.

Throughout the 1880s, the writings of these four – d'Arpentigny, Desbarrolles, Carus and Vaschide – did much not only to heighten the public's awareness of the value of hand reading but also to spread its popularity. Undoubtedly, though, it was the Victorian hunger for knowledge, pioneering instinct and desire to stretch the limits in every field of human understanding which fuelled the massive revival of interest in chirology that occurred in the latter half of the nineteenth century. But although countless books on the subject were printed, many of them have not stood the test of time.

At this time, too, an important development which was to have far-ranging consequences for us all was taking place. This involved the work of Francis Galton who, in cataloguing and classifying hundreds of skin ridge patterns, was able to demonstrate the uniqueness of fingerprints. It was his pioneering study which eventually led Scotland Yard in 1901 to adopt fingerprinting for forensic purposes in the identification of criminals.

The swell of interest was carried over well into the first half of the twentieth century. At the turn of the century William Benham put together a learned and scholarly book on the subject entitled *The Laws of Scientific Hand Reading*, a work which is still highly respected to this day.

But it was the colourful figure of Count Louis Hamon, or Cheiro as he was more popularly known, that was to dominate the field of palmistry around that time. Cheiro achieved huge recognition and a wide following. His clients came from far and wide to consult him and amongst them numbered politicians, heads of state, writers and a multitude of influential notables in positions of authority. He is said to have predicted, on examining the hands of Oscar Wilde, the sensation the author was to cause several years before the scandal surrounding his homosexuality erupted. In another of his dramatic predictions, so the story goes, he foretold the assassination of William Whiteley, owner of the famous department store in Queensway, London.

Undoubtedly he was a clever man and it is true that he helped to popularize the subject. However, he did claim occult powers, which tends now unfortunately to confuse the scientific validity and credibility of his practice of hand analysis. Of his many books some are still in print today and, although not the best introduction to the study, are often amongst the first books that a student of chirology is likely to pick up. Like so much of the literature in this field published in the late 1800s, some of the information is inaccurate and has a fascination for the macabre. A murderer's thumb, for example, head lines of the criminally insane, predictions of death by drowning, by hanging and a host of other conclusions on deviant behaviour were the sort of morbid aspects somehow drawn from the structure and composition of the lines that seemed to appeal to the late-Victorian mentality.

It was at the beginning of this century, with the rise of the scientific method, that the anatomists turned their gaze to the hand as a potential indicator of health.

Of the anatomists, Professor Frederick Wood-Jones wrote a definitive book about hands, *The Principles Of Anatomy As Seen In The Hand*, which, though first published in 1919, remains unsurpassed to this day. And though a distinguished professor of anatomy at the University of Manchester, he was not above believing that some connection existed between the hand and the workings of the mind.

Some twenty years later two American anatomists, Harold Cummins and Charles Midlo,

published the new findings of their genetic studies. Their work conclusively confirmed a link between abnormal skin patterns and chromosomal aberrations which cause mental and physical abnormalities. Their pioneering studies have given rise to a great deal of research on the hand with particular emphasis on its patterns. This 'new' branch of medical science is known as **dermatoglyphics** – *derma* meaning skin, and *glyph* a carving.

The development of psychology, too, at the beginning of the twentieth century, has had its impact on chirology, influencing a more complete analysis of personality through the structure of the hand in conjunction with the interpretation of its lines. Three names in the field of experimental psychology with particular reference to hand analysis stand out.

Julius Spier, a German who worked under Jung, developed a method of interpreting the hand which he termed psycho-chirology. His research into hand analysis was thorough and meticulous but as a consequence he published only one book on his findings out of a proposed three, entitled *The Hands of Children*.

The second is Dr Charlotte Wolff, also German, who worked with the mentally disturbed both in Paris and in London. She published several papers on her research but unfortunately little of her data now seems to meet the rigorous methodological criteria that modern psychological research demands. Of her books, however, three – *The Human Hand*, *The Hand in Psychological Diagnosis* and *Studies in Hand-Reading* – are perhaps her best and still of value to hand analysis today.

The third of the trio is the Swiss psychologist Dr Hugo Debrunner, whose work with primates and behaviour led him to study the psychology of gesture, a forerunner, no doubt, of the recent interest in body language and non-verbal communication.

The influence of both the scientific process and the psychological approach to analysis produced a transformation in chirology during the early part of the twentieth century.

Any superstitious or folkloric traditions that may have built up around the reading of a hand had, by this time, been discarded. Chirologists, working with a more dynamic and scientific approach, honed the subject into a valuable tool for self-discovery and self-knowledge.

Working diligently towards this end were Dr William Benham and Noel Jaquin. Benham was an American who took up medicine in order to study health patterns in the hand. His *Laws of Scientific Palmistry* is one of the first 'modern' books on chirology.

But it is Noel Jaquin who towers head and shoulders above all others for his pioneering work in the application of psychological techniques to the subject which brought chirology bang into the twentieth century. His books, invaluable to anyone interested in hand analysis, are a delight to read not only because of the scholarly erudition they contain but also because of his understanding and humanity. The love and respect he had for the subject come through in his many books, of which *The Hand of Man, Practical Palmistry* and *The Hand Speaks* are of especial value to the modern application of hand analysis.

Moreover, it was Noel Jaquin who founded the Society for the Study of Physiological Patterns, an organization dedicated to promoting hand analysis, to encouraging research and establishing its importance in physical and psychological diagnosis.

Beryl Hutchinson, disciple of Jaquin, took over from him at the SSPP with the same dedication and enthusiasm for the subject and for the aims of the society. Her book, *Your Life in Your Hands*, is perhaps *the* modern classic which any self-respecting hand analyst should not be without.

Of the practitioners in the second half of the twentieth century Fred Gettings, Mary Anderson, Peter West, David Brandon-Jones and, more recently, from the antipodes, Andrew Fitzherbert, are each exponents whose work has furthered the advance and reputation of the new scientific approach to hand analysis.

And what of the future? It has to be admitted that, despite its long history, hand analysis is still not recognized as an orthodox mainstream subject. Indeed, many regard it as superstitious 'mumbo-jumbo' and reject it wholesale without even considering its potential as an analytical tool. Hard-line scientists disregard its claims because these have not been substantiated in the laboratory. If it can't be replicated, under double-blind conditions, they would say, its theories cannot be validated.

And yet they are reluctant to even try putting those claims to the test because to accept hand analysis now would be to undermine long-held beliefs, to admit shortsightedness in the derision and scorn that has been poured upon the heads of its practitioners for so long. And if they were to even suggest that there could be some validity in the subject, what would it do to their reputations, to their scientific standing?

It is a salutary lesson to remember that once it was the clever thing to believe the earth was flat. Only village idiots said it was round. Galileo was persecuted for daring to say that the earth revolved around the sun. Harvey was laughed at for his theories on the blood circulatory system. And Darwin was scorned and censured for his ideas on the origins of the species.

Nevertheless, this obdurate attitude is hardly surprising considering chirology's chequered pedigree. Its association with charlatans, its scurrilous predictions that delighted in the macabre, its links with fairground, end-of-the-pier fortune-telling and its persecution by an intolerant Church have all left their inevitable tarnish.

Yet, blemished though chirology might be, a testimony that its knowledge contains at least a core of truth must lie not only in the fact that hand reading has existed for thousands of years, but also in that it has survived despite severe persecution and periodic purging. And still does thrive in the East where palmists are consulted daily on every aspect of life.

And surely the fact that so many learned and scholarly men in the past have seen its intrinsic value can neither be disregarded nor denied. Could they all, separated by centuries, by culture, by religion, have been misguided?

Perhaps, then, it is time for a reappraisal of the subject which, in the last eighty years or so, has made a quantum leap. Like psychology's metamorphosis from metaphysics, chirology has similarly undergone a transformation from palmistry into hand analysis.

Its practitioners have proved that in our changing universe they are prepared to update their knowledge, to stretch the boundaries of their understanding. Yesterday's truths are not necessarily those of today. Today's common sense is not that of tomorrow. Quantum mechanics, black holes and the theory of chaos all tell us how little of our universe we have so far understood and how much there is still to know.

In the past, palmists tended to work on intuition and with knowledge that apparently had no firm empirical basis. Now, hand analysts are more keenly aware firstly of the psychological relationships between the hand and the mind, and secondly of the need for a more objective approach and overview of their techniques. Perhaps this new rationalization will place hand analysis in a new light and will establish it, in the twenty-first century, as a core reflector of human personality; as a mirror of the individual's nature, potential, motivation and drives; and as a very valuable aid to medicine in the diagnosis of both physical and psychological ill health.

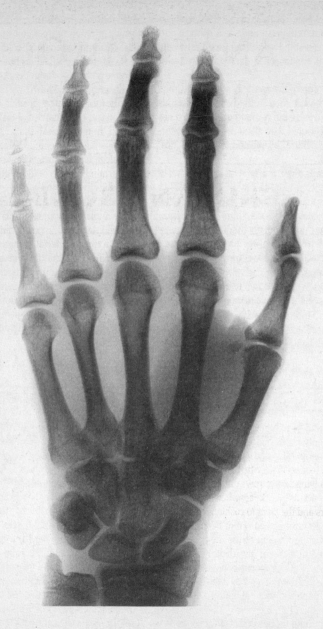

Figure 1

ANATOMY OF THE HAND

CHAPTER TWO

SKIN AND BONES

As early as the fourth week of pregnancy, the tiny arms and legs of the foetus begin to appear. In the next two weeks flat, plate-like extensions start to form on the end of the limbs. These will rapidly develop into hands and feet but at this stage there is little to differentiate between the two. It won't be for another four weeks that the digits form – those of the forelimb into fingers and of the hind-limb into toes. By the end of the second month the hands are well developed with fingers and thumbs clearly defined. And one month later still the fingernails will form.

THE SKELETON – STRUCTURE AND FORMATION

The hand, together with the wrist, is made up of twenty-seven bones. Figure 1 is a photograph of an X-ray of a hand. At the base of the hand, connecting with the wrist, are eight bones lying in two rows of four. These effectively act as shock absorbers between the fingers and the arms to cushion the impact of any pressure applied. From here, five metacarpal bones fan out across the palm to connect with those of the digits. Each finger consists of three separate bones except for the thumb which contains only two. The bones in the fingers and thumbs are called *phalanges*.

At birth the bones in the hands are made of tough elastic tissue which is known as *cartilage*. Some of the smaller bones like those of the wrist start to ossify, or harden, within the first few months of life. This process of ossification, however – turning the cartilage of the hand and fingers into bone – continues for many years and may not be complete until around eighteen or nineteen years of age.

The bones are connected from wrist to fingertips by a series of powerful muscles and tendons which give the hand its movement and grip. By holding the palm of one hand between the thumb and fingers of the other it is possible to feel these tendons at work when flexing and stretching the digits.

A complex network of veins, arteries, joints and nerves are all neatly packaged together to bring life, mobility and sensitivity to the hand.

But it is the thumb, that essentially human development, with its opposing action to the fingers and palm that gives human beings their manual dexterity and allows them their wide range of manual skills. To facilitate this movement the thumb alone has three muscles and it is these that form the fleshy pad at the base of the palm known as the *thenar eminence*, or more popularly referred to as the Mount of Venus.

Another group of muscles link with the little finger whilst a third set service the remaining middle digits. The whole lot is wrapped in skin.

THE SKIN

Skin is a major organ in its own right, possessing some quite extraordinary qualities and performing crucial functions. First of all it acts as a protective barrier preventing bacteria from entering in and salts and other vital body fluids from leaking out. Amongst its other complex functions it can insulate and regulate body temperature, excrete wastes, breathe, produce Vitamin D, is able to absorb chemicals and can even change its pigmentation. On top of all this, because of the thousands of nerve endings that it contains, the skin is a vital sensory organ transmitting a variety of sensations to and from the body and the outside world.

The skin is composed of two layers and comes in two types, a factor which is especially pertinent to the hand. The two layers are known as the *epidermis*, which is on the surface, and the *dermis* which lies beneath. Both rest on a bed of fatty tissue and this helps to cushion and insulate the body. As many of us know to our horror, this fatty layer can be inches thick in various parts of the body – especially around the buttocks and thighs. But in other places, such as the fingers, it can be as thin as a mere fraction of an inch.

The epidermis, or outer covering, is made up of several thicknesses of dead cells. These flake off and are replaced by new cells which are manufactured by the dermis below. This layer is at its thickest on the palm because it has to resist and sustain pressure and friction.

It can take about two months for a cell to travel through the layers to the top of the dermis where it is then shed, and a good deal longer where the skin layers are thicker, as on the palm.

It is the dermis, or bottom layer, which is the living part of the skin containing, as it does, blood vessels, elastic fibres, sweat and oil glands, nerves and proteins, and which also provides the environment for structures like nails and hair to grow. It is here, too, that the ridge and furrow patterns, so characteristic of the palm, are formed. These patterns are better recognized as fingerprints although they do occur all over the palm, (and also on the soles of the feet), where they may sometimes be referred to more technically as **papillary** or **epidermal ridges**.

There are two types of skin, both of which are conveniently to be found in the hand. The first type, which covers most of the body, is thin, quite fine and covered in hair. This skin covers the back of the hand. The palm, though, is covered in the second type, which is much thicker and hornier and only found in two places in the human body – the palms of the hands and the soles of the feet. The **palmer** and **plantar** skin, as it is known, is very special and unique to these areas and, unlike the other type, it is hairless and does not contain oil glands. And just to show the comparison, the epidermis on the palm can be as thick as one twentieth of an inch as opposed to one two-hundredth of an inch on the lips.

· SKIN RIDGES

The skin ridges which make up the familiar fingerprint patterns are formed as part of the dermis layer and not on the surface of the skin as might at first be assumed. On reflection, this would indeed seem logical given that fingerprints never change but remembering that the top layer of skin is made of dead cells which are constantly being shed and replaced.

Cases of bodies where the cause of death has been either through drowning or burning have led to the confirmation of this fact. Forensic scientists have discovered that in cases where the top layer of skin has been damaged through fire, perhaps, or simply deteriorated with age, a positive identification can still be made from the ridge markings on the dermis layer beneath.

Skin ridges, although widely recognized as producing patterns on the fingertips, actually form themselves into patterns all over the palm as well. These patterns are developed very early on in the foetus around the end of the third month of gestation. As they are being formed they are susceptible to abnormalities and any genetic hiccup will not only impair their growth but will stamp in certain abnormal features. The fingerprint patterns on the hands of someone with Down's Syndrome, for example, will be quite specifically different to those in a normal hand.

On close inspection the ridges look rather like a sheet of corrugated metal, or perhaps like a field that has just been ploughed. These ridges are, on average, something like 0.4mm wide. They appear continuous but are, in fact, punctuated by thousands of tiny sweat glands. Once formed they never change throughout the individual's life, although they can become rather faint, especially in occupations where friction may cause excessive wear. Years of typing or of playing the piano, for example, can smoothe the fingerprints to such a degree that it becomes almost impossible to make them out with the naked eye. In certain illnesses, too, the ridge patterns can actually break down or become 'smudged' by fine lines developing on the skin surface.

The actual ridges or furrows travel in parallel lines and then, in certain places such as on the fingertips, break away and form themselves into patterns, sweeping and swirling before meeting up again to regain their parallel paths. There are three main categories of patterns – **loops, arches** and **whorls** – each of which are further subdivided to form eight or so different types.

The function of the papillary ridges on this highly specialized skin is to enable firmer contact and grip. The sweat glands, too, depositing a layer of dampness across the palm, add further adhesion, ensuring a more secure bond.

Only monkeys and the higher primates have this special skin on the palms of their hands and the soles of their feet. Interestingly, though, some apes also have it on the backs of their fingers because they walk with both hind- and forelimbs, placing down their fisted hands as they do the soles of their feet. Even more fascinating is that some monkeys, such as the Woolly Monkey, for example, have this skin running some three or four inches down the backs of their tails. The tails, which are prehensile, are used like hands for both grasping as well as for touch.

THE FINGERNAILS

The nails develop between the ninth and twelfth weeks of pregnancy. Their function is to protect the tips of the fingers and to facilitate the picking up of objects. They are composed of densely packed keratin, a substance which forms itself into a horny layer on the backs of the fingertips. The germinative part of the nail penetrates deeply into the skin where the living cells produce the root. The milky white half moon, often seen more clearly on the thumbs than on the other digits, is the external part of the growing root. It is surrounded by the cuticle which acts as a waterproof seal preventing germs from invading the nail bed.

As the nail grows out from the root it is firmly attached to the bed on the tip of the finger where living cells provide the constant supply of blood that gives nails their characteristic pinkness. Once it grows out and frees itself from the nail bed it loses its blood supply and then turns a cloudy whitish colour and, being composed of dead cells, it may be cut or filed without fear of pain.

How fast a nail grows depends on several factors. In general, fingernails take between four to six months to grow from base to tip but there are all sorts of exceptions to the rule. Interestingly, nails on the toes are 25 per cent slower at growing than those on the fingers, so that toenails would take a month to grow the same amount that fingernails do in one week.

Another interesting factor is that the longer the fingers the faster the growth. People with short fingers, then, will find that their nails are slower growing than those with longer digits. Equally, nails on the middle fingers grow faster than those on the little fingers. They also grow quicker in young people than in older folk, faster in hot weather than in cold, and there are other conditions and environments besides which have an effect on the growth rate of the nails.

Healthy nails should be springy and slightly convex in shape, from pink to beige in colour, depending on race, with a milky-white moon. The moons should not be too big nor too small. They should have an overall lustre or sheen to them. Any abnormalities or deformities may directly correspond to illnesses or to damage of the growing root.

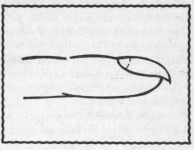

Figure 2

One condition that has been recognized for thousands of years is known as the **Hippocratic nail** (Figure 2). Often starting with the left index, it is easily spotted as the nail curves right around the top of the finger. It has become association with bronchial problems but straightens up again as soon as the illness is cured.

More commonly, white specks, once believed to be caused by a lack of calcium, may now be indicating an imbalance of zinc. Horizontal grooves (Figure 3), also called **Beau's lines**, may indicate a shock to the system, nutritional problems or just simply damage to the nail bed. Pitting, too, may be caused by nutritional deficiencies but could also point to the skin disease psoriasis. All these markings grow out at the same rate as the nail so that a keen eye can judge when the damage or ill health took place.

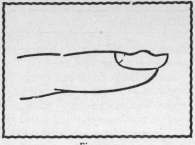

Figure 3

It can be seen, then, that the nails provide valuable diagnostic clues to all manner of disease and ill health.

It is the elaborate arrangement of veins and bones, of muscles and tendons and of joints and skin that gives the hand its outstanding flexibility, enabling it to grip and grasp; to hold and manipulate objects with exact precision; to feel and gather information from the surrounding environment.

Think of the wide range of movements a hand makes in the course of a day: holding and turning door handles, for instance; pressing light switches; manipulating buttons through tiny button holes; unscrewing faucets or lids of jam jars; testing the temperature of water from the tap; holding an egg at just the right pressure; picking up a cup of tea; turning the page of a newspaper; picking fluff off a jacket lapel; carrying a bag; inserting keys into locks – all this and a good deal more even before setting off to work in the morning!

And, given the agility and sensitivity of the hand, it is not surprising that the number of brain cells that deal with messages to and from the hand far exceed those that communicate with the whole of the arm. It is interesting, too, that at least half of those brain cells are dedicated to the thumb alone. Just a reminder of the key role that the thumb plays as part of the hand.

PSYCHOLOGY OF THE HAND

CHAPTER THREE

FINGERPRINTS

THE ORIGINS OF FORENSIC FINGERPRINTING

One doesn't need to be a follower of whodunnits to know that many a careless fingerprint has often convicted the unwary villain. The science of fingerprinting is now established world-wide as a method of detection because, as is well known, fingerprints are unique: no two people, not even identical twins, possess similar patterns. They are our very own personal signatures, our calling cards, irrefutable marks of our identity.

Interestingly, that eminently successful Victorian writer Sir Arthur Conan Doyle, whose finger was on the pulse of new scientific trends, was so advanced in his theories on forensic techniques that he had his famous detective, Sherlock Holmes, use fingerprints to solve criminal cases at least twenty years before fingerprinting became accepted standard practice in the police force.

But, contrary to popular belief, it wasn't that intrepid detective from Baker Street who pioneered the use of fingerprinting for investigative purposes. How this practice of criminological detection ever came into being in the first place reads like a detective story in itself. It's a story that begins with a series of coincidences in the Far East and ends, in 1901, at Scotland Yard.

The Orientals have, for centuries, recognized the uniqueness of the skin patterns. Whereas illiterate Europeans, when faced with official documents, would make their mark with a cross, their Eastern counterparts would use a print of their thumbs as a sign of their personal identity.

Towards the end of the nineteenth century this practice was observed and noted by William Herschel, a British district officer in India, whilst supervising the payment of pensions to government workers. He soon realized the important implications this practice could have for the identification of criminals.

Meanwhile, unknown to him and in another part of India, Edward Henry, a police Inspector-General in Bengal, was already collecting fingerprints and was busily devising a system by which to classify them. And at the very same time in Japan, a medical missionary digging for prehistoric pottery noticed that some of the shards he was finding had thumbprints pressed into them. He concluded that this must have been a means by which potters, through the centuries, signed their work. The discovery prompted him to write to the great anthropologist Charles Darwin who, in turn, passed on the information to his cousin Francis Galton.

As it happened, Francis Galton had just been commissioned by the Home Office to find a foolproof method of establishing identity. Up until then, suspected criminals were being identified by the measurement of their bones – hardly a satisfactory method at all. The news of the fingerprinting possibility, therefore, brought great excitement and a flurry of scientific activity. In 1901, fingerprinting was finally adopted by Scotland Yard as a reliable method of personal identification – a system which was completely to revolutionize police work world wide.

Scotland Yard, or rather the National Identification Bureau, has in the region of three million sets of fingerprints currently in its files. Some of the work of collecting, classifying and matching is now computerized but it is still essentially a task which is done by hand. It is a laborious process which takes many man-hours and a good deal of perseverance by teams of highly skilled and dedicated experienced people.

The process is two-fold. The first part is the actual taking of the fingerprints from a suspected criminal, classifying them and then filing and storing them away. The second is the lifting of fingerprints, or 'latent marks' as they are now called, left behind at the scene of a crime, classifying them and cross-matching for identification purposes.

The first part is comparatively simple and straightforward. Charged individuals are fingerprinted at the police station. Occasionally, depending on the practice of the constabulary, not just the tips of the fingers but an imprint of the whole hand may be taken. These are then sent to the fingerprinting team to record and file away in their library according to whatever classification system is used. They are, at this point, also cross-matched and cross-referenced against any outstanding latent marks found at the scene of a crime but as yet unidentified.

The second part is the more complex. The finger-marks which we leave on the surface of an object we touch are made up of tiny beads of sweat that come from the rows of pores running all along the top of our papillary skin ridges. Lifting these latent marks is the easy bit. Aluminium or graphite powder is brushed over the mark and then a transparent adhesive strip applied on top. When the strip is peeled off it brings with it the pattern which is now traced out by the powder. The strip is then securely stuck on to a sheet of see-through plastic, carefully labelled and photographed ready for classification and identification.

So much for the easy part. It is the classification and identification of the marks that takes the skill and the long man-hours. Latent marks left at the scene of a crime are not, as one can imagine, neatly placed on an object. Skin, being elastic, has a tendency to stretch when it comes into contact with a hard surface so that a good deal of distortion of the pattern takes place. Nor indeed need the marks be found whole. In many instances the patterns may be only partially laid down so that the fingerprint team have barely a fragment of print to work with.

So, whilst the actual defining of the pattern can have its difficulties, matching it to existing prints in the files can be mind-boggling. In order that a latent print can be accepted as admissible evidence in a court it has to match the defendant's own fingerprint by what is known as the 'sixteen-point match' – that is, that at least sixteen separate characteristics must be exactly alike. (Figure 4).

The matching is done by hand. With a magnifying glass and a sharp pencil, the ridges in the latent print are counted and measured and then the searching begins. Each mark has to be individually compared to similar fingerprints in the bureau's files. If working with a good latent mark, a skilled operator can compare it with five hundred fingerprints in an hour. With a poor one even the most

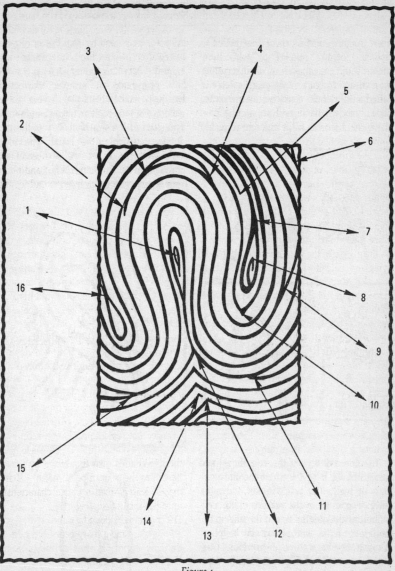

Figure 4

experienced operator would be lucky to compare and eliminate just twenty.

Technology may have moved on since Sherlock Holmes, but the man with the magnifying glass still has a vital role to play!

FINGERPRINTS IN CHARACTER ASSESSMENT

Apart from the forensic use of fingerprints to establish identity chirologists, who have known about the uniqueness of fingerprints for thousand of years, have incorporated the patterns into their character assessments. Today, modern hand analysts ascribe particular characteristics to the different patterns.

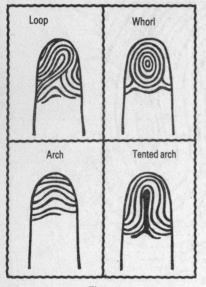

Figure 5

example, it's a good bet that one or more of her children will too. Each pattern type highlights distinct character and personality traits. Some people may have just one pattern on all ten digits whilst others may have a combination of several scattered about. Six similar prints out of ten would make that the predominant pattern in the hand. Otherwise, each print has to be analysed separately according to the finger on which it occurs.

As Figure 5 illustrates, there are three basic categories: the loop, the whorl and the arch, each of which has subdivisions, making a total of about six major patterns – although other unusual varieties do occasionally occur. The loop types can always be detected because they have only one **triradius**, a triangular formation of ridges, at the side of the pattern. The whorls have two whilst simple arches have none, although it must be added that tented arches do have one.

Patterns tend to run in families so that if a mother has a predominance of whorls, for

Figure 6

THE LOOP

Loops (Figure 6) are invariably found on flexible, adaptable and versatile people. They are a sign of open-mindedness, tolerance and fair play. These people need change and thrive on challenge. Excitement and stimulation are food and drink to them. A boring, dead-end, nine-to-five type of existence is their idea of hell. It is almost impossible to meet an individual with a majority of loop fingerprints who doesn't have a vast number of interests and hobbies. If they become bored with one hobby, they can always leave it and turn to the next to amuse them, returning when their interest has been rekindled.

Communication is their thing. They are at their happiest and best when in the company of others, working in a free and open environment where they can exchange news and views and opinions. The sort of job where they have to think on the hoof, to be constantly one step ahead, suits them right down to the ground.

No matter upon which digit it is found, the loop is the mark of creativity, of an open, amenable approach and, above all, of a love of new ideas.

THE WHORL

Of all the patterns, the whorl (Figure 7) is the most individualistic. Whenever it is found it highlights inflexibility and fixed, rigid attitudes. People with a predominance of whorls need to be in charge and in control. This applies particularly in the work place if the whorl is found on the thumb or on the index of the dominent hand. When it occurs on the index of the other, or passive, hand, the need for control is centred around the home so that, for instance, the individual might feel undermined if not able to make all the major domestic decisions. Whether at home or at work, people with whorls on either thumbs or forefingers hate anyone

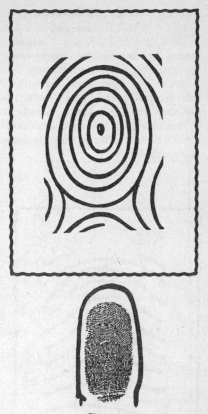

Figure 7

looking over their shoulders and telling them what to do. They are best left alone to use their initiative, carry their responsibility and do the job on their own.

Creative appreciation and a good artistic eye go with whorled ring fingers. This pattern is not often seen on the little finger except when part of a full set. When found here it reveals the quiet, reflective thinker, those who like to research their facts before giving their opinions. Start them on a subject dear to their hearts, however, and it will be almost impossible to get them to stop talking again!

People with six or more whorls on their fingertips are invariably fairly entrenched in their ideas and philosophy on life and they find it very difficult to change their outlook. Moreover, they tend to be slow to respond because the 'whorled' types are far from impulsive. They need time to process information, to think things over and rationalize their answers. Never expect a quick reply from them, however frustrating this might be, but leave them alone for a while and they'll come back with their answer in their own good time.

Figure 8

THE SIMPLE ARCH

People with arches (Figure 8) have a practical, sensible and down-to-earth attitude to life. They are always prepared to help others, to step in when needed for they are known as the 'salt of the earth'. Sometimes sceptical, sometimes suspicious, but always firm realists, they are definitely not prone to flights of fancy and their conversation is usually based on everyday subjects, or is about concrete, material topics. They have masses of common sense, are thoroughly trustworthy and reliable and, as such, tend to attract people with problems who find arched individuals infinitely patient and excellent shoulders to cry on. When it comes to their own problems, though, they find it very difficult to put their deeper feelings into words and are often in danger of repressing their emotions.

Arches may be found on the first three digits but, unless as part of a full set, it's unusual to find this pattern on the little and ring fingers. When found on the thumb or first and second fingers, the inability verbally to express themselves is enhanced. Such people should try to find other ways of expressing their feelings; perhaps by writing them down or keeping a diary. Alternatively, they could try to paint, do pottery or anything constructive that will help to vent their emotions.

THE TENTED ARCH

The tented arch (Figure 9) resembles the ordinary arch but looks as if it has a ridge pole through the centre. This pattern is usually only found on the index or second finger, very rarely on the third and hardly ever at all on the thumb or little finger. When present it denotes enthusiasm and a need for challenge to fire the inspiration. Whenever a new interest grabs their imagination, people with this pattern throw themselves into it with single-minded fervour and intensity. Life would be very dull

Figure 9

Figure 10

indeed if these people didn't have at least three or four dozen things to busy themselves with in a single day – otherwise what would be the point of getting out of bed in the morning?

When present on the middle finger it highlights those who tend to be staunch followers of religion or of ideological movements, for it is the sign of the great idealist. Although rare, when it does occur on the ring finger it tells of either musical talents or creative flair. When several tented arches occur in the hand they highlight a sensitive individual who needs a harmonious environment in which to live.

THE COMPOSITE

Although composites (Figure 10) are also known as twin loops, they actually belong to the whorl category because they have two triradii. Studied closely, they look like two loops pulling in opposite directions. It is rare to find them anywhere other than on the thumb and forefinger. When present, this fingerprint shows an ability to appreciate all points of view, to see all sides of a problem. In any occupation where it is necessary to understand a situation from all its angles – that of a judge, a lawyer or a teacher, for example – this pattern is certainly an advantage. It's jolly useful, too, for mothers dealing with children and their problems, especially when their youngsters are going through those turbulent teenage years.

But when it comes to personal decision-making, the composite can be a definite drawback, a spanner in the works. Because people with this pattern tend to spend so long considering the alternatives, weighing up the 'pros' and 'cons', analysing their problems from every aspect, they tend to complicate the matter and end up totally confused, unsure which way to turn or which road to take. 'Shall I, shan't I? . . . But what if . . .?' These are the questions that owners of composite patterns are always asking themselves.

In order to make things easier for themselves, or to succeed in life, these people have to find a way of making firm decisions and commitments. Otherwise, their constant vacillations will mean they'll just miss out on opportunities. Perhaps when they find themselves in two minds, one of the best ways of dealing with it is to simply let their intuition guide them through.

THE PEACOCK'S EYE

The peacock's eye (Figure 11) isn't really a category in its own right but it is listed because of its unusual qualities. It is a compound pattern consisting of a tiny circle, or whorl, inside a closed loop. This fingerprint is more usually on the ring or little fingertips. It is a fairly rare marking and when found it represents an odd sense of preservation, a certain amount of luck especially when it comes to dangerous or tricky situations. This

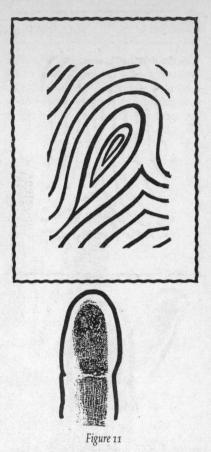

Figure 11

pattern has been found on the hands of survivors, people who have been picked off the top of a burning building, for example, or who have miraculously crawled out of the wreckage of an aeroplane – people, that is, who have come within inches of their lives and who have been saved by the very skin of their teeth! It's certainly a lucky pattern to possess!

PALMAR SKIN PATTERNS

Just like those on the fingertips, the skin ridges on the palm can form themselves into patterns too. Directly beneath each finger is a triangular pattern of ridges known either as an apex or a triradius; and interdigitally, or between the bases of two fingers, loops may sometimes be found as well.

Triradii and a variety of other patterns may also occur elsewhere on the hand, especially on the thenar eminence or Mount of Venus,

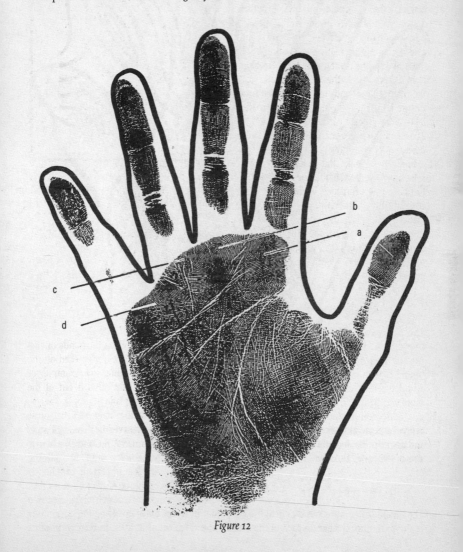

Figure 12

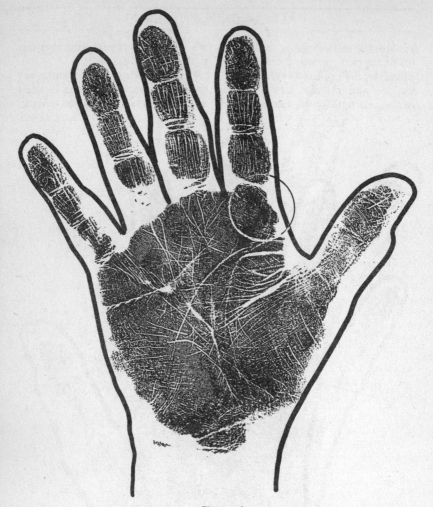

Figure 12A

that area encircling the base of the thumb, and also on the hypothenar, or percussion side of the hand, better known as the Mount of Luna.

TRIRADII

The triradii patterns are found right at the top of the palm directly beneath each of the four fingers (Figure 12). In medical and scientific works these are termed A, B, C and D, where A occurs beneath the index and D beneath the little finger. Another important triradius is found on the palm and is referred to as T. A great deal of medical research has been carried out in recent times involving the positioning and ridge count of these in relation to other

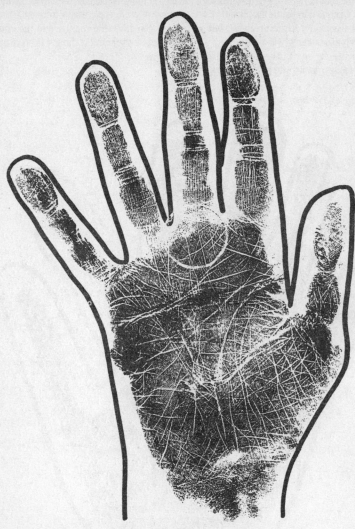

Figure 12B

important triradii patterns in the palm. Though rarely found in the normal hand, the research has shown that certain specific malformations and misalignments of these patterns correspond to particular congenital or chromosomal abnormalities in the individual.

THE INDEX FINGER

When the point of the triradius is found centrally aligned beneath the index finger it denotes a well-balanced, sensible and responsible individual.

Should the triradius be skewed towards the thumb, as illustrated in Figure 12a, it shows a need for challenge and adventure in life. Individuals with this marking will always show a daring, pioneering spirit. There is a certain unpredictability about them. Sometimes living on the very edge of the law or taking themselves off to explore new frontiers, they possess the drive, the courage and the guts and need a certain hint of danger to spice up their lives.

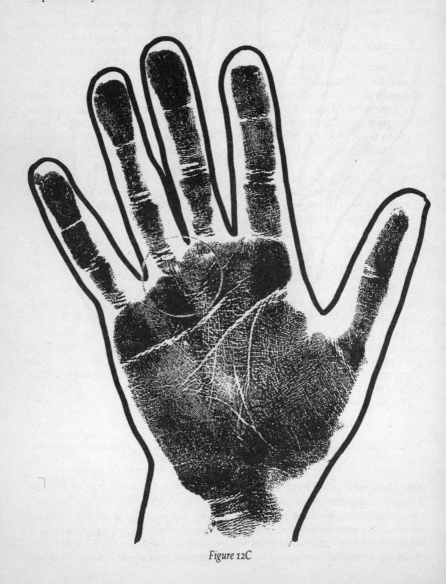

Figure 12C

If it is skewed towards the middle finger it means quite the opposite to the above, for these people are extremely timid and cautious. They have an absolute horror of taking risks and much prefer to tread the same groove than expose themselves to unnecessary hazard.

THE MIDDLE FINGER

If the point of the triradius lies directly beneath the mid-point of the finger so that it is centrally aligned, it reveals masses of common sense and good judgement. Values and morals are strongly upheld.

It is so extremely rare to find this pattern skewed towards the index that it is hardly ever seen.

Those who possess the pattern displaced towards the ring finger, as in Figure 12b, tend to lack sound financial understanding. Those who let money simply slip through their fingers often have this skin marking.

THE RING FINGER

The triradial patterns beneath the ring finger can be a little more complex than those of the other digits. In some cases a normal, neat, triangular formation may indeed exist. At other times, however, the ridges may be elongated into a loop or even formed into a half-ring encircling both the base of this finger and reaching right over to Saturn (Figure 12c).

If the pattern doesn't appear to have a clear point but seems to be stretched downwards into a long loop it is the sign of an innate rapport and understanding of animals. I first came across the pattern in the hands of a well-known zoologist and writer who has devoted his entire life to working with animals.

A semi-circle of ridges that surround the base of this finger and that of Saturn is often found on the hands of people who tend to be a bit of a wet blanket. They cannot seem to appreciate the lighter side of life but tend to take a rather gloomy view. They are always expecting the worst and this attitude tends to cut off their spontaneous appreciation of fun and enjoyment. Those who possess the marking but who have managed to change their attitudes – who have forced themselves to appreciate the sunshine in their lives – develop an Apollo line (*see* p.168) that cuts right through the semicircular ridge pattern.

THE LITTLE FINGER

The normal position for the triradius here is with its point displaced towards the ring finger. Now and again it may be found centrally placed beneath the digit, in which case it always highlights someone with a passion for words. I have seen a marked example of this in the hand of one of Britain's leading poets. Another example was found in the hand of a person who was an absolute wizard at crosswords.

INTERDIGITAL PATTERNS

Skin ridge patterns can be found on the palm between all the digits and have significant meanings according to their locations. When patterns occur in these areas they are, more often than not, loops. Just occasionally a tiny whorl may be seen, but this is rather rare – so rare in fact, that not enough records have been found to make any valid assessments.

THUMB/INDEX

Occasionally, as seen in Figure 13, a loop may

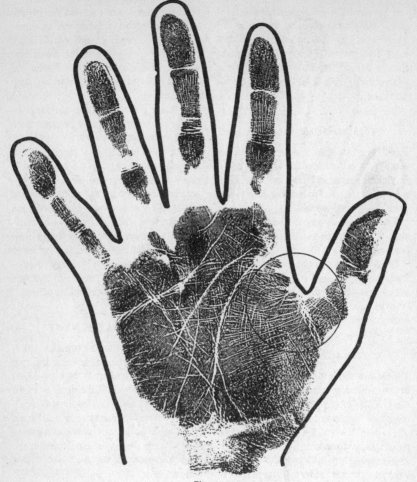

Figure 13

be found just above the base of the thumb lying on the Mount of Mars. Here it is a sign of a strong admiration of courage and indeed, at times, of bravery itself.

INDEX/MIDDLE

A loop in this position is known as the **Rajah Loop** (Figure 14). It is not commonly found, but when present reveals a charismatic per-

sonality; someone who is looked up to, who can carry responsibility and who is a leader amongst men. Anyone with this marking is said to possess executive abilities and should work in a managerial capacity in any position that carries authority and responsibility.

It was the Oriental tradition of palmistry that gave it its name because it was originally thought to be a mark of nobility. Curiously enough, I have found it on the hands of

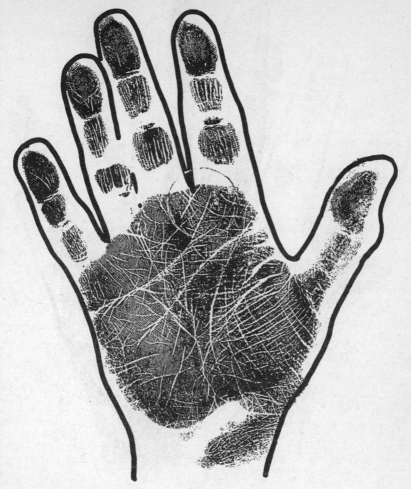

Figure 14

people with a strong Celtic ancestry and have often mused whether this implies a lineage stemming back to ancient royal clans!

Certainly, one lady I once had the pleasure of meeting fulfilled all the categories. As a distinguished actress, she did indeed possess a charismatic personality, she was respected not only by her fans but also by her contempories in the profession. Her whole bearing

and manner spoke of dignity and, although her accent didn't betray her nationality, she was indeed of Irish descent!

MIDDLE/RING

A loop in this position (Figure 15) is often referred to as the **vocational** loop. It is more frequently seen than the two former loops

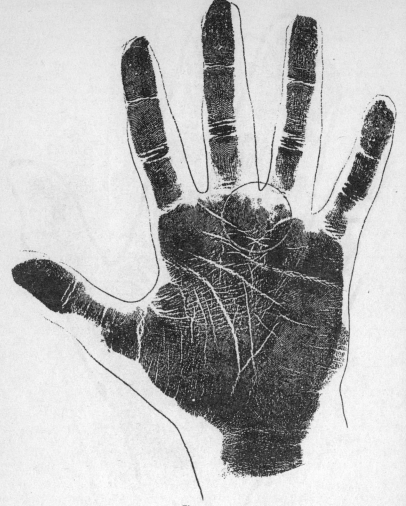

Figure 15

and reveals a strong vocational urge, a need to be of help to others or to the community at large. People in vocational occupations – teachers, health workers and clerics, for example – often have this marking. The loop characterizes someone who is serious and has a responsible attitude to life; who is a hard worker and thus is likely to become fairly successful at whatever is undertaken, especially in business.

RING/LITTLE

This pattern, as illustrated in Figure 16, is known as the loop of humour. It reveals an ability to relax, to enjoy oneself, to see the

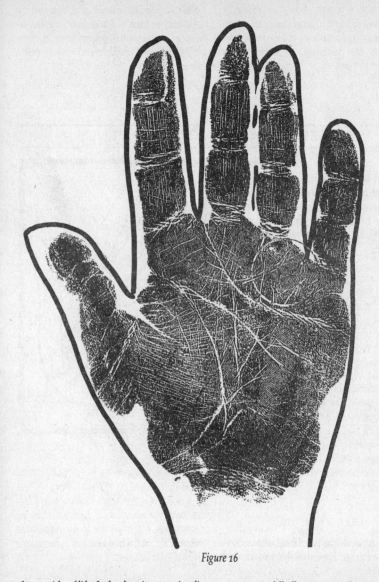

Figure 16

funny side of life. Indeed, as its name implies, it is a sign of a good sense of humour, but one that is rather odd – not the normal kind but the sort that tends to laugh at unusual things – the sort of humour that might be described as wry, oddball, even macabre at times. At the cinema one can always distinguish those with the loop of humour because they're the ones who laugh 'in all the wrong places'.

But one important significance of this

marking is that it also shows an ability to laugh at oneself and at one's own mistakes and foibles. These people, then, don't take themselves too seriously, a factor which makes them much more tolerant and easy-going in life.

Now and again, instead of a loop, a tiny whorl may be seen in this position. Beware of those with interdigital whorls here for they can be extremely scathing and very sarcastic indeed.

PATTERNS ON THE MOUNT OF VENUS

Patterns on the Mount of Venus, or thenar eminence, are fairly uncommon but, although rare, there are two particular patterns which may sometimes occur. These may be seen in Figure 17. Both show an appreciation and, in some cases, an aptitude for music.

THE LOOP

On some hands a loop pattern may be seen entering the area from low down towards the wrist and up on to the mount itself (17a). When it does occur it indicates an ear for music, especially for that of the brass section.

I once came across the marking in the hand of an industrialist and, although he didn't play an instrument as such, he did admit to enjoying music played by big brass bands. It was also remarked, at the time, that much of his working life had been spent in factories and steel works of one kind or another where the metallic rhythms of clanking machinery were not too dissimilar from the rhythms of a brass band!

Figure 17

BEE STRINGS

The pattern known as **Bee Strings** is a curious marking of ridge lines contained in an oval shape on the Mount of Venus (17b). When present it, too, highlights musical talent but this time the attraction is towards stringed instruments. I have seen it in the hands of a violinist, a guitarist and also in the hands of a pianist.

THE MOUNT OF LUNA

Patterns may quite frequently occur on the Mount of Luna. A variety of arches, loops, whorls and composites can all be found here.

THE ARCH

When an open arch is found on this mount, as in Figure 18, it reveals a practical, constructive imagination. Ideas are fairly materialistic and inspiration may be limited.

Figure 18

A tented arch may sometimes occur. When found, it shows an enthusiastic imagination. The owners possess drive and initiative and when fired with an idea feel compelled to put it straight away into motion.

THE WHORL

A whorl on this mount denotes heightened imagination. A whorl on the Mount of Luna is illustrated in Figure 19. As with the fingertip whorls, ideas are formed slowly but in meticulous detail. The imaginative powers here are so sharp, so vivid that individuals with this marking can make themselves identify so strongly with their own ideas that they can convince themselves that their fantasies are, in fact, reality.

Figure 19

The whorl in this area is helpful to artists and all those in creative occupations. It is especially useful in the hands of actors and performers who have to take on the role they are playing. However, all those who possess this pattern must learn to listen and be more open to other people's ideas.

THE COMPOSITE

There is a confusion of ideas when the composite, or twin loop pattern, is present on the

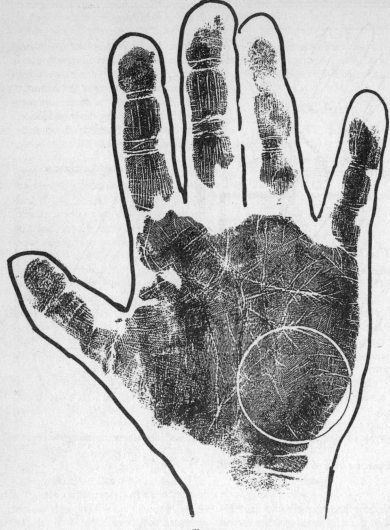

Figure 20

Luna mount (Figure 20). The imagination gets tugged and pulled in opposite directions so that the individuals tend to vacillate, changing their minds from one day to the next and finding it hard to maintain a single direction in life.

THE LOOP

Various loops may be seen on the Mount of Luna. One enters from the percussion edge, one sweeps down from the direction of the Head line and another shoots straight up from the wrist (Figure 21).

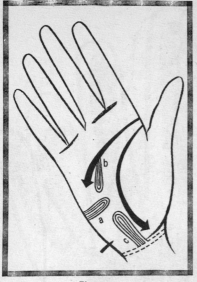

Figure 21

A loop that enters from the percussion side of the palm and lies horizontally across the mount (21a) highlights a special gift with flora and fauna. It shows an unusual, instinctive rapport with Nature in general; an ability to feel the 'vibes' of a place or a situation; a deep understanding of the rhythms and cycles of the earth.

If a loop sweeps into the mount from the direction of the Head line (21b) it has several meanings. Some hand analysts believe it shows a vivid memory of the 'collective unconscious'. Others maintain it represents telepathic powers. Perhaps both these meanings are valid in certain cases but in my experience I have found it denotes something quite unusual. People with this formation seem to have an affinity to water. Either they like living by the sea or by a river, enjoy water sports more than the average, or find themselves constantly drawn to a favourite beach, river bank of sea shore.

They find, moreover, that if they have problems or decisions to make, a walk along a river or seashore will refresh, inspire and invigorate them. If it's not possible physically to get to the seaside then, strange as it may sound, a bath or a shower can have the same effect. Although at first it may sound quite implausible, many people with this marking really find that it works! Scientifically, there could well be a connection here with a response to the invigorating effects of negative ions.

Very rarely one comes across a loop which takes root from the wrist and shoots upwards (21c). It lies in the area known as the Mount of Neptune, right between the mounts of Luna and Venus. It is found in the hands of sensitive people, writers, poets, artists, musicians, and it represents inspiration.

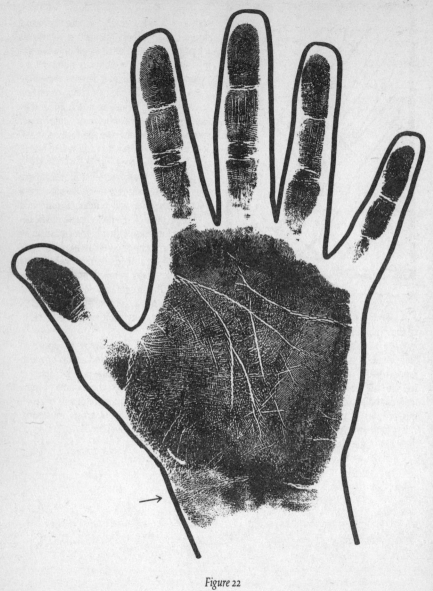

Figure 22

CHAPTER FOUR

THE BACK OF THE HAND

Whilst the palm of the hand is covered in its distinctively thick, ridged skin, the cutaneous layer on the back of the hand is of a much finer and rather elastic texture.

Apart from the rascette (Figure 22) at the base of the hand, which acts as a boundary between palm and wrist, there is no noticeable demarcation line between one type of skin and the other. Each simply blends into the other and it makes quite a fascinating few minutes' study trying to work out where, along the edge of the palm and down the side of the fingers, one type of skin begins and the other ends.

On close inspection, the skin on the back of the hand has the appearance of what might be described as finely crazed china – an effect which is produced by tiny wrinkles known as **cleavage** or **tension lines.**

TENSION LINES

Insignificant though they might seem, these tension lines perform a very important function. Without them our hands would lack their ease of flexibility, for it is this very system of tiny wrinkles that enables the skin to stretch across its framework, facilitating every tiny movement that is made by our fingers and thumbs.

Indisputably, the way this fine skin functions is quite ingenious. The whole surface is crinkled by the criss crossing of the tension lines so as to produce a mesh-like effect in the skin similar to a net. A net has a much greater degree of flexibility within its structure than, say, a closely woven piece of fabric, for the net has a good deal of give when pulled and stretched in different directions.

On the back of the hand the mesh-like effect flows roughly in a sweep from thumb to percussion, allowing the skin its 'give' in several different directions as the thumb moves in opposition to the fingers or as the digits are clenched into a fist (Figure 23). But the fingers, unlike the back of the hand, bend

Figure 23

in one single axis, so skin that stretches in all directions is not required here. On the backs of the fingers, then, the tension lines are laid horizontally, so that when the skin is under tension due to the flexion of a digit it stretches smooth, and when the finger straightens again the tension creases take up the slack. This is particularly noticeable across the joints.

Another interesting factor about the skin on the back of our hands is that, if we cut ourselves so that the wound is in line with the directional flow of the tension lines, it will heal much faster and leaves less of a scar than a cut that is made across them. This is because the crinkled pattern effect has what might loosely be called a nap, rather as one may imagine a piece of velvet. Tear the velvet along the nap and the cut may be mended almost invisibly. However, if the tear is made across the nap, it will not only be difficult to mend but is likely to stand out fairly noticeably too. Surgeons, aware of this factor, will, for these reasons and wherever possible, make any necessary incisions in the skin in the same direction as the flow of the tension lines.

BENEATH THE SURFACE

Beneath the skin covering of the hand there is a very thin layer of subcutaneous fat, laid down in a sponge-like arrangement which is very specific to hands and which is not found elsewhere in the body apart from the foot. It is interesting to note that in general this fatty layer is thicker in European hands than in those of Asiatics. Oriental hands are noticeably leaner and finer than those of Europeans.

A lean hand, however, is no reflection on the corpulence of the rest of the body. Many well-built people are found to have surprisingly thin and bony hands. In general, thinner hands are more inclined to wrinkle earlier on in life than fuller, fatter hands.

But every day activities in our modern way of life can leave their effect on the skin of our hands. Exposure to chemicals and to detergents can dry the skin and cause premature ageing. And so too can excessive sunbathing.

These effects apart, because the texture of skin can change throughout life, it can be possible to estimate the age of an individual simply by considering the texture and condition of the skin on the back of the hand.

A baby's hand is invariably podgy with smooth skin dimpled at the knuckles. With age, though, the skin starts to lose some of its moisture and elasticity and begins to wrinkle. So, damage caused by exposure to chemicals and to sun notwithstanding, it is possible roughly to estimate an individual's age by the condition of the skin on the back of the hands.

The well-known 'pinch' test is also another guide to age. When a youngster's skin on the back of the hand is pinched and then released again, it springs back almost instantly because it is so elastic. But the same test on an elderly person's hand will show that the skin takes a few seconds to return to its normal position. And the pinched skin on the hand of a much older person may remain in its 'pinched' position for a considerable time.

The actual texture of the skin on the hands is significant as it reflects character and disposition. A fine texture, for instance, tells of a sensitive nature, whilst a coarser-grained skin denotes someone of a more robust make-up. The finer-texture types tend to be more refined, often highly cultured, their interests of an urbane nature. The coarser the texture of the skin, so that the hand feels rather leathery, the more 'fibrous' the personality and the more the interests are centred on outdoors or rural-type pursuits.

SKIN PIGMENTATION

Next to texture, the pigmentation of our skin can yield valuable information about ourselves – not only about our genetic inheritance and geographic roots but also about our state of health. It may even hint at character and personality traits too.

The agent responsible for colouring skin is **melanin**, a genetically inherited dark pigment which gives people from different parts of the world their distinctive racial colouring and shows how, in terms of evolution, people have adapted to their different environments.

Judgements derived from the colour of the skin on the hand, however, should be arrived at only in the context of the natural pigmentation of the rest of the body; although palms, it must be remembered, are usually lighter than the back of the hand. A black hand, for example, will have a pinkish-beige palm.

There is a general feeling that the better the colour of the skin, the more robust the individual. For instance, hands with very pale, almost transparent skin suggest physiological debilities, whereas coarse, brown-as-a-berry hands reflect strong, energetic people with a love of the outdoors.

A milky-white skin, it has been observed, often goes with a self-centred disposition: selfish egocentrics are associated with this pigmentation. Blue- or red-tinged skins may point to organic disorders, as long as, of course, the colour has not been affected by the ambient temperature of the environment.

Bluish skin might point to circulatory problems. So too might a very red skin and this, incidentally, can also denote a fiery, irascible temper. A yellow skin may allude to liver dysfunction. The skin of young babies who develop jaundice, for example, tends to take on a yellowish hue, the colour also affecting their nails.

Yellowish-brown patches rather like large misshapen freckles that occur on the back of the hand are known as liver spots and are associated with ageing. Some beauty therapists recommend vitamin supplements, notably Vitamin A, for curing liver spots on the skin.

HAIR

Much, in the past, was made about hair on the hands – too much, too little, too dark, too light, all would have been interpreted with what amounted to superstitious beliefs. Modern hand-analysts take into account the general hirsuteness of the individual in relation to the hair that is found growing on his or her hands.

The one reliable indication in this respect is where a discrepancy occurs between the texture of the skin and that of the hair. Fine skin with coarse, stubbly hair or coarse skin with silky hair may each, in certain cases, be pointing to a hormonal disorder.

SHAPES AND SIZES

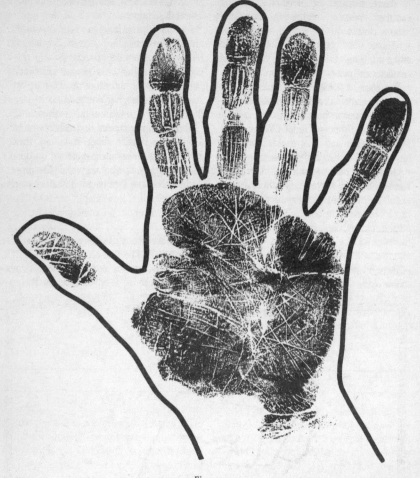

Figure 24

Determining character from the size and shape of the backs of people's hands is not only good practice but also helps to while away an amusing quarter-of-an-hour stuck at the bus stop or waiting in the check-out queue at the local supermarket. Any observations made can be matched to the behaviour of the individual or to the contents detected in her supermarket trolley!

People with small hands and short fingers are generally of the impatient type. They will fiddle and fidget the whole time they are waiting for the bus.

Long-fingered people pay a great deal of

attention to detail which will be reflected in the way they carry themselves, in their clothes and in their accessories.

Large, broad hands belong to active types, so they might be expected to wear casual or sporty clothes.

Those with square, blunt-fingered hands take a 'no nonsense' approach to life. Their trolleys, then, are likely to be filled with good, wholesome, nourishing foodstuffs. Products in their baskets will reflect value for money.

Longer, leaner hands will go for the more aesthetically packaged goods. They have a refined palate and their baskets will reflect quality as opposed to quantity.

Podgy hands reveal a touch of indolence and their owners adore luxury and the *dolce vita*. Their shopping trolley, then, may well contain convenience foods amongst the choice delicacies with which they like to treat themselves and their families.

Thin, small and very narrow hands are a sign of selfishness. Owners of this type of hand tend to be fastidious, a factor that is reflected in their bearing and general behaviour.

Long fingers with prominent joints are a sign of careful thinkers. They have discerning tastes and will spend a considerable time comparing products for quality and price.

People with fingers which have only the basal joints pronounced, as in Figure 24, will be very particular about how they dress. Orderliness is extremely important to them. Consequently, these types will always appear neat and tidy, well groomed with not a hair out of place.

THE KNUCKLES

The back of the hand exposes the knuckles to view, particularly when the hand is at rest or formed into a fist. Just as the finger joints highlight a sense of tidiness and method, so

Figure 25

the shape of the knuckles confirm and even magnify that need for order in the individual's life.

Neatness in personal appearance together with a coordinated sense of dress are of paramount importance to those whose first knuckle is noticeably pronounced. But if it is the second knuckle that stands out in relation to the rest, as in Figure 25, then the emphasis is laid on a need for a tidy environment and surroundings in which to live and operate. People with this formation may be considered houseproud.

The talent for putting just the right finishing touches that gives everything that little *je ne sais quoi* is revealed by a large knuckle at the base of the ring finger. With the little finger knuckle pronounced, the need for neatness and order will pervade all areas of the subject's life. These people may be compulsive 'tidy-uppers', for theirs is an instinctive need which cannot resist straightening the crooked picture, for example, or methodically rearranging the objects on a table.

CHARACTER IN THE NAILS

Chapter 2 described the growth, development and composition of the nails from the anatomical standpoint. Over the centuries, however, chirologists have observed that certain shapes of nails are associated with particular behaviour and character traits.

Both the size and shape of the nails should be proportionately in keeping with the fingers and hand in general. A long and slender finger requires a long, slender fingernail. A short, blunt finger is in harmony with a small, square nail.

Large nails on a small hand or, conversely, tiny nails on a big hand are noteworthy because such a discrepancy would highlight the existence of contradictions within the character and temperament of the individual.

Equally, a discrepant nail within a whole set, either because of its size or of its shape (though bearing in mind its relative size to the finger), would focus attention on the particular sphere of influence denoted by the digit on which it occurs. For example, a smaller nail on the ring finger might suggest a blockage in the creative expression of the individual.

Just as hand shapes may be classified as basically square or oblong, long or short, so

Figure 26

too, do nails fall into the similar fundamental categories of wide or narrow, long or short. Length, of course, does not comprise the white tip in this case for when the nail is assessed only the pink, living part is taken into consideration. And the shape, too, is determined by the pinkish quick, irrespective of its white tip which may be manicured and filed according to fashion.

The best type of nail to possess is one preferably with parallel sides (Figure 26) either square or oblong in shape according to the finger it is on, and with a neat white moon. Its colour should match that of the palm, topped with a natural lustre or sheen. There should be a gentle curve from side to side and from the root to the top of the quick. For a well-balanced nail in good proportion to the finger, the pink living part should be roughly half as long as the top phalanx on which it sits.

In general it is recognized that small nails reflect a critical outlook. Perhaps this is because small nails normally accompany short fingers and the shorter the fingers, the quicker, the more active and intuitive the individual.

Large nails, just as implied by a broad hand, indicate a more steady and easygoing temperament. A set of these nails denotes a calm and placid disposition, someone with good judgement and good sense.

The four categories of wide, narrow, long or short may occur in permutation so as to produce several basic, well-documented nail shapes.

Broad nails, with a wide, square base denote a strong, robust character with a well-balanced outlook and disposition (Figure 27a). It is the solid square base of the nail that confers the sense of strength and stability to the subject.

When the nail is broad, so that it is much wider than it is high, it usually denotes a temper that is easily roused (Figure 27b). But, though volcanic, once the anger has flashed there is no smouldering moodiness or lasting resentment with these types. The short broad nail tends to be seen more often than not on the thumb.

Another in the wide category is the shell or fan-shaped nail (Figure 27c). Here, the sides slope to a pointed base weakening its

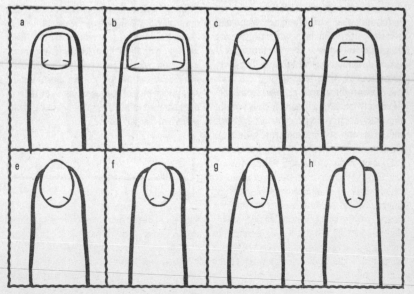

Figure 27

strength and balancing influence thus associating it with a certain nervous instability that goes with a highly-strung disposition.

Small square nails, where quite a lot of the finger is seen above and to the sides of them, warn of narrow-mindedness (Figure 27d). People with this nail shape are highly critical types, lacking warmth and love for their fellow men. The bigoted, narrow views implicated here are associated with fanaticism and fundamentalism.

Filbert-shaped nails have a romantic nature (Figure 27e). They are, in general, placid types with a slow temper, for they require a peaceful and harmonious environment in which to live. In fact, they actively run away, whether mentally or physically, from any situation that threatens to undermine that balance and harmony in their lives. People with this nail shape have a habit of sulking – perhaps a strategy for shutting themselves away from, rather than confronting, unpleasant situations.

Almond-shaped nails (Figure 27f) are slightly narrower than the filbert shape and are usually found on the hands of people who are gentle and refined. They are dreamy and sensitive, kind and loyal to those they love. When roused, they tend to be cross with themselves rather than angry towards others.

People with long but narrow nails are not physically active types for they lack robustness and physical energy (Figure 27g).

They do, however, possess a sensitive nervous system and are keenly intuitive types.

In extreme cases, the nail becomes very narrow, pointed both at the root and the tip (Figure 27h). When all the nails in the hand tend towards this shape they imply a grabbing, calculating disposition verging, at times, on the neurotic.

THE COLOUR OF NAILS

Just as white skin represents egocentricity so, too, a very white nail will point to selfishness. Such people can be cold and aloof with a rather cynical attitude to life.

Similarly with redness of skin, red nails denote an irascible disposition. Those who possess such nails as a matter of course tend to be impulsive types with unpredictable and fiery, angry tempers.

A warm, even temper goes with a healthy-looking pink nail or, in African and Asian races, with a nail whose colouring closely resembles that of the palm.

But although the pigmentation of the nail does play a small part in the assessment of character, any discoloration of the nail, together with its lustre or lack of it, is more an indication of the state of the individual's health. So too are blemishes, the condition and prevalence of the moons and any defects or general abnormalities in the normal growth pattern of the nail itself.

CHAPTER FIVE

HAND TYPES

It was d'Arpentigny in the nineteenth century who first devised a practical classification system of hand shapes. Having studied thousands of hands, he came to recognize that similar shapes tended to recur. Moreover, he discovered that particular personality traits were associated with each kind of shape and that these characteristics differed markedly from one category of shape to another.

His research led him to deduce that all hands could be classified into a mere half-dozen categories – six pure types plus one other which was to include all hands that simply did not comply with any of the other six. He named the pure types **Elementary**, **Square**, **Conical**, **Spatulate**, **Psychic** and **Philosophical**. The seventh category, which was to be the catch-all for any nonconformist hands, he labelled **Mixed**. The seven different shapes are illustrated in Figure 28.

The value of recognizing to which category a hand belongs is that it lays down the fundamental characteristics of the individual. It is, if you like, the foundation – the bottom line – upon which the rest of the analysis is based. Types of fingers, quality of lines, nails, skin markings and the rest, all consequently embellish and refine the picture of the individual that is slowly being constructed.

That only a few basic similar shapes do recur may seem obvious to us now; it appears however that this fact was not historically

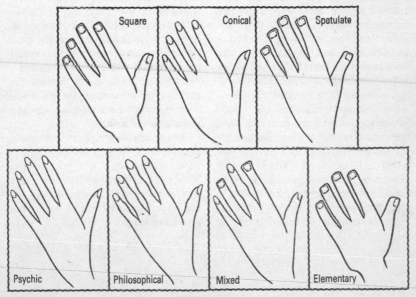

Figure 28

recognized, or at least if it was, it has not been documented. The d'Arpentigny classification system was a landmark in its time and was quickly accepted and widely used throughout the nineteenth and early twentieth centuries. Indeed, many chirologists and modern hand analysts still use it to this day.

And yet, despite its intrinsic value, d'Arpentigny's system has posed certain difficulties, not only amongst beginners who find it almost impossible to match hands to the six pure types, but also amongst the modern, more scientific practitioners of the study who find some of the categories arbitrary and specious.

It is the Elementary category in particular that has caused a good deal of disquiet in recent times. For, whether it is that hands subtly evolve, or whether we are constantly refining our ideas, it would seem that the Elementary hand no longer belongs to a world that is fast approaching the twenty-first century.

The Philosophical hand has likewise been rejected as a pure type because the features that represent a philosophical turn of mind may be found to exist across all the categories.

And, although the other categories that d'Arpentigny has described do indeed occur, very few hands actually conform exactly to the pure types so that most hands are now relegated to the miscellaneous bag that has so appropriately been named the Mixed hand.

THE ELEMENTARY HAND

This hand is characterized by its thick, coarse appearance. The fingers are extremely short and stiff and the thumb is invariably described as bulbous or 'clubbed'.

The Elementary character is described as basically unintelligent, an atavistic type who works mainly on instinct. These people are not conferred with powers of higher reasoning, as ascribed to the Philosophical category, nor thought capable of aesthetic sense or lofty ideals, such as the Conic or Psychic types might possess. But they operate on the material level, very often with primitive astuteness and cunning. Emotionally touchy, they can be docile one moment and fly off the handle the next. In general, they are prey to their own passions and tempers, which can make them prone to sudden bursts of violence, particularly if they feel misunderstood.

The damning negativity attributed to this type has, in recent times, brought the whole category into question and in fact discredited it as a product of the nineteenth-century's rigid class system. Even the Evolved Elementary type – an attempt to attribute at least a few higher qualities to the basic character – seems to cast many doubts.

And yet, despite its Victorian imputations, instances of the hand do still occur. In particular, evidence would seem to suggest that when found in the West, this hand shape tends to exist amongst a few mentally subnormal types or those who suffer from certain genetic malformations.

THE PHILOSOPHICAL HAND

This hand has a large palm topped by very long, bony fingers with characteristic protruberant joints which are the hallmark of the Philosophical type. The second phalanx of the thumb, being unusually long, especially stands out.

The Philosophical category, just as its name implies, is associated with the deep thinker, with those who possess excellent powers of reason and logic. They are born with inquiring and investigative mentalities – unable to leave a thing or a concept alone without minutely scrutinizing and analysing it. But their constant need to process information suggests they can be slow to respond or to show a reaction which can be somewhat frustrating to others around them. Seekers after truth, they are the great sceptics of the world and yet perhaps belong to the most fair-minded and tolerant of all the categories for they are ever prepared to weigh up the merits and defects of any system or situation.

This category has now noticeably been dropped as one of the pure types amongst both modern and traditionalist practitioners who still follow the d'Arpentigny system.

In terms of characterization, the Philosophical temperament is indeed valid, but it is the characteristic 'knotty' fingers which highlight that personality rather than the type of hand *per se*. Moreover, the Philosophical fingers may occur on any of the other shapes of palms where they would confer the same power of deep, analytical thought to the mentality on whichever hand they appear.

THE MIXED HAND

The Mixed hand is instantly recognized for its mixture of fingertip shapes, possessing a collection of square, conic and spatulate tips. This category contains a mixed bag of different-shaped palms and fingers and anything that doesn't belong to the pure categories is dumped into here. No wonder, then, that it has always been considered the most common type!

The mixed elements that are contained in this hand reflect the variety of interests that attract these subjects. Consequently, they may be described as multitalented people, Jacks of all Trades, able to tackle a wide range of subjects and skills. But, because of this very diversity, they may lack the specialization required to bring any one of their talents to ultimate success. Nevertheless, they are happy to take a broad approach, contented to scatter their nets widely, for it is their very diversity that makes them flexible and tolerant so that they can easily adapt to varying situations and circumstances. And it is their adaptability, too, that keeps them optimistic and cheerful no matter what vicissitudes life has to offer.

Though doubt has been cast on these three categories, it does not detract from the fact that a classification system is valuable and one cannot get away from the premiss that certain shapes can and do recur. For this reason some hand analysts still continue to use the d'Arpentigny categories although, it would seem, in a modified form. More recently, it appears, many who still adhere to this system have refined the categories to just four, concentrating only on the Square, the Conic, the Spatulate and the Psychic.

THE SQUARE HAND

The palm is as broad as it is long. The fingers are the same width all the way up and the fingertips are squared off giving the whole hand a square, rather blunt appearance.

Essentially, people with this type of palm are hard, steady workers. They are practical and level-headed with masses of common sense. Earthy by nature, they are the doers and never afraid to roll up their sleeves and pitch in when needed. Routine is important to them and so is law and order. They work best in the outdoors rather than cooped up in an office all day long. At work, they have a tendency to go by the rule book and to work steadily if not a little ploddingly. So perhaps they tend to lack imagination but they more than make up for it with their industry and practical expertise.

THE CONIC HAND

The hand has a rounded palm with tapered fingers and gently rounded fingertips. It is a much more fluid, rounder type than the square hand. The fingers are a little longer than the palm giving it the appearance of a cone shape.

In comparison to the Square hand this is a much more sensual hand and reflects feminine qualities. Those who possess it tend to be creative and imaginative. They are enthusiastic, adaptable, lively people who need plenty of variety for stimulation. Unlike the square-handed people, they hate the tedium of routine but need to be kept buzzing about always one step ahead. Highly intuitive, they can read between the lines, catch on at a glance and are fast learners. They are excellent at organization but not so good at sticking to the same thing day in, day out.

THE SPATULATE HAND

Palms and fingers are slightly elongated. The fingertips are bulbous, especially the middle fingers, although the tips of the index and little fingers may not be quite so pronounced. The hand gives the appearance of a spatula.

There are two versions of the spatulate palm. One is characterized as very broad and heavy at the base and tapering up towards the fingers. The other is wider at the top and narrows down towards the wrist. Both are signs of energy and activity. The first shows physical power and strength and many sportsmen have this formation.

The second shows an active mind, often people whose thinking is well ahead of their time – and because of it are sometimes considered a bit cranky! This is the sign of the inventor, the creator, the explorer and the pioneer. They too work hard and are always on the go, whether physically or mentally but, unlike the Square, they like to generate their own ideas, for their minds are extremely inventive, with a rich and fertile imagination.

THE PSYCHIC HAND

The Psychic hand has an oblong palm and very long tapering fingers that end in rounded tips. It is unmistakable for its general leanness and for its length, making it the most elegant of all the types.

Despite its name it doesn't necessarily mean that these people have psychic powers although they do tend to be very sensitive folk indeed. And because of their sensitivity they can be anxious, highly-strung individuals. These are the dreamers, the poets and the artists among us. Invariably, they are elegant and refined types with a strong eye for beauty. Often impractical in the extreme, they seem not to be of this world at all but live in the clouds. They are not really suited to the nitty-gritty of everyday living and need someone more worldly to help them with the realities of life. But, without the beauty they generate and inspire, this world would be a much duller place.

Modern hand analysts, however, have adopted a new approach. Taking their cue from Noel Jaquin, one of this century's greatest hand analysts, they have simplified the whole classification system.

From years of observation they have concluded that hands are either short and broad or long and narrow. The broader the hand, the more solid and stable the character; the more active and outgoing the personality. With a long, narrow hand the nature is more internalized, more introspective and, at the far end of this scale, the very thin, narrow hand denotes a completely self-centred individual.

Fingers, they deduced, whatever shape they come in, are either long or short in comparison to the palm. The longer the fingers, the more patient, methodical and analytical the mentality. The shorter the fingers, the sharper the mind and the more instinctive and spontaneous, though less patient, the behaviour.

So the new classification system is based on two simple dimensions: whether the palm is square or oblong and whether the fingers are long or short. Using this formula, four permutations are derived which have been named after the four ancient elements of Earth, Air, Fire and Water (Figure 29).

Incidentally, character-wise and in appearance, these are not too dissimilar to the d'Arpentigny refined system of Square, Conic, Spatulate and Psychic. The **Square** type corresponds to the **Earth** hand, the **Conic** to the **Air**, the **Spatulate** to the **Fire** and the **Psychic** to the **Water** type.

THE EARTH HAND

The Earth hand is recognized by its **square palms and short fingers**. The palm contains only the barest essential major lines, which are clear and well chiselled. Loop or arch fingerprint patterns are mainly associated with this type.

Earth is an excellent analogy for this type. From rich fertile plain to barren wilderness, from mountains to valleys, from rock to mud, from soil to lava, earth reflects in its many forms the solidity and immovability, the permanence, denseness and implacability, the stodginess, grip and fertility of the Earth individual. But beware benign Mother Earth for she can, when forced, show the power that's locked beneath the surface with its undercurrent of slow, rumbling menace that builds up and builds up until at last it volcanically explodes.

So Earth individuals are characterized as solid as a rock. Like the fertile soil, they like to produce, which means they are great makers, doers and menders. They are sensible and emotionally stable people. Earthy or down-to-earth are expressions commonly used to refer to these types. Hard workers and practical, they like working with their hands and tend to work at their own pace, stolidly and routinely. Indeed, they like to live and work to a set pattern, becoming rather disgruntled if their routine is upset. At work, they plod along persistently and methodically, unperturbed and unflappable.

They are conservative in life, especially so as they get older, and are great believers in discipline and in the status quo, maintaining and upholding law and order. Security, too, is very important to them.

Earth types make steady and loyal friends but, should they feel a serious injustice has been done to them, they will rumble and smoulder for a long time. Then, one day when they are ready, they erupt with the sort of ferocity that would match anything that a Vesuvius or a Mount St Helen may have to offer.

THE AIR HAND

The Air hand is recognized by its **square palm and long fingers.** Its lines are clear and well formed. The fingerprints are usually loops.

Air is invisible but all pervasive. It is the gentle breeze that scatters the seed, that fans the flame, that cools the heat on a summer's day. It is the oxygen we breathe, the carbon dioxide we expel, the hydrogen that violently explodes. It is the blustery winds of March, the mistral that chills the bones, the thick simoom that chokes and suffocates, the tornado that rips out trees by the roots, sweeps them to the heavens and hurls them crashing back to earth again.

Like the element, Air types are characterized by their changeableness. But it is this very mutability that makes them not only fascinating people but also fascinated in everything that is going on around them. They have a deep and burning curiosity, always needing to know, to investigate, to find out.

And it is this curiosity about life that gives them such a buzzing mentality and inquiring mind. Because of this they can be bookish, enjoying school and academic life to the full. And they're quick learners, too. Their minds, fast as quicksilver, pick things up in a flash. Sometimes, however, their desire for information may be so widespread that their knowledge can end up rather superficial.

People belonging to the Air category are lively, talkative, social individuals who enjoy being surrounded by people. Communications are their great joy in life and because of it many are attracted to the media, to writing in general and to anything connected with travel. Work must be stimulating. Anything dull and monotonous would bore their socks off and have them screaming all the way to the nearest employment office.

Emotionally they are well balanced and well able to control their passions and their tempers. Like the element from which they take their names, though, they can appear rather cool at times and somewhat standoffish.

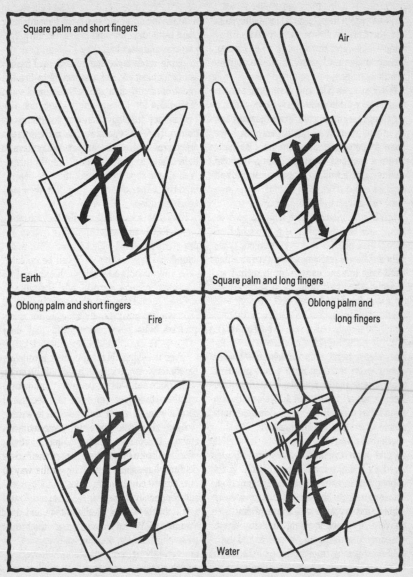

Square palm and short fingers

Air

Earth

Square palm and long fingers

Oblong palm and short fingers

Fire

Oblong palm and long fingers

Water

Figure 29

THE FIRE HAND

The Fire type is recognized by its oblong palm and short fingers. It normally contains many lines which are strong and well formed. Whorl fingerprint patterns figure prominently with this type.

Fire generates heat and warmth and light. In darkness it can show the way, in gloom it provides comfort, in cold it can thaw the ice. From vital spark to candle flame, from fierce blaze to glowing embers, fire takes its many forms. Contained, it can produce power and energy. Uncontrolled, it can consume and devastate, indiscriminately laying waste anything that may stand in its path.

Just like the element from which it takes its name, the Fire individual is a dynamic live-wire. These people are active, energetic types who are always on the go. Fairly sporty, they like adventure and excitement in their lives.

Indeed, life is very busy and bustling for these types and they tend to live it to the full.

Warm and friendly, they have a knack of inspiring others with their boundless enthusiasm and magnetic personalities. Fun-loving and uninhibited, they can be the life and soul of the party.

They are intelligent and as bright as a button. They make good leaders and excellent organizers with their positive outlook and their ability to motivate those around them. Well able to cope with stress, they are happy to carry responsibility in any sort of managerial position.

They may act impulsively for they possess an excitable and volatile nature which is prone to emotional display and flashes of temper.

THE WATER HAND

The Water hand is unmistakeable for its oblong palm and long fingers. It is instantly recognizable for its abundance of fine lines looking for all the world as if a spider has spun its web across the palm. This type commonly sports loop fingerprints.

Without water there would be no life. It soothes and refreshes, washes and cleans, assuages thirst and ends the drought. From babbling stream to cascading torrent, from gentle rain to torrential flood, from silently glistening snowflake to a storm of hail that can destroy a harvest overnight. It may lie on the surface glacial cold or, foaming geyser, well up steaming from the belly of the earth. Indifferent to form, it takes its shape from the vessel into which it pours itself. And, drop by drop, it can in time wear away even the hardest stone.

Of all the types this is the most sensitive. Emotionally tender, they have soft, limpid eyes which seem never far away from tears, whether of sorrow or of joy, for they are people who are easily hurt but just as easily pleased. They tend to live very much by their emotions, prone to changes of mood, often swinging from the heights of happiness to the depths of despair. But if they feel hurt or misunderstood, they can become moody and sulk for days at a time.

Water types are especially known for their dreamy, poetic natures, living all too often with their heads in the clouds. They are of a quiet and thoughtful disposition, passive and contemplative, ever gentle and caring towards both man and beast. Highly cultured, they are passionate about beauty, music and all forms of the Arts. And they are noted especially for their good taste, their refinement and urbanity.

At work, they tend to gravitate towards the creative and artistic fields, happy in their infinite patience to bury themselves in the most minute and detailed work. When it comes to the nitty-gritty of life, they can be somewhat impractical, and tend to run away, if not physically then psychologically, from any thing or situation that displeases them or which they feel unable to deal with. For happiness and peace of mind, the Water types need to find a peaceful, harmonious environment in which to work and live because they cannot really cope with the pressures and stresses of modern life.

Just as water has no shape of its own, so the Water type is impressionable and easily led – and all too often, easily taken for a ride.

CHAPTER SIX

DIVISIONS OF THE PALM

An analysis of the hand is built on the premiss that different areas of our palms represent different aspects of our lives.

Classically, it has been held that the hand may be divided into specific sections, first horizontally, then vertically, and finally into discrete zones according to the topography of the hand itself.

By sectioning the hand in this way it is possible to gauge which areas predominate and which, perhaps, are deficient. Any sector that stands out, whether because it dominates by its size, or is noticeably weaker than the rest, will throw the spotlight on those outstanding aspects in the individual's life which are represented by that particular area.

Dividing the hand into sections is also a clever device for assisting the interpretation of the lines in the palm. Imagine that the lines are like rivers that carry energy and that flow from one part of the country to another. Supposing that one of those rivers rises from a predominantly peat-laden terrain so that its waters have an acid quality to them. Wherever it irrigates, the river will leave behind that acidic deposit. But if it rises from a chalk-based source, its predominant quality will be alkaline, tainting its waters with a limy residue.

In just such a way, then, it is possible to deduce that the qualities represented by a certain line will be coloured and influenced by the particular sector from which the line originates. Thus it can be seen that to localize the various centres in the palm is of great intrinsic value, firstly because this provides a means of focusing attention on individual characteristics and, subsequent to that, as a guide to the interpretation of the lines.

These basic divisions fundamentally separate out the mental from the physical qualities, and the conscious from the subconscious.

The horizontal division cuts the palm into two just above the root of the thumb thus separating the physical, at the base of the hand, from the mental, which is located across the top beneath the fingers (Figure 30).

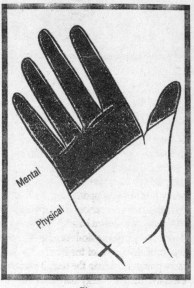

Figure 30

With a vertical dividing line (Figure 31), cutting down from the centre of the middle finger to the wrist, the rational, conscious world is differentiated from that of the subconscious and instinctive.

If the two divisions are then superimposed one on top of the other, the palm is then subdivided further into quadrants as in Figure 32.

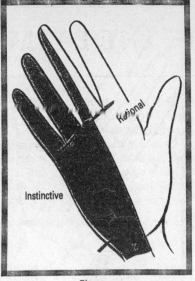

Figure 31

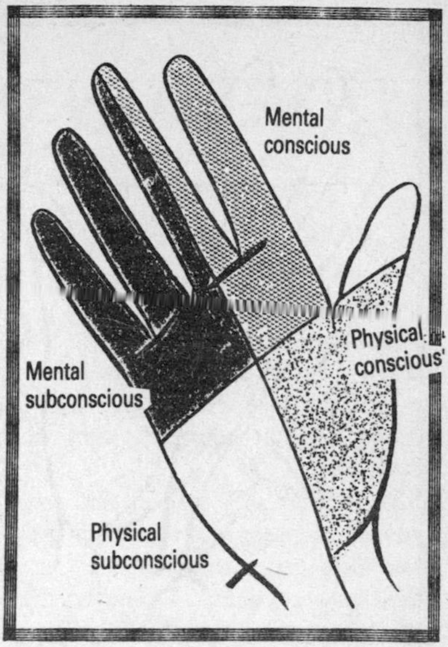

Figure 32

The two basal quadrants of the palm together represent the energy store, the power house of the body. Here, the *physical* qualities of the individual, the energy and vitality are assessed. To possess a well-developed base to the palm is indicative of physical strength. Many athletes and sporty men and women have this area pronounced in their hands.

A poorly developed base to the palm, then, denotes a lack of physical stamina. When the top, or mental part, of the hand is markedly more pronounced than the base, it warns that excessive mental energy may force the body to work well beyond its physical capabilities and dangerously deplete its energy resources.

The principle line to be found in this area is the Life line, appropriately dealing with physical aspects in our lives (Figure 33). Beginning as it does in the mental/physical sector, it shows our awareness of the quality, or tenor, of our lives in relation to our physical strengths and weaknesses.

The Health line, too, takes root from this area, corroborating the Life line and reflecting aspects of our health and well-being.

Here, too, is the normal beginning of the Fate line before it powers its way upwards into the mental domain. It takes its influence from the physical source, describing our early roots and how we each materially interpret these for ourselves in terms of our standing in relation to the outside world.

Also from the base of the hand, but from the subconscious area, springs the line of Intuition, bringing our innermost instinctive thoughts to light.

The area across the base of the hand incorporates the Mount of Venus in the physical/conscious sector and the Mount of Luna in the opposite sector of physical/subconscious. The area that connects the two is known as the Mount of Neptune. Figure 34 maps these three basal mounts on the hand.

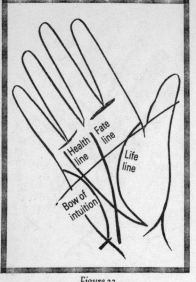

Figure 33

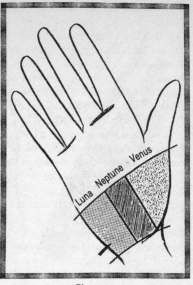

Figure 34

THE MOUNT OF VENUS

Because the Mount of Venus is located in that quadrant which comprises both the conscious and the physical, it represents energy, vitality and strength. Interestingly, the whole area is bounded by the longitudinal curve that is known as the Life line thus corroborating the physical symbolism of this mount.

Anatomically, it is known as the **thenar eminence** and is the padding, or fibrous tissue, that covers muscles and tendons to the thumb and the radial artery entering from the wrist. The fleshier the mount the more muscle and better protection to the blood vessel. The leaner the area, the less muscle tissue there is and the more vulnerable and exposed the artery. It is this muscular development that in hand analysis symbolizes the measurement of strength and vitality of the individual.

The Mount of Venus is also referred to as the ball of the thumb. Easily recognized, and perhaps the most well-known mount in the hand, it is that fleshy pad at the root of the thumb that extends across to the centre of the palm and down to the wrist at the base of the hand.

As seen in the previous chapter on fingers, each digit is composed of three separate phalanges whilst the thumb appears to be made up of only two. In fact, it also has three sections and it is this mount which, in effect, isn't really a mount at all but in essence the third phalanx of the thumb.

PSYCHOLOGICAL CHARACTERISTICS

The appearance and condition of this mount is most revealing for it is considered the reservoir of the individual's life energies, sexuality, health and general enthusiasm for living.

A thick, well-padded area here denotes physical strength and plenty of sexual drive. Those with a large Mount of Venus are healthy, robust types with a good deal of vitality. Magnetic and charismatic, they have a love of life, a *joie de vivre*, that pervades all they do and colours all their relationships.

Usually this type will enjoy robust good health. They have excellent recuperative powers which help them to shake off most illnesses whether of a physical or psychological nature.

But if the mount is underdeveloped, looks pale and vapid so that the Life line tightly encircles the thumb, it denotes a lack of vitality and low physical resources. Their personality seems to lack warmth and empathy and they have been described as cold and aloof, withdrawn and either unable or unwilling to project themselves outwards.

Health-wise they tend to be physically delicate, often prone to whatever infection is doing the rounds. And when ill it takes them much longer to recover than their colleagues with the fuller mount.

Named after the Greek goddess of love, the Mount of Venus represents the instincts of love and sex. When this area is full and extensive it points to a need for physical gratification and sexual pleasure. When firm and springy, love is paramount but when flabby and spongy it is pure sensuality that is sought with a strong desire for the pleasures of the senses and what religious ascetics might refer

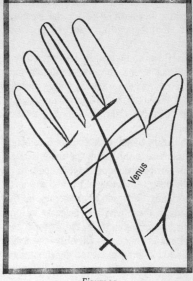

Figure 35

to as 'the gratification of the flesh'. Too firm, however, so that the padding feels rock hard, is a sign of steely self-control.

But Venus was not only the goddess of love, she was also the goddess of beauty, so this mount gives information about one's aesthetic tastes. A high, well-padded mount will reflect a cultured individual, someone who needs to be surrounded by beauty and who prefers to live and work in a beautiful and harmonious environment. A love of music and of the arts in general is usually highlighted by this type of mount.

THE MOUNT OF LUNA

The Mount of Luna, or **hypothenar** to give it its anatomical name, is found on the opposite, percussion, side of the palm. It lies at the base of the hand where the palm meets the wrist.

Just as the Venus area in the first quadrant is the powerhouse of physical or active energy, so here this sector is the powerhouse not of active but of the passive energy that comes from the unconscious mind.

The Mount of Luna, or moon, is associated with the imagination, with racial memory, with the hidden processes of the subconscious.

Creativity and originality are denoted by a large mount when the area forms a generous curve on the percussion and bulges over the wrist. When full and also firm to the touch, it highlights the ability to generate creative ideas.

A narrow mount with a pronounced bump at the base overhanging the wrist is often seen on the hands of sensitive, perceptive individuals with keen intuition and powers of prescience. This formation occurs in the hands of those who are somehow in tune with Nature, receptive to the rhythms and cycles of Mother Earth. They have the ability to pick up vibrations, to feel the atmosphere of a situation or of a place, to read between the lines.

A corollary to that receptivity to rhythms is that people with this formation often make excellent dancers. Models, too, with their poise and feel for movement may also possess this feature.

A hand which noticeably lacks the development of this mount denotes a dearth of imagination and impoverished subconscious powers. Creativity here is very scarce.

A soft, flabby area here, and one which is very pale in colour, may point to a need for escapism either through alcoholism or the abuse of drugs. Moodiness, too, and a changeable, vacillating temperament is denoted by this feature.

Lunacy and lunatics derive from Luna, the Latin word for the moon, because historically it was believed that it was the moon that

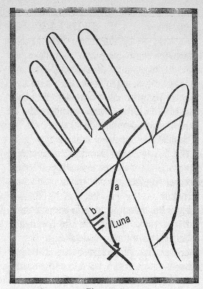

Figure 36

caused insanity. Interestingly, a highly anxious disposition, a wild imagination (one that runs out of control) or the inability to differentiate between fantasy and reality are all highlighted by a large Luna mount which is either heavily crossed with fine lines or which has a steeply sloping Head line (Figure 36a), dipping right down into its depths.

The moon's association with fluids and its gravitational pull upon the tides is yet another aspect which is reflected in this mount linking it to journeys and voyages overseas. Deep horizontal lines in this sector (Figure 36b) indicate journeys, as do any branches from the Life line that sweep down in this direction and usually denote movement of some kind or other.

THE MOUNT OF NEPTUNE

In between the two mounts, just above the wrist, lies the Mount of Neptune. This is a comparatively new addition to the mount divisions and, because it is not found in traditional palmistry, many hand analysts still refuse to acknowledge it as a mount in its own right.

Straddled by the two basal giants, it is located in the physical band of the hand but part of it lies in the conscious and part in the subconscious quadrants.

In many hands the Mount of Neptune is barely noticeable at all, the palm forming itself into a cleft between the two major mounts. In others, it is almost indistinguishable from the Mount of Luna, appearing as a continuation of that area.

But when it is well developed so that it stands out, it always throws the spotlight on someone who has a charismatic personality, who seems capable of fitting in right across the social strata with confidence and ease. Such people leave a lasting impression and are both admired and well loved by all who come into contact with them.

The top of the palm represents the *mental* or intellectual power of the individual. Just as the basal areas are the physical powerhouses, this part of the hand is the storehouse or reservoir of **mental** energy.

Well developed, this area points to a strong intellect. When this band is the most dominant – larger, fuller, wider than the base of the hand – it suggests that the intellectual energy is more powerful than the physical resources. Such individuals tend to be more intellectual, or spiritual, types. Physical jerks are not their idea of fun. As children, they are the ones who loathe sports and would go to almost any lengths to find an excuse to sit in the library and read rather than run around on the football pitch, or have to sweat it out in the gym. Armchair sports are much more

Figure 37

their style.

Those, however, with a pronounced bulge on the percussion just below the little finger have what is known as a 'fidgety' mind. Here, the mental energy is overactive, always on the go, never tiring or willing to shut down.

Such people can't sit still or watch television without thinking and planning, turning things over in their minds, working out tomorrow night's menu, next week's activities, the annual family holiday. And they have difficulty, too, switching off at night, the day's events intermingling with tomorrow's plans, revolving endlessly round and round in their minds.

It is this formation that warns against overtaxing one's physical reserves. Intellectually, these individuals are amazingly active and tend to push their bodies beyond their natural limits, often to the point of sheer physical exhaustion. Mental relaxation exercises, yoga

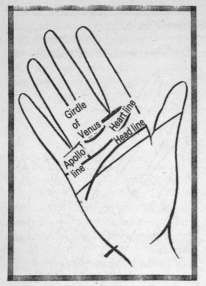

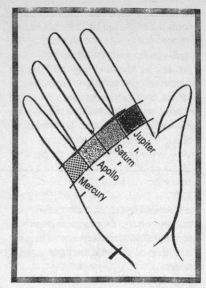

Figure 38   Figure 39

or any pastime that helps to slow down the mind and give the body time to rest and recoup will be greatly beneficial to these types.

As Figure 38 shows, the two lines that are predominantly located across the mental sector are the Head and Heart lines. For the Head line this would indeed be its natural environment and it is interesting to note that the higher up the line occurs the more logical, rational and pragmatic the individual. Sometimes the line dips down into the Luna area, where the physical/subconscious sector would imbue it with inspiration, imagination and expansive vision.

The Heart line, however, high in the mental sector, would seem out of place here. But, unlike the Head line, it takes its roots from the mental/subconscious area and travels out towards the mental/conscious side of the hand thus representing how we become aware of our deeper emotional feelings and drives, and showing how we outwardly express those feelings to others and to

the world in general.

Some hand analysts would argue, too, that the higher sublimation of the intellect is the spirit and it is the topmost band across the palm that represents the spiritual aspects of the individual's life. The Heart line here, then, is expressing the more spiritual values of the mind.

This argument would hold true when considering the Girdle of Venus which is also located in this area and which denotes heightened sensitivity. But more so, it would explain the Apollo line's representation of contentment and self-fulfilment, especially so when it occurs above the Heart line.

The area across the top of the palm incorporates the Mounts of Jupiter and Saturn in the mental/conscious quadrant and the Mounts of Apollo and Mercury on the opposite side in the mental/subconscious quarter (Figure 39).

These four top mounts reflect the characteristics and attributes of the Roman gods of mythology from which they take their names.

And it is the way in which each of the four mounts across this top band are individually developed that focuses on how the individual uniquely expresses that mental energy.

Just as it is important to take note whether the top band of the palm is more pronounced than the basal area, or the ulna (subconscious) more dominant than the radius (conscious), so it is important to note if any of the top mounts appear more or less developed than its neighbours. A dominant Mercury, for example, would suggest that the qualities represented by that mount are salient in the character of the individual. Similarly, a deficiency in any of the mounts would immediately point to a weakness or a lacking of those attributes in question.

THE MOUNT OF JUPITER

The Mount of Jupiter is situated beneath the index finger and is located in the mental/conscious quadrant. Named after Jupiter, the Roman god, or Zeus in Greek mythology, it represents the conscious awareness of the self or of the ego.

As Zeus was the supreme deity, the leader of all the other gods, so leadership is one of the qualities associated with this area. Ambition and pride in oneself are also both represented here. So too is a sense of personal power.

A large expanse here may denote keen sociopolitical interests with a strong awareness of environmental problems and issues.

When normally developed, so that the mount looks well proportioned in relation to its neighbours, it shows that all the Jupiterian attributes are held in good balance. The qualities of leadership, one's sense of power and personal pride are all kept within reasonable bounds.

But if the mount is overdeveloped so that it seems to swamp all the others, it reveals an egotistical nature. Pride deteriorates into arrogance, and ambition becomes overweening. In extreme cases, such people are domineering, especially so in positions of power where they rule with a fist of iron, despotic and tyrannical towards others.

When the mount is weak in comparison to the others it tells of a lack of pride in oneself, in one's appearance, work or achievement. A deficiency here would highlight a general lack of drive and impetus in the individual's life.

THE MOUNT OF SATURN

Theoretically, the Mount of Saturn is located in the conscious/mental quadrant, although – bridging the two top quarters as it does – part of it may take some influence from its neighbouring mental/subconscious sector.

In ancient Rome the god Saturn was worshipped as the patron of corn for he took his name from the Latin word for sowing. Thus grew the symbolism of this area, and that of the middle finger above, as denoting the basic wherewithal for living. From Kronos, Saturn's Greek counterpart, comes the association with time, with learning and with contemplation that sometimes, being inwardly directed, degenerates into gloom and despondency.

Because of its position beneath the middle finger, this mount is associated with balance and stability. Normal development here in relation to the other mounts tells of a well-balanced individual who takes responsibility seriously and philosophically. A love of study and research, one that goes with an inquiring mind, with scientific investigation and with a serious approach to life, is also denoted here.

Traditionally, it has always been held that a slight deficiency of this mount is preferable to one that is overdeveloped. For when the mount is too full it highlights a lugubriousness in the nature, a morbid disposition that might label its owner as a thoroughly wet blanket.

Conversely, a nonexistent mount tells of the sort of fecklessness that results from a deficient sense of responsibility and seriousness in life.

THE MOUNT OF APOLLO

The Mount of Apollo is situated beneath the ring finger in the mental/subconscious quadrant. Taking its attributes from the Roman sun god, this mount is associated with aesthetic appreciation, so creativity and the Arts are represented by this mount. But, in addition, it also deals with one's sense of happiness and contentment together with that sense of accomplishment that goes with the fulfilment of one's talents in life.

When of noticeably larger proportions in comparison to the rest, this mount denotes a sunny and happy disposition. There is a leaning towards creative and artistic talents and interests. The appreciation of beauty and the need for an aesthetic and harmonious environment are of great importance.

If this area is dramatically overdeveloped it highlights a narcissistic inclination. There will be pretension and affectation in the nature, and conceit and snobbery may result. Much about this individual will be larger than life and the behaviour will be markedly extravagant and showy.

Should the Mount of Apollo be conspicuous for its absence, it denotes a lack of refinement and a certain Philistinism when it comes to artistic or cultural matters.

THE MOUNT OF MERCURY

Situated beneath the little finger, the Mount of Mercury is firmly located in the mental/subconscious area.

In Roman mythology Mercury was the messenger to the gods, hence the association with communications, with verbal expression, indeed with all matters concerning the media.

Often this area merges into that of Apollo so that the two mounts blend into each other. As both are a form of communication, one personally creative and the other verbal, the idea of projecting the self through personal expression applies to both and may be interpreted together in this way.

A large area highlights a magnetic warmth of personality that attracts others and is able to communicate with them with ease and understanding.

With a full mount, the urge is towards verbal expression – but, too full, points to sheer garrulousness.

Apart from messenger, Mercury was also the patron of merchants and, interestingly, of thieves. It is this connection that adds the association with business and commerce

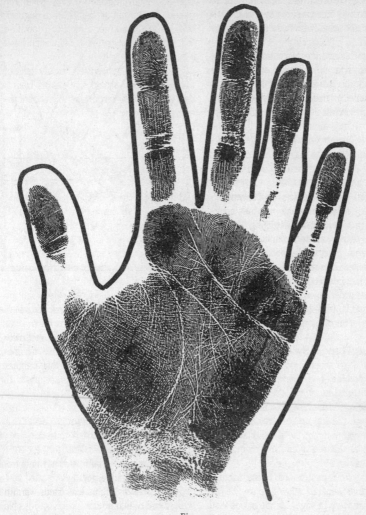

Figure 40

here, so that a good mount would denote excellent commercial skills and interests.

But his association with thieves adds the negative tendency, in any hand with too full a mount, towards cunning and deception. Double-dealing in business affairs and an inclination to mendacity are also reflected by this formation.

Deficiency of the mount, however, points to a block in one's ability to communicate with others. As sexual relations are also a form of deep personal communication, a deficiency here may equally suggest a problem when it comes to one's sexuality, especially so the inability sexually to express oneself satisfactorily.

In some hands the percussion edge here, just beneath the little finger, noticeably curves outwards (Figure 40). This is the sign of an individual who might be described as highly strung. It reveals a hyperactive mentality, a mind that finds difficulty relaxing but pushes the body to the very limits of its physical resources. When the basal sectors are also full, the individual can resist and withstand the mental pressure that is being exerted. But, should the base of the hand be deficient, it is possible that the excessive nervous tension would produce strain, depleting the little reserves of the body and eventually leading to mental and physical exhaustion.

The salient message with this formation is that the individual needs to learn mental relaxation in order to give the body time to regenerate its batteries and generally replenish its reserves of energy.

The central band of the palm, known as the zone of Mars (Figure 41), is that grey area which combines both physical and mental in the horizontal plain and the conscious and subconscious in the vertical plain.

In effect, the area acts as a balancer, giving passage and filtering the physical processes through to the mental and the instinctive to the conscious.

On the subconscious side, along the ulna edge above Luna but below Mercury, lies the Mount of Mars Passive. On the opposite, or radial, side of the hand, the Mount of Mars Active may be found above the Mount of Venus. Straddled by the two mounts is the flat central area that is known as the Plain of Mars.

In Roman mythology Mars was the god of war, so the attributes of courage, of drive and of resistance are reflected in these areas.

As with all the other mounts in the hand these, too, may be described as reservoirs of

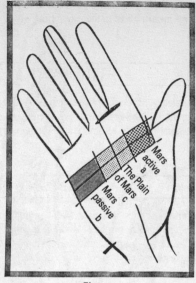

Figure 41

energy. The Zone of Mars, which takes in the central third of the palm reflects the practical, worldly abilities of the individual, mediating, combining and bringing to reality those physical and mental attributes that are represented by the basal and top sectors of the hand.

When this band is well developed it highlights basic worldly knowledge, clever managerial talents and a shrewd understanding of how to execute one's talents for best effect. Practical business skills in the commercial world of affairs are especially indicated when both the basal and middle bands are well developed together.

But if it is the top, together with the middle bands, of the palm that are better developed than the basal areas, the expertise would be of a mental nature, with intellectual rather than physical drive.

When, however, this middle area right across the hand is underdeveloped so that it appears squeezed out by both the top and bottom sectors of the palm, it suggests that the individual is somehow disorganized, perhaps inexperienced in the ways of the world, and thus unable to marshal his energies into productive output.

THE MOUNT OF MARS ACTIVE

Located by the tuck of the thumb (41a), this mount, when large and full, represents physical courage, resistance and strength. If developed to excess, however, the courage degenerates into pure aggression. When deficient, the mount may denote cowardice.

THE MOUNT OF MARS PASSIVE

Mars Passive is that area that lies in the middle third of the palm towards the ulna edge (41b). A well-developed mount here suggests strong powers of resistance, an inner, passive courage that goes with moral fortitude. A poorly developed area here reflects a lack of constancy and perseverance.

THE PLAIN OF MARS

Strictly speaking this area is not a mount at all; it is that flat, often hollow part in the centre of the palm that lies between Mars Active and Passive and should be treated and interpreted as an integral part of the two (41c).

When this central area feels well padded it reflects practical and worldly ability. Such an individual might be described as capable, well able to put into practice whatever talents are represented by the other salient mounts.

But when the central Mars area feels thin and bony to the touch, it suggests a certain impracticality, a worldly ineptness when it comes to putting into practice whatever mental or physical attributes are being reflected in that individual's hand.

Now and again, a development of the ulna edge may occur at this level so that the percussion noticeably curves outwards, giving the outside edge of the palm a central bowed effect (Figure 42). When this formation is

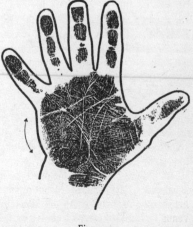

Figure 42

prominent it reveals heightened creative powers. It is, in fact, known as the creative curve. Occurring on the instinctive side of the hand as it does, it also highlights supreme intuition. Vivid and prophetic dreams are often experienced as an outcome of the prescient powers of the individual.

CHAPTER SEVEN

THE FINGERS

Our fingers mediate between our thoughts and the material world. With them we probe and feel our environment. Through them we make, manufacture and translate our ideas into concrete reality.

Whilst our palms reveal our innate abilities and talents, the fingers show how we express that potential through our ideas via our character and personality.

Each finger deals with a particular sphere of interest according to its position in the hand. Depending on its shape, development, condition and appearance, the finger will yield information about how we express ourselves within that realm.

NAMING THE FINGERS

Because of their prominence in our lives, the fingers have been referred to by a variety of names throughout history and according to different circumstances or fields of specialization.

In medical circles, the clinical reference to the digits incorporates the thumb into the system as the first digit, the forefinger is the second digit and so on to the littlest finger or fifth digit.

A little confusing perhaps for those who prefer to consider the thumb as a separate entity, distinguishing it from the four fingers so that the index, rather than being considered the second digit, is actually the first finger, right through to the little finger which is not then the fifth digit but, in fact, the fourth finger.

The most familiar system is to call the first the forefinger. The second, the middle finger as it is strategically placed in the centre of the hand. The next is the ring finger because this is the one upon which the wedding ring is worn. And the last, due to its size, is referred to as the little finger.

In the time of the Romans, the fingers were named according to their function, a nomenclature that perhaps reveals the more prosaic side of one of the most civilized nations in history, and which for us may now hold some amusement.

It is from the Latin that we derive **index** for the first finger because this is the finger that is spontaneously used for pointing. The middle finger was referred to as the **obscoenus** or **impudicus**, not only because of its association as a tool for grooming the more intimate parts of the body, but also because of its phallic, genital or anal implications and connotations. Moreover, in Roman times this finger was employed in a gesture of insult and is still used today as a very rude sign when sharply stabbed up into the air – often to the accompaniment of 'up yours!'.

The ring finger was interestingly called the **digitus medicus**, for this was the one that was used by doctors to apply ointment and by apothecaries to mix and stir their compounds and distillations presumably because, being the weakest of the digits, it does not tend to be used for grooming and thus was believed to be the cleanest finger in the hand.

The Romans called the little finger the **auricularis**, again for its toiletry purposes, this digit being the only one that will comfortably fit into the ear when required to do so.

For the purposes of Western hand analysis, however, the digits were named in ancient times after Greco-Romano gods as a form of shorthand, instantly recognized symbolism that encapsulates the sphere of interest of each finger. They share the same name as the mounts beneath them which act as their roots, providing the environment from which the fingers take rise. The index is called the finger of Jupiter, the middle becomes the finger of Saturn, the ring is the finger of Apollo and the little one is known as the finger of Mercury.

Careful observation through the centuries has led to certain judgements regarding the appearance of the fingers so that now we are able to correlate specific psychological characteristics with the particular formation of each digit. An assessment of personality, drive, inclination, motivation and attitude may be made by analysing the strength and weakness of each finger in turn, its size and shape, how it appears in relation to its neighbours, how it sits in the hand.

Essentially, each finger has to be studied in two ways, firstly as part of the whole hand, and secondly on its own merit. But, when it comes to the fingers as a set, there are several initial generalizations that can be made. Overall length is the first consideration whilst others concern shape, flexibility and the prominence of the joints as a whole.

LENGTH

The length of the fingers is considered in relation to the length of the palm. This is ascertained by measuring the middle finger from its tip to the join line where it meets the palm (Figure 43). The palm is then measured from this point to the top rascette. If the length of the finger is three-quarters of the length of the palm, or even longer, then the fingers are judged to be long. Any shorter than this and the fingers are described as short.

Long-fingered individuals are patient. They have a good eye for detail and can immerse themselves in minutiae. Very long, though, and the individual tends to become pedantic. Short-fingered people, on the other hand, are impatient, especially when it comes to dealing with the finer points in life. They prefer to see things on a grand scale, to take in the overall picture.

Short fingers are a sign of inspiration and quick wit. They pick things up in an instant but may be accused of being a touch slapdash in their approach. This is because they are

Figure 43

forever in a hurry to complete their tasks and arrive at their goal, whereas long fingers prefer to linger and take their time, losing themselves amongst the myriad trivia they encounter on their way. But those with long fingers will do the job thoroughly and well, meticulously dotting every 'i' and crossing every 't'.

People with short fingers are best employed in any managerial position where they can make plans and initiate projects, but, once the work has been put into motion, they like to turn their attention to the next item on the agenda. Their longer-fingered colleagues, however, are at their happiest when they can concentrate in depth on the piece of work in front of them, getting their teeth into the nitty-gritty of the project, digging into the research required, turning things over and over in their minds until they are satisfied that their job has been done well.

Any task that has to be done urgently, that requires a little touch of inspiration, that won't spoil for cutting the odd corner or two, is best tackled by someone with short fingers. But if a task requires meticulous precision or punctilious attention and there is no urgency for its completion, the long-fingered individual is best suited to the job.

Generally speaking, the fingers as a whole should look well balanced in relation to the palm. When the palm is large so as to swamp the fingers, it is a sign that the baser instincts, or the animal passions, dominate. But when the palm is tiny in comparison to the fingers so that they completely overshadow it, it is the intellect or the spiritual side of the personality that predominates.

KNOTTY FINGERS

Prominent joints or 'knotted' fingers, as they are called, further slow the action. When, as in Figure 44, both top and bottom joints are markedly pronounced the fingers are known as **philosophical**. These reveal the thinker, the person who needs time to process information, who likes to ponder and reflect before coming to any conclusion.

So it is the thinking, or cogitative, processes that predominate when the majority of joints are pronounced, especially when the top ones are also prominent. With this formation the individual has a mind which likes to marshal facts into order, mentally storing and analysing the input of information that is received. Retrieval of the information may often require much reflection, for the mind has a strong tendency towards a contemplative, philosophical outlook that requires it carefully to consider and weigh in the balance any statement the individual is likely to make.

People with knotted fingers often gravitate

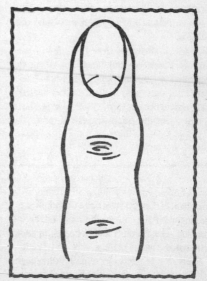

Figure 44

towards any occupation that requires analytical thought, gathering of information, discussion and debate. They make excellent philosophers, scientists and researchers and, even in their spare time, any hobbies they prefer will be of a mental or intellectual kind such as chess or cryptic crossword puzzles, rather than strenuous physical or sporty activities.

It is extremely rare to find only the top joints pronounced and the basal ones smooth. Indeed, it is the opposite that is generally the rule. The need for mental order and method still applies even if only the bottom joints are prominent, although it is believed by some that this feature applies solely to material order rather than to analytical thinking.

In general, people with this formation do not seem to be at all scrupulously tidy. But, though outwardly others might find such people untidy, they, nevertheless, know precisely where everything is in their home or in their office and are most put out when a kindly friend or colleague tries a spot of spring cleaning for them because that throws their whole 'mental filing system' into total confusion.

Now and again, however, one comes across those few individuals for whom the pronounced second joints do emphasize a need for order and method in their material environment, sometimes even to obsessional limits. This formation singles out those who

are houseproud, who like to live and work in neat and tidy surroundings. An untidy room, for example, would make them feel uncomfortable and depressed. In general, they abhor mess and need to make order out of chaos.

On the personal side, too, the need for neatness and tidiness is carried through to their clothes and to the way in which they present themselves. More often than not impeccable dressers, it is unusual to find this type untidy or unkempt, badly groomed or, even worse, with dirt under their fingernails.

Whereas knotted fingers take time and trouble over their deliberations, smooth fingers which, when traced around onto a sheet of paper show no signs of prominent joints, have a mind that works like quicksilver. They seem to grab impressions out of the air, formulate their ideas and make instant analyses and decisions on the spot. No hanging around to think things out at leisure; these types act intuitively and often impulsively too.

They dislike protracted analytical thinking, delving into the minutiae, working through the convolutions of a problem. If they can't respond by gut-reaction they simply aren't interested. In fairness, though, longerfingered types with the smooth digits will take a little more time for reflection; owners of short fingers won't.

WIDTH

To look at, fingers may appear thick or thin. The thicker the fingers the more earthy the nature. Thick fingers that appear strong and muscular denote manual skill and practical ability. But when they are podgy they highlight a love of sensual pleasures. Owners of such fingers are often indulgent types with a taste for luxury and ease in life.

Thin, firm fingers show a more spiritual approach. Intellectual pleasures take those with thin fingers above the purely physical and mundane for they can live quite contentedly without the shackles of our materialistic society. Very thin fingers are particularly a sign of austerity. And, if necessary, it is the people with thin fingers who fare much better, when belts need to be tightened, than their thicker-fingered friends for whom going without material comforts would be such a sacrifice. Very thin, however, with a rather bony feel to them may suggest a rather dry and cynical disposition.

THE DROPLET

Whilst considering the width of the fingers, in some hands there is a marked thickening of the fleshy pad on the top phalanx which in appearance looks like a little drop of water just about to drip off the finger, hence its name of 'droplet' (Figure 45).

When droplets occur in a hand they are a sign of tactile sensitivity and show that their owners have a strong sense of touch. They derive a great deal of pleasure in the feel of different objects and textures. Such sensitive fingers are often found amongst musicians who have that special feel for their instruments. They are also found in the hands of people noted for their gentle touch.

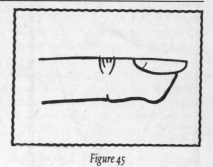

Figure 45

FLEXIBILITY

Some fingers are extremely supple, fluid and expressive in their movements whilst others are markedly stiff. Supple fingers, those that slightly arch backwards along their length, highlight flexibility of mind and acceptance of and adaptability to new ideas.

Stiff fingers are quite the reverse. They denote mental inflexibility together with an inability to adapt to new situations and changing circumstances. With stiff fingers there is a blocking of the energy flow which leads to rigidity in the personality.

FINGER SETTING

The set of the fingers, or how the digits are joined to the hand, yields important behavioural information. In some hands the fingers are each attached to the palm on the same level, forming an almost straight line at the top of the palm. In others they form a neat arch whilst, in still others, the index and little fingers are both set markedly lower down than the middle ones, giving the appearance of a sharp 'v' formation. Figure 46 illustrates the three settings.

The straight setting reveals a forthright, assertive manner. People with this hand tend to be confident types – sometimes, though, so

Figure 46A

Figure 46C

Figure 46B

much so that their self-confidence spills over into arrogance.

The neat arch is the normal setting and shows a well-balanced approach to life – not too overweeningly confident at one end of the scale, nor unduly self-effacing at the other.

The sharp 'v' setting suggests a serious lack of self-confidence together with a classic inferiority complex. The lack of confidence is revealed by the low-set little finger whilst it is the low-set index which highlights the deep-seated feelings of inadequacy. Moreover, this formation may also be seen in the hands of those who go through life with what appears to be an enormous chip on their shoulder.

FINGER SPACING

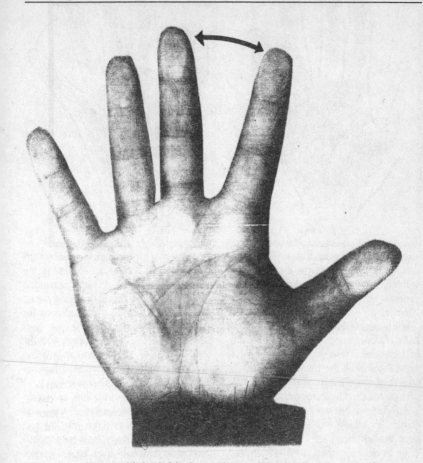

Figure 47 is a photocopy of the hand of the singer and actress, TOYAH WILLCOX. Notice the wide space between her first and second fingers, highlighting strong intellectual independance.

Patterns of finger spacing can produce notable differences from hand to hand. When at rest the norm is for the fingers to fall, gently flexed and only barely apart, all more or less equidistant one from another. In some cases, however, the fingers may be held fairly tightly together, whilst in others they are widely separated. Gaps may also occur between fingers, throwing digits out of line or conferring prominence to some, which makes them stand out amongst their neighbours.

When the fingers are held tightly together it

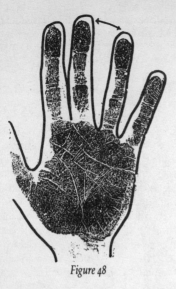

Figure 48

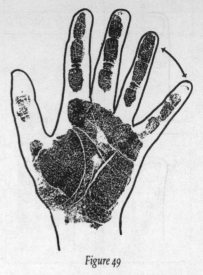

Figure 49

suggests a closed nature, a dependent individual; someone who accepts the status quo without too much question and who generally tends not to think openly or laterally.

With widely-spread fingers the individual has a tendency to extroversion. Individuality and freedom of thought are essential requisites. People with this formation are usually frank and open, always ready to give their opinion and share their thoughts.

A wide space between the first and second fingers (Figure 47) highlights the independent thinker. Here, the individual likes to think for himself, make his own decisions and arrive at his own conclusions.

The second and third fingers widely spaced is a sign of self-resourcefulness (Figure 48).

People possessing this formation enjoy their own company. There is an element of the antisocial about them, perhaps manifesting itself as extreme shyness in childhood, whilst as adults there will be a marked need for one's own space. Generally, these types need time to themselves, time to get away from the hurly-burly of life, time for quiet and solitude in which to recharge their spiritual batteries and regain their mental composure.

With a space between the third and fourth fingers (Figure 49) there is a need for physical independence. Just as those with the gap between their first two fingers need mental freedom, so these individuals have to feel free physically to come and go as they like. Any enforced restriction of their movements is anathema to them.

THE TIPS OF THE FINGERS

Not all fingertips are the same shape. Indeed they vary, not only from person to person but also from finger to finger within the same

hand. Generally speaking, there are four different finger shapes which determine the tip ending and which emphasize the method of

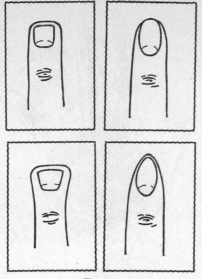

Figure 50

Square fingers, with their blunt straight endings, denote a methodical worker with a practical, logical outlook. A square Apollo finger, for example, would suggest a pragmatic approach to art and creativity – anything that is produced would necessarily be of practical use.

Conic fingers are tapered and gently rounded at the top and are the most common type of fingertip to be seen. The form the expression takes with these fingers is easygoing affability. There is a creative approach to all things, a receptive and responsive attitude to life.

The third type of finger is the spatulate shape, easily recognized by its wide or splayed tip. This is always the sign of activity and invention. A strong adventurous and experimental streak is associated with this type.

The last in the category is the pointed or psychic finger, sharply tapering to a pointed tip. Such fingertips are not so commonly found, but when they are they suggest a spiritual, intuitive, dreamy approach to life. Diametrically opposed to the square, this type is impractical.

expressing the individual's talents. By rights, each finger, because of its individual shape, should be analysed separately according to the sphere of interest it is said to govern. Figure 50 illustrates the four different fingertip shapes.

THE PHALANGES

Each finger is made up of three sections known as **phalanges.** Just as the digits govern a specific sphere of interest, so each phalange, according to its length and appearance, focuses on a particular aspect of those qualities.

Because of the differing lengths of the digits, each section across the fingers will also differ in length, a factor which must be taken into account when a comparison of the individual phalanges is being made.

The top, or nail phalange, describes the mental aspect. Managerial and business skills, together with practical ability, are all denoted by the middle phalanges. Bottom phalanges point to a basic, earthy or material point of view according to the qualities described.

Taking a general look at the sections across the fingers, when all the top phalanges are long they reveal an intellectual approach to life. When the middle phalanges predominate in length, it suggests executive or administrative powers. Long basal phalanges allude to a strong materialistic streak.

When these basal phalanges are also podgy, there is a good deal of self-indulgence

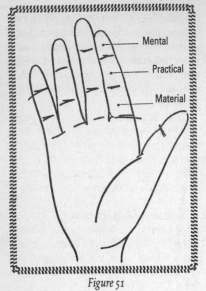

Figure 51

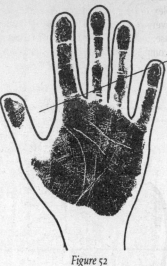

Figure 52

implied, possibly even greed. But, when thin and narrow at the very base of the phalanges so that light shows through when the fingers are held together, it is quite the opposite to self-indulgence as it shows discerning and discriminative tastes, verging on fastidiousness.

An interesting situation occurs when both the top and bottom phalanges are long and well developed at the expense of a short middle section. This shows an excellent ability to come up with ideas and to formulate plans and projects but unfortunately, because the practical inclination is poor, the plans tend not to be put into practice and the ideas remain purely speculative. People with this arrangement of phalanges are, in short, basically dreamers.

The sections are divided by the joints which are marked on the fingers by flexure lines or digital creases. The first joint, separating the top from the middle phalanges, has one single flexure line across the underside of the fingers.

The second digital crease normally consists of two sets of lines each of which are composed of several smaller, finer lines. Only one of these, however, wraps around the side of the finger and it is this one that is used for the purposes of measurement.

In the case of the second digital crease there is an exception which does occasionally occur. In certain cases of mental abnormality, such as Down's Syndrome, chromosomal abberations may leave their distinctive mark on the second crease of the little finger. Here, instead of the normal composite set of lines, the crease is made up of one single flexure line, thus resembling more closely the creases of the top phalanges.

The basal digital crease varies from finger to finger. That of the index finger is complex. It is made up of a single chained line at an oblique angle to the digit. Extend this crease line, as in Figure 52, and it will be found to cut right through the pad of the little finger.

The second and third fingers have double basal creases, perhaps in general those of the middle finger being more obvious and more faithful to the rule than those of the third.

Similar to the index, the basal crease is as complex on the little finger too. This one, however, is wider than that on the index because, instead of being made up of a chain, it is composed of several short, interwoven lines that together produce a wide crease.

Vertical lines may, from time to time, occur on some of the phalanges. Those on the top sections are believed to reflect certain conditions of the endocrine system and as such will be discussed in the section on health, Chapter 21. A few, deeply etched lines on the middle

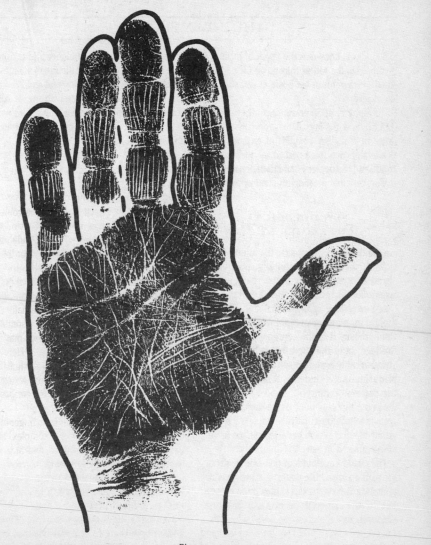

Figure 53

phalanges show an ability to shoulder responsibility.

But if there are many strong lines running down the whole length of the fingers it is a sign of tiredness and stress (Figure 53). With these markings the individual has obviously been overdoing it and should make a point of taking things easy and resting until the lines fade away again.

THE INDEX FINGER

The index is known as the finger of Jupiter. It symbolizes the self or the ego and the individual's idea of his or her position and standing in society.

Its sphere of interests includes religion, politics and the law. Thus from the appearance of this digit qualities of authority and leadership may be assessed, as well as self-pride and the degree of ambition and aptitude for success that the individual may possess.

PSYCHOLOGICAL CHARACTERISTICS

In the division of the palm, the Jupiter finger falls in the mental/conscious quarter of the hand so that it comes under the conscious control of the individual, and thus represents the power and influence that the subject is able to exert on her environment and on those around her. It is the condition, appearance and length of this digit that will reveal how much assertion and personal power the individual feels she possesses and how she uses, or abuses, that power.

In the assessment of psychological characteristics according to this finger, the digit itself must be considered in relation to the type of hand in which it occurs. Because an Earth hand by nature represents a strong, solid individual, the qualities symbolized by the index, even though it may appear short, will always be reflected in a positive, even forceful, way.

The same will hold true for the Fire hand whose owners are active, enthusiastic types so that they are able to influence and inspire others with the strength of their personalities.

But Air types are not so forceful and Water-handed people are the least strong of all. Long indexes on these individuals, then, will have the same impact as the shorter Jupiter fingers have for the other two.

LENGTH

Gauging the length of this digit according to the second finger can be misleading as Saturn in some hands may be unusually short. For this reason the index is always considered relative to that of the ring or Apollo finger and ideally they should be roughly equal in size.

Degree of intelligence may be assessed here for a long finger indicates awareness and sharp perception. Indeed, studies have shown that no cases of mental deficiency occur when this finger is longer or as long as the ring finger.

Long index fingers are seen on those who sense their own power of control and are able to use this power to change or influence their immediate circumstances.

A good strong index is the sign of self-discipline, of confidence and authority. It is the mark of the leader, for its owner possesses a natural ability to take charge and to be in control of situations. Consequently, those with this formation seem to gravitate towards positions of power.

Figure 54 is a rare example of a long, strong and dominant index finger. But, too long, and the finger suggests a tendency to egocent-

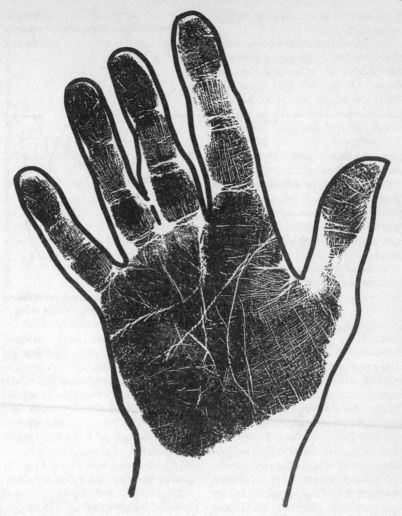

Figure 54

ricity. And when it appears dominant in size so as to overshadow the rest, it can be a reflection of an overinflated ego which may run to conceit. In extreme cases such an exaggerated sense of self can produce the bully, the despot or the tyrant.

Short fingers detract from that sense of personal power so that the individual feels unable to exert his influence. If the long finger is the sign of the leader, the short finger is the mark of the follower.

When noticeably short, there is a marked reticence about the personality due to a lack of self-confidence. People with small index fingers doubt their ability and suffer from low self-esteem. This sense of personal insecurity is exacerbated if the index bends towards the second finger.

Lack of confidence and poor self-esteem are also denoted by a weak index finger or one that appears to be swamped or over-shadowed by the other digits in the hand. This may be logically deduced by considering that this sector of the hand is the area concerned with conscious power and control. Any weakness here, then, will show a marked inability to project one's influence outwards into the world.

A weak Jupiter finger will also reveal a lack of self-discipline and concentration. Such people will be easily distracted and deflected from their goal, so will be less likely to be as high achievers as their longer-fingered colleagues.

Occasionally, however, if the rest of the hand shows strong physical tendencies, there may be an inclination to mask any shortcomings in the character with aggressiveness. Jealousy and a strong possessive streak may also result.

These tendencies are emphasized when the Jupiter finger is low set – that is, when it sits noticeably lower in the hand than the other digits so as to make the finger look very short. Traditionally, a low-set index has been the mark of an inferiority complex (Figure 55).

In some hands the index is the straightest of all the fingers. When it is long and held vertically it is invariably a sign that the individual is morally upright. Religious conviction and spirituality are also suggested by this formation. Religious leaders very often possess this characteristic, especially so when the finger is not only long and straight, but also tapered and conic in shape.

Ambition is characteristically portrayed by an index which stands away from its neighbours and leans out towards the thumb. Owners of this formation, particularly if the finger is also long, are noted for their independence, especially so when it comes to

Figure 55

formulating ideas and making decisions. Indeed, these are the sort to question established, orthodox thinking; to throw into doubt the sacred cows of conventional beliefs; for they have a strong compulsion to think for themselves, to question and debate and finally to arrive at their own conclusions.

A markedly bent index, one that is curved towards Saturn, is another sign of a lack of self-confidence and here there is a need to shore up one's ego. Mainly this is done by seeking security and positively avoiding change or unknown situations. These people work very much on the principle that 'the devil you know is better than the devil you don't'.

When the index is held close to the middle finger it suggests a dependent individual, someone who has a timid, conventional attitude to life where the status quo is never questioned.

THE PHALANGES OF THE INDEX FINGER

The individual phalanges will bring the spotlight even closer on the psychological characteristics represented by this finger. The size, appearance and formation of each section will focus the attention on very specific aspects of the personality.

A long top phalange highlights the intellectual faculties of the individual. Here the long section denotes a good spiritual and theoretical grasp. These people have high ideals and aspirations in life. But, very long, may bring in a touch of the bombastic about them.

Short top phalanges on these fingers are a sign of scepticism and caution. They denote that their owners are less interested in spiritual or theoretical issues and have a preference more towards mundane, materialistic interests and concerns. When the phalange is not only short but also thick, its owner may be rather a possessive and grabbing type, selfish and ungenerous over her possessions.

Intuition is represented by a flexible tip. An individual with this formation is a sound judge of character with a keen ability to read between the lines.

The middle phalange reflects the practical application of the qualities symbolized by this finger. Those who possess a long section here need to feel influential, to be sought out for their advice. They like to pull strings, to feel they have personal power. For this reason they often gravitate towards positions where they are able to use their authority and influence over others.

A short second section here will betray an unwillingness to shoulder responsibility. Such people will prefer to work in a supporting role rather than be up front in the glare of the spotlight. With a short middle phalange on the index finger there is a marked lack of ambition and drive.

A full, fleshy middle section is a sign of

Figure 56

dynamic push and vigour in order practically to achieve one's ambitions and goals in life, whether this means the acquisition of personal power or that of material gains.

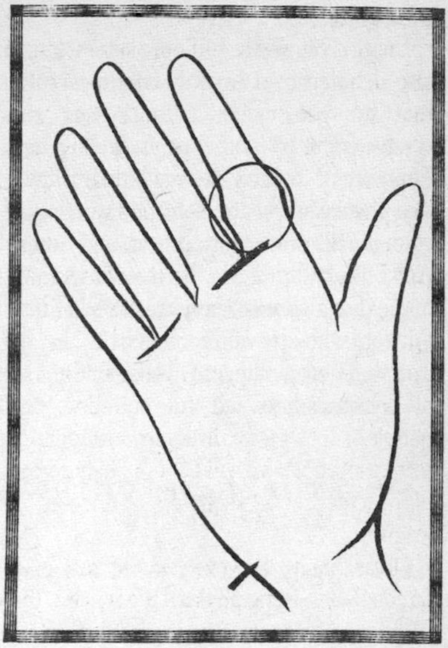

The third phalange deals directly with the physical aspects implied by the finger. Jupiterian appetite and a sense of the *bon viveur* are reflected in this part of the index finger. This is particularly so when the third section is podgy, thus showing a love of food (Figure 56). Often good cooks, restaurateurs or people in catering possess this formation. That holds true if the area is firm; but when it is flabby, with no spring or resilence to it, it suggests indolence and a penchant for an easy life.

Conversely, a thin phalange here reveals a more ascetic type. There is something rather prim and starchy about those who possess this formation. Invariably they have a refined palate. Whilst banquets were invented with the owners of podgy third phalanges in mind, nouvelle cuisine must surely be aimed at those with this lean and narrow development.

A noticeably long third phalange, longer than each of the other two sections, reveals a dominant personality. Because this area represents the physical aspects, when it predominates it reflects an individual with a large physical presence, someone who is able to project his personality over that of others. Whilst this can produce the charismatic individual, it carries with it a sense of power that, with other negative characteristics in the hand, can degenerate into overweening pride and aggressiveness.

FINGERTIP SHAPES OF THE INDEX FINGER

Excellent organizers often share a square-tipped index finger. This is the sign of practical executive expertise; owners make good planners and good administrators. They're sticklers for convention, though.

Conic tips show that their owners work intuitively with a butterfly mind that needs to take in everthing that is going on. The more pointed the tip becomes, the more inspirational but also the more impressionable the individual. This shape also highlights curiosity, sometimes to the point of downright nosiness.

A spatulate tip to the index adds energy and drive. Enthusiasm is a marked characteristic when this formation occurs. There is a dynamic force to the personality that pushes its owner into the thick of any action and to the very front of any situation.

THE MIDDLE FINGER

The middle finger is also known as the Finger of Saturn. It symbolizes balance and, linked to a sense of justice, it represents the understanding of right and wrong.

Its sphere of interest covers a fairly wide brief from morality through self-discipline and responsibility to matters concerning property and possessions. The size, appearance and development of this digit throws light upon one's sobriety and powers of reflection; it reveals the individual's needs regarding personal stability and security; it encompasses one's aptitude for philosophical thought and highlights the individual's ideas about property and the general requirements of existence.

PSYCHOLOGICAL CHARACTERISTICS

Because the middle finger falls between the two sectors of the conscious and sub-conscious division of the palm, the qualities revealed here act as the fulcrum between the two. Thus the digit has come to be known as the balance or steadying influence between reason and instinct and, as such, it may be said to represent one's conscience.

At its best, this digit should be substantial looking and in good proportion to the rest of the hand. Developed like this, it reflects a solid, stable individual – morally, mentally, emotionally and spiritually. This is someone who can be relied upon, who stands on her own two feet and who has a well-balanced attitude to life. It is the sign of one who takes responsibilities seriously and who has due regard for the proprieties of life.

People with well-developed Saturn fingers are often involved with property and real estate. Their interests draw them to the land, as farmers and agriculturalists at one end of the scale, through land agents, to landscape designers at the other end. The rest of the hand would show creative tendencies.

A weak finger would be interpreted as indicative of a careless, frivolous and superficial nature belonging to a person whose understanding of right and wrong is somewhat blurred around the edges and thus for whom pretty crime is an easy recourse.

A long, strong thumb in cases where the middle finger is short would add enough self-control and strength of character to give moral strength to the personality so as to offset the negative tendencies.

Strong middle fingers harmonize well with Earth hand characteristics. Each confirms and supports the other, from the interest in the land to the responsible nature with which both are associated.

Strong middle fingers also help to stabilize both the Air- and Fire-handed individual, whilst weak middle digits here would encourage irresponsibility.

Too strong a middle finger in a Water hand would add too much gravity and lugubriousness to an already impressionable nature, easily prone to emotionality and mood swings.

LENGTH

The length of the finger is determined by the length of its two neighbouring digits, Jupiter and Apollo. In the ideal hand these two would be roughly equal to each other with Saturn standing approximately half a phalange longer. A very long middle finger would tower above the tops of these two whilst a short one would be almost level with them.

A long middle finger reveals a serious attitude to life. The disposition is introspective, with much time spent on reflecting upon the philosophical condition of existence and mankind. Here is the mark of the scientist, the scholar and the researcher, especially when the finger is not only long but also thin and bony.

But when the finger is overlong the indivi-

dual becomes too serious. There is little time for humour and even less time for frivolity. Indeed, morbid and obsessional tendencies may predominate. These people are considered lugubrious, wet blankets or downright miseries to have around.

People with short middle fingers are unable to handle responsibility. Bohemian and non-conformist, they flout all the rules, cocking a snook at rigid orthodoxy and at the Establishment. In general, they have little regard for the conventions and proprieties of life and are invariably described as society dropouts.

As with the weak digit, if a short middle finger is supported by a strong thumb the irresponsibility may be counteracted, giving the individual a greater sense of stability.

Austerity is denoted by a very thin finger of Saturn, whilst a fat one indicates quite the opposite. It is greed that is suggested by a full and fleshy finger here, and those who have this type of middle finger usually like to feel the security of lots of possessions around themselves.

When the finger stands straight and apart from all the rest it tells of a sober and serious individual who is upright and upstanding. Moral balance is in evidence here, the finger standing as a fulcrum between the other digits.

A middle finger may lean towards the index thus turning away from the subconscious, instinctive sector and towards that part that deals with the conscious, rational part of the hand. By thus favouring the ego, the emphasis is put on ambition and the pursuit of the development of the self. Another characteristic of this formation is that the individual positively seeks and enjoys the company of others.

Some people hold their hands with a marked space between the middle and ring fingers whilst others hold these two constantly together.

The wide-spaced formation as seen in Figure 57, denotes an ability to stand on one's

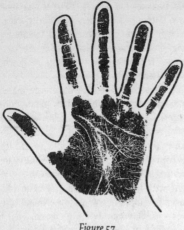

Figure 57

PHALANGES OF THE MIDDLE FINGER

An inflexible top phalange is the sign of a strongly principled individual who takes his work very seriously indeed. A rigid first joint here suggests scepticism and a certain intolerance and inflexibility when it comes to other people's beliefs and philosophies.

When it is supple it tells of a more flexible nature, an ability and readiness to accept the ideas and opinions of their fellow men.

Organizational ability is marked by a long second phalange. An aptitude for technical or scientific work and financial dealings is also associated with this formation. Classically, a long second phalange has been the sign of husbandry, or of careful management; those who have this development are born managers. They make excellent housekeepers, too, capable of running their households with great efficiency.

The third section of the Saturn finger is usually slightly longer than the other two. But

own two feet. Best at working on their own, such people are self-resourceful types, possibly shy as youngsters and needing their own space as adults – even a short time spent on their own each day is enough for them to recharge their batteries both spiritually and psychologically.

When the two fingers are held closely together it reveals a need for security – one's sense of stability is very much tied up with instinctive creative happiness and fulfilment.

When all the fingers lean heavily towards Saturn, even to the point where they bend inwards towards the palm, the emphasis is taken away from the natural expression of the qualities reflected by each of the digits and placed firmly on the shoulders of Saturn – that is, on the security represented by the middle finger. Thus, this picture reveals a subject who suffers with fundamental feelings of insecurity.

In the case where the middle finger dominates and overshadows a weak ring finger, there is often a conflict between moral responsibility and artistic ambition.

Figure 58

one that is noticeably long is associated with mining and farming. It is the sign of green fingers, that wonderful gift with plants and gardening in general.

When the basal phalange is podgy it emphasizes farming or agricultural interests and abilities. If the hand is also artistic, this development may suggest a good eye for landscape gardening.

Well developed, the section also denotes an interest in property (Figure 58). Interior designers, people who deal in property or those who like doing up old houses come into this category. So too do those who deal in furniture – collectors of antiques or furniture restorers, perhaps.

In some hands the base of the Saturn finger is markedly narrow, seemingly pinched in just as it joins into the palm. This invariably denotes a love of learning, of research and of gathering knowledge. It is, in fact, the sign of the eternal student.

FINGERTIP SHAPES OF THE MIDDLE FINGER

Square tips to Saturn fingers suggest practical ability in all the affairs governed by this digit. Discipline and self-control would be characteristic, and so too would a methodical approach to work. Similar to a strong thumb, a square tip here would also help to offset any of the negative tendencies denoted by a shortness or weakness of this finger.

A conic tip may detract from the solid common sense implied by Saturn, giving the character an impulsive nature with perhaps a touch of recklessness now and again. But this ending does soften the austerity of the Satur-

nian characteristics, giving a broader outlook and a sunnier, more hopeful, more optimistic disposition to its owner.

Spatulate tips enhance the desire for knowledge and feature strongly in the hands of inventors and of serious students. This makes for a solitary individual, with a somewhat jaundiced or pessimistic turn of mind, who pursues a rather austere or monkish type of existence.

But on a short or weak middle finger the spatulate tip would add a sense of adventure so that the individual may be prone to speculate. Perhaps the stock market might take his fancy, if he can afford it; or else he might be tempted to have more than the occasional flutter at the races.

Pointed Saturn fingers would be unusual to find except as part of a set where they denote an emotionally sensitive but intuitive nature together with a generally impressionable disposition. On this finger in particular the pointed tip would suggest that its owner might be somewhat gullible and even easily taken in by superstition.

Cross lines or tiny dashes across the top phalange point to tension and worry regarding one's security. Problems with housing or with the purchase of property may produce these markings.

Vertical lines either running down the second phalange or down the finger as a whole show that the problems are so stressful as to lead to extreme tiredness or even exhaustion in dealing and coping with these matters. A quick resolution, a change of attitude or at least a rest away from the problems would be greatly beneficial.

THE RING FINGER

The ring finger is also known as the Finger of Apollo and symbolizes art and creativity.

Its sphere of interests encompasses the Arts – design, music, the more spiritually aesthetic side of life. The size, appearance and development of this finger reflects the individual's appreciation and abilities in all the creative and artistic fields. Moreover, it reveals one's feelings about happiness and contentment, one's sense of accomplishment and of self-fulfilment in life.

PSYCHOLOGICAL CHARACTERISTICS

The Finger of Apollo is located in the upper ulna sector of the hand which governs the mental, instinctive side of the personality, and as such represents how an individual brings to light his subconscious feelings and how he expresses those to the outside world.

Strongly developed, this finger highlights talents in the Arts such as painting, drawing, designing or music. When other indications in the hand also show a technical or scientific slant, the individual may gravitate towards technical drawing or architecture.

LENGTH

A comparison between this digit and the index determines its length. When it is as long as, or even longer than, the first finger, Apollo may be considered as long. Obviously then, the converse holds true – that any shorter than the index and the digit is considered short.

People with long Fingers of Apollo are invariably attracted to the Arts and will be at their happiest in any of the creative fields. When the finger is long, the suggestion is that the individual feels that the expression of his creative talents is far more important to him than the pursuit of ambition or money.

A very long third finger – one that is as long as, or even longer than, the middle finger – is a classic sign of a gambling instinct.

Short ring fingers, which are fairly rare, suggest a lack of a creative soul and also tell that Art and creative interests do not play a

fundamentally central role in the individual's life. Should any creative talent exist in this hand, its owner would employ it to obtain tangible material results.

WIDTH

A very thin ring finger is a sign of a person who can be awkward and hard to please for they have a strong perfectionist streak. Those who possess a noticeably thin digit in comparison to the rest are prone to an over-anxious imagination which may, at times, verge on the hyperactive. Emotionally, they may also be highly strung.

Thick and well developed, though, identifies those who are open and gregarious and full of *bonhomie*. Emotionally, they are good natured and much more stable than their thinner-fingered colleagues.

FINGER SPACING

When the third finger leans towards the middle one (Figure 59) it shows that the Apollo qualities need the shoring provided by

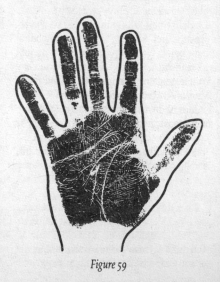

Figure 59

those of Saturn. Here, the character is turning to the stabilizing influence represented by Saturn in order to seek support for the expression of his own inner feelings. Happiness, contentment and fulfilment, then, are heavily interdependent with the individual's sense of security. Take the security prop away and the individual possessing this formation will feel that his life lacks stability and consequently his happiness and well-being are threatened. This formation, then, is the classical sign of a need for security.

Conversely, when the finger leans in the other direction towards the little finger, thus forming a wide space between itself and the middle finger, it is always a sign of someone who is self-resourceful and self-reliant. Often not particularly good at mixing socially with others, such people are happy working and living on their own. They need their own space and in general it may be said that they prefer their own company to that of others'. In this formation the digit is aligning itself firmly in the instinctive, subconscious side of the hand thus reflecting the needs to express oneself through one's deeper imaginative abilities, through one's inherent creativity.

PHALANGES OF THE RING FINGER

With a long top phalange to this finger there is an intellectual appreciation of art and literature. Many artists possess this long section on the top of their Apollo fingers.

Short top phalanges denote a critical eye.

The thicker the top phalange, the more artistically practical and skilled the individual, whereas a thin section here reflects the more creatively ascetic personality.

When the fingertip is stiff it shows a rigidity and inflexibility in one's musical appreciation and creative abilities and ideas. Response to music and art may be somewhat limited in certain respects as the imagination and interests here seem to follow rigidly set patterns.

A flexible tip, though, shows creative adaptability and artistic broad-mindedness. One's tastes in the music and artistic fields may be described as 'catholic'.

A long, well-developed middle section is a sign of practical expertise in artistic fields. In some hands this section is narrower than the top one; and when both long and narrow it reveals a good analytical eye for line, for perspective and proportion. Graphic, fashion or interior designers, architects, draughtsmen and even musicians do well to possess this feature.

Another side to the long middle section is the ability to negotiate with other people. This, then, is the sign of the diplomat, the mediator and the middleman. Agents in particular are brought to mind when this feature occurs and, considering the nature of the Apollo finger, perhaps it is to the fields of literary or theatrical agencies that owners of this formation are drawn.

A good eye for colour is suggested by a thick middle phalange but a thin, short section here will show little inclination towards the pursuit of artistic interests.

The basal phalange on this finger reflects the individual's creative expression through the image he presents of himself, both in his dress and in the status symbols with which he surrounds himself and adorns his home. Long, thin third phalanges, then, highlight good taste and finesse. It is one of the signs of the stylist and the designer.

When the bottom phalange is long and thick there is a hint of ostentation about the individual. Poseurs and those whose style has a tendency towards affectation may belong to this category.

Lack of good taste, however, may be suggested by a short phalange here.

A full and fleshy but firm basal section is known as the 'collector's urge' and is found in the hands of such people as art collectors,

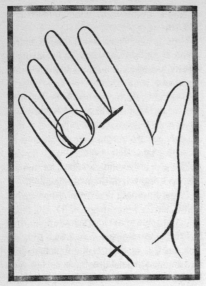

Figure 60

those who deal in the antiques business and anyone who has a passion for collecting *objets d'art* (see Figure 60).

But when the section is full and soft, rather than a passion for art, these subjects have a pure and simple instinct for hoarding.

A thin basal phalange on this finger is a sign that the individual eschews materialism and prefers to live without unnecessary clutter in her life.

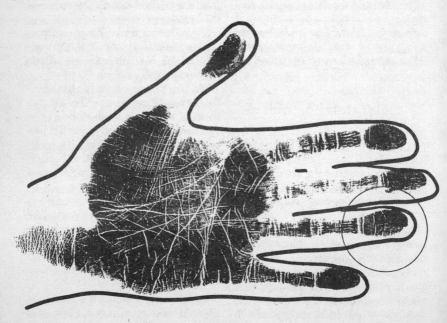

Figure 61

FINGERTIP SHAPES OF THE RING FINGER

Apollo fingers that end in square tips are representative of people who are prepared to work hard and systematically at their art. They put in long hours and work doggedly to achieve the results they require so their output, though perhaps lacking in innovation can, nevertheless, be prodigious.

Conic-tipped ring fingers belong to people who are artistically gifted. It is a sign of style and of savior-faire, and as such is often a feature of the hands of dancers and models. With this fingertip goes a touch of pizazz. The boredom threshold, though, is low, so these individuals need lots of pots on the boil at the same time, lots of friends and acquaintances to maintain their interest and keep their inspiration alive.

Those with spatulate tips are at their best working with other people and are quite often to be found in the media and in the world of entertainment. The spatulate tip here highlights an inventive mentality, a mind capable of far reaching ideas, innovative and sometimes well ahead of their time. People with this formation are inspired and tackle their creative work enthusiastically. But it is also a sign of histrionics, of a tendency for exagger-ation and over-inventiveness. As such it is often the mark of the actor.

Very pointed tips reveal the eccentric, someone with avant-garde and sometimes utterly outrageous ideas and modes of behaviour. On a practical level they may not be the most constructive people in the world but, when it comes to ideas, they are likely to be very progressive. Emotionally they can be slightly unstable for they are highly impressionable individuals, bending and flowing with the prevailing trends and easily influenced by people and situations around them.

When cross lines or a series of fine dashes are seen to lie across the tip of the ring finger it tells that not all is well in the garden – that one's sense of happiness or of self-fulfilment is being undermined (Figure 61). When the cross lines occur more heavily on this digit than any other it is a hint that the individual feels she is creatively underachieving or is artistically blocked in some way.

More often, however, these lines are seen in conjunction with cross lines on the Saturn tip. When both occur together it is a tell-tale sign of domestic or marital problems – either that there is some difficulty in connection with the home-life, or that the individual's relationship is, at that time, going through a somewhat rocky patch.

THE LITTLE FINGER

The little finger is also known as the Finger of Mercury. It symbolizes everything to do with communications.

Its sphere of interest is wide. Language, literature, broadcasting and the media all come under its realm. But so too do science, business, and commerce. And, because it is also a form of self-expression, sexuality comes under this rulership too. The size, appearance and development of the finger reflect how the individual is able to express himself in these differing contexts. The digit accordingly reveals talents for wheeling and dealing, for negotiating and persuading, for putting one's ideas across to others.

PSYCHOLOGICAL CHARACTERISTICS

Adjacent to the ring finger, the Finger of Mercury is located off the farthest corner of the hand in the sector governing the mental/

instinctive side of the personality and, as such, it reflects the individual's ability to express both verbally and sexually his innermost thoughts and feelings.

LENGTH

The Mercury finger is measured against that of Apollo to determine its length. The ideal length is for the digit to reach at least half-way up the top phalange of the ring finger. But because the tendency for the little finger is to be set low it may, in many hands, be mistakenly considered shorter than it actually is. Measuring both fingers with a ruler and comparing one with the other, then, is the most reliable method for judging the true height of the little finger.

People with long Mercury fingers have a flair with words, either in the written or spoken form. Writers, politicians, diplomats, entertainers and after-dinner speakers often possess long, well-developed little fingers. But so too do clever salesmen, with their excellent powers of persuasion.

Oddly enough, Earth hands may often sport a long Mercury finger which, unless otherwise corroborated elsewhere in the hand, should be treated simply as an exception to the rule and not accorded the same significance as described above.

Very long, however, so that the digit nearly reaches the tip of the Apollo finger, suggests excellent communicative abilities and powers of speech. There is a tendency, though, for owners of such long Mercury fingers to be perhaps just a little too fond of hearing their own voices!

Those with short Mercury fingers may find it difficult to express themselves verbally and perhaps in some cases there may even be little desire or effort put into academic self-improvement. Emotionally, they may show signs of immaturity, which can reflect adversely in their relationships because many of them have a block when it comes to talking about their innermost feelings.

But with those whose little finger is short, straight and well developed there is a wonderful naïveté of life which shows itself in the Peter Pan quality they exude. Ever youthful, both in ideas and appearance, they seem to embrace life with a child-like wonder and excitement that breathes a breath of fresh air into whatever company they find themselves in.

When the finger is thin there may be a cynical, sarcastic disposition whilst a full, well-developed little finger is the mark of good humour.

FINGER SPACING

A straight Mercury finger highlights a scrupulously honest individual. But it is fair to say, however, that this digit more often than not has a tendency to curve slightly towards the Apollo finger; this slight degree, however, would not detract from the sincerity of the individual.

The slightly curved finger shows an altruistic spirit, an individual who is prepared to sacrifice himself and his ambitions for the sake of those whom he loves. Such people are often found in the vocational professions, where they care for and look after others.

There is a goodly element of shrewdness or worldly-wisdom in an individual whose little finger is curved towards the finger of Apollo. But beware deception and dishonesty when the digit is crooked and sharply bends towards the ring finger, especially so if it is also short.

When the digit is straight but leans towards the ring finger it is a sign of timidity. Straight-laced and starchy, though, are often the characteristics which go with the little fingers that stand in front of those of Apollo.

A wide space between the little and ring fingers shows a need for personal freedom. This is the mark of individuality and independence. People possessing this feature need to feel they are free to do things in their own way, free to come and go as they please – they may, of course, choose not to use that freedom, but if the possibility of it were denied to them they would suffer enormously from feelings of constriction and limitation.

When the finger is held close to Apollo it tells of a conventional attitude, especially so to sexual mores. Such individuals seem to be contented with their lot, with the status quo and with whatever dictates society is currently imposing upon its people. They are often conventional and dependent types, especially dependent upon their partners whom they regard as the more dominant of the two and with whom they are quite happy to play a passive role.

The majority of little fingers sit slightly lower down on the palm than the other three. Sometimes, however, the digit is considerably lower set so that it appears extremely short (Figure 62). When measured, though, it is surprising just how long the Mercury finger may be in this sort of case and how deceptively short the low setting will make the digit appear.

These low-set Mercury fingers are a sign of a fundamental lack of self-confidence. Those possessing this feature may have poor self-esteem and lack belief in themselves and in their abilities. The lack of confidence portrayed by this feature invariably stems from events in early childhood or from family expectations which the subject felt unable to meet.

A flexible finger will show a mind that interests itself in a wide range of subjects. Its owner, then, is able to converse on many topics and paint life on a very broad canvas.

When stiff, the finger denotes traditionalist and conventional views.

PHALANGES OF THE LITTLE FINGER

Communication and the ability to talk or successfully to put one's point across go with a long top phalange to this finger. Salesmen with the power to charm the birds off the trees or those who tend to talk the hind leg off a donkey are reputed to have a long top phalange on their Mercury fingers.

A long middle section here is the sign of cleverness and astuteness. It is interesting to note that doctors often possess this feature. Lawyers, too, many have a long middle phalange, especially so if the index is also well developed and strong.

Short second phalanges reveal a lack of organizational ability whilst unscrupulousness, especially in business dealings, is associated with a wide middle section here.

Sensuality is a strong characteristic in a hand where the basal section is full and fleshy.

People with long third phalanges can talk plausibly on a wide range of subjects but, scratch the surface, and their knowledge will be only skin deep.

Those who are easily taken in and rather

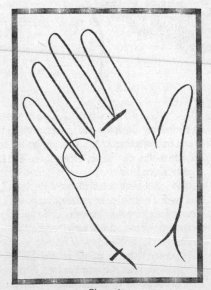

Figure 62

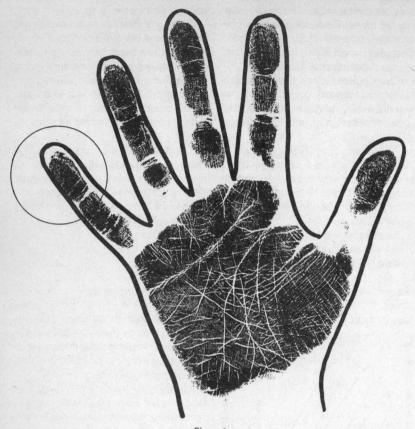

Figure 63

naïve in the ways of the world often possess a short third phalange on this finger.

FINGERTIP SHAPES OF THE LITTLE FINGER

A square tip on this digit shows an understanding of the formalities and conventions that are required in personal conversations and negotiations with other people. Businessmen, women and diplomats do well to possess the square-tipped Mercury finger. A square tip here accompanied by a spatulate tip on the ring finger are two features which often occur together in the hands of actors and actresses.

Little fingers with conic tips show a mentality that is quick-witted and a disposition blessed with a good sense of humour. When a long top phalange with a conic tip is seen on the finger of Mercury, beware the charmer!

A spatulate tip to the little finger is unusual to find unless it occurs as a part of a set. When it does occur it reinforces the inventive mentality coupled to manual practicability.

When the finger has a markedly pointed tip it suggests that the individual could well have a caustic tongue. Blisteringly sarcastic might be one way to describe such people. Downright bitchy is another!

Horizontal lines across the tip of the Mercury finger pinpoint a time of stress. Usually these occur on the little finger when all the other digits show the markings too and thus are part of the general problems the subject is undergoing at the time (Figure 63). But, when the lines are particularly emphasized here, they show that the individual is experiencing problems either in connection with her own powers of communication or perhaps in connection with her sexual relationships.

Either way, the conflict suggests some form of blockage or feelings of inadequacy in these areas. When the problems are resolved the lines should fade away.

CHAPTER EIGHT

THE THUMB

If the hand is considered a feat of engineering, the thumb must be its *tour de force*. It is the action of the thumb, set in opposition to the fingers, that gives the hand its unique gripping capability.

Although monkeys and apes do possess a shortened, stubby thumb, it is Man alone, of all the primates, whose thumb is developed to such a sophisticated degree.

And because this digit is so uniquely important to Man it is given special significance in the study of hand analysis. In fact, in the Indian tradition, investigation of the thumb takes up the better part of an analysis as practitioners there base the majority of their findings on the shape and development of this digit alone.

Unlike the other four digits, the thumb is composed of two phalanges. The third is buried inside the thenar eminence, otherwise known as the Mount of Venus, and as such

has been described in the chapter on mounts.

Just as the mounts of Jupiter, Saturn, Apollo and Mercury provide the root or powerhouse for each of their respective fingers, so the Mount of Venus is the foundation and energy store for the thumb. It is the development of this mount, with its symbolic representation of dynamic vitality, of physical energy, of enthusiasm and sexual virility, that imparts its influence on the thumb. And the whole area of both mount and digit, located as they are in the physical/conscious sector of the palm, denote the energy and power of the individual and the charismatic presence of the personality.

The shape, size and development of the thumb reveal important information about the individual's drive and strength of character. It determines resolution, persistence and grit.

PSYCHOLOGICAL CHARACTERISTICS

The thumb, then, can be said to be the indicator of the individual's motivation and staying power, its strength or lack of it directly corresponding to its owner's strength or weakness of character, enabling him or her either to win through or to submit and give in to more negative qualities.

A strong thumb has the power to rectify

any personality defects, to reinforce any weak links, to bring to fruition any talent inherent in the nature.

A weak thumb reflects a will that is undermined; that vacillates; that lacks reason and logic; that is incapable of shoring up any character breaches in the individual's line of defences.

SIZE

In the ideal hand the thumb would appear harmoniously in balance with the rest. If it is too large it would swamp the palm and digits. Too small, would make it appear insignificant.

Over-large thumbs suggest a dominant and forceful personality whose drive and determination overrule logic. But if the thumbs appear disproportionately small it would suggest a lack of guts in carrying through one's plans and ideas.

If a thumb appears small in comparison to the fingers it confirms a lack of will-power and a reluctance to take control of one's own destiny. The stronger fingers denote a good deal of potential and talent but a block in the character prevents these from reaching fruition. The weakness of the thumb here would reflect a fundamental weakness in the nature, characterized by a lack of drive and tenacity that in practice thwart the qualities represented by the fingers.

Length is usually gauged by measuring the thumb against the side of the index finger. A long thumb, it is said, reaches up to the bottom phalange of the first finger. Any lower down than this would deem the digit as short. However, this determinant can be misleading because of the thumb's setting, or its point of attachment to the palm.

SETTING

Some thumbs are set low, that is, joined to the hand low down close to the wrist; and when the digit is closed against the palm, it may appear short. Others are attached higher up so that they reach well up against the Finger of Jupiter. See Figure 64 for a comparison of the two settings.

When the thumb is set high up on the palm

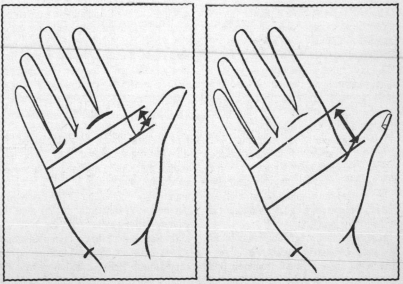

Figure 64

it denotes an original turn of mind. But, when set lower down, innovation rather than creative originality is the key.

Perhaps, then, there are only two criteria to use in judging the ideal thumb. The first is that the digit should look as if it complements the rest of the hand, well proportioned and harmoniously in keeping with all the other features. And the second is that its top phalange, representing will and determination, should be longer than any other phalange in the fingers, thus denoting that the individual has enough power and control to fashion and hone the talents and character traits symbolized by the other digits.

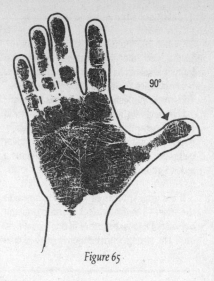

Figure 65

ANGLE OF OPENING

The setting of the thumb is not only important in the ascertaining of its length, it also suggests the sort of angle the digit is likely to form as it opens away from the hand.

Low-set thumbs are more likely to open out to form a wider angle than higher-set ones, which tend to be held more rigidly close to the hand at an acute angle.

Oriental teaching has it that a ninety-degree angle to the palm reflects a well-balanced nature and a harmonious disposition (Figure 65).

A good angle of between forty-five to ninety degrees is the norm in an ideal hand where it would denote an open, frank and generous nature. It is the mark of a warm, affable and easygoing character.

Tighter than a forty-five degree angle, however, hints at an individual who is cautious and reserved, someone who doesn't want to give too much away but plays her cards close to her chest. Narrow-mindedness, inhibition and introversion are the qualities often associated with this formation.

In some hands the tight angle may be due to a natural, inherent reticence. In others it may result from personal emotional difficulties such that, in order to protect his vul-

nerability, the individual feels he has to hold himself in and present a tough and capable exterior to the outside world.

Often, this is a transient state of affairs and, as the situation improves – as the subject learns to trust again and to loosen up and unwind – so the thumbs begin to open out again and to form the wider angle once more.

A thumb capable of forming a very wide angle, one that stretches to greater than ninety, is the sign of the extrovert. This individual is extremely generous to the point of extravagance. The nature is expansive and the character inclined to work spasmodically. Lack of discipline seems to characterize this type together with the sort of irresponsibility that borders on immaturity. There is a marked difficulty in applying one's concentration here due mainly to a lack of persistence and determination. The tendency with this type is to constantly put off until the morrow – a true *mañana* syndrome.

The way in which the digit is carried reveals a great deal about the individual's mood and temperament. Held out and away from the hand, it tells of a spirited character, someone with a sense of adventure and who enjoys a challenge in life.

But when the thumb is held tucked inside the palm with the fingers tightly wrapped around it, research has shown that it is a sign of inner conflict and deep depression. Effectively, what this gesture symbolizes is that the individual no longer wants to use her powers of control, to influence her situation and environment but chooses instead to withdraw inside herself, to shut herself away from the world around her.

LENGTH AND BREADTH

The first two dimensions that need to be considered when studying the thumb are length and breadth.

The width of the thumb is a gauge of the amount of power and resolve the subject possesses, whilst the length reveals how that will-power and determination are put to use.

By combining these two elements it is possible to establish whether a thumb is weak or strong.

When the thumb is both long and wide it reveals a strong personality with plenty of vitality and staying power. Such an individual will actively pursue her ambitions not only with guts and determination but also with reasoned logic.

Wide but short again suggests masses of energy and determination to get there in the end but here there is a lack of reasoning power so that the individual attains her goals through the force of her will alone – her ambition may not be logically thought through but she won't let anything stand in the way of her progress.

A thumb that is long and narrow shows elegance of thought and ideas. This thumb belongs to the intellectual, the tactician, for it is the sign of the thinker: one who may not have an excess of physical energy or staying power but who logically works out her plans and progression until she succeeds at reaching her desired goal.

A long lean thumb looks refined and thus represents elegance both in terms of the way the mind works and in the physical appearance of the individual. Such people are invariably cultured and refined, preferring quality to quantity every time.

A short, narrow thumb shows indecision and vacillation. Easily influenced and victims of their own uncertainty, those who possess this type of thumb lack motivation and tend to be swayed by situations and the mood of people around them.

A further dimension may be added to the equation: the thickness, the padding or cushioning, of the digit. To assess whether a thumb is full and fleshy or thin and bony from base to tip is best achieved by looking at the digit sideways on.

The thicker the thumb the more insensitive, outspoken and direct the individual. People with this type of thumb come across as strong and forceful. There's power and energy and a sense of solidity about a well-padded thumb.

Those who possess thin thumbs, however, tend to use a more subtle approach in life. They may not exactly appear to pack a punch but they are clever and calculating and get to their destination just the same – albeit circuitously. Here, the lack of padding suggests less physical strength but this is compensated for by a more active intellect. The lack of padding, though, in this digit detracts from the feeling of solidity about the individual and gives a more jumpy, nervous, bird-like approach to the nature.

When considering length and thickness there is an unusual type of thumb which occasionally puts in an appearance and which is recognized by its thick, stubby, bulbous development. In the past it was named 'the murderer's thumb', possibly because of its connotation of physical strength which, when frustrated, can result in aggressive and violent behaviour. This is also referred to as the 'clubbed thumb' because of its short but excessively wide nail phalange. People possessing this type of digit are prone to changeable moods. Often irascibly temperamental, they can suffer from bouts of passion and extreme emotion at the drop of a hat.

PHALANGES OF THE THUMB

Figure 66 is the hand of the internationally acclaimed romantic novelist, CATHERINE COOKSON. Note the elegant thumb with its two well-proportioned phalanges

Of its two phalanges, the top represents will-power and strength of character whilst the second section symbolizes reason and logic (Figure 66). A well-balanced thumb should have both sections of just about equal length with perhaps the nail section a fraction longer than the second.

When the two phalanges are thus well proportioned, reason and will are in harmony producing a well-balanced personality, one who is well adjusted, fairly self-assured and confident.

A long top phalange represents strength of will with plenty of determination and persistence. How this strength is used, however, will depend very much on its shape and on how it corresponds to the length of the second phalange.

When this top section is much longer than the second phalange it suggests that the individual is impulsive and has a tendency to jump in at the deep end before logically having worked out all the consequences of her actions.

Those whose top phalanges are shorter than the second are endowed with more rational powers than strength of will to carry through their plans. What this means is that they have a tendency to replay their thoughts in their minds over and over again, to over-rationalize problems and decisions. The consequence of this is that by thus going over old ground they may not leave themselves enough time or energy to act on their decisions. Perhaps, then, what is required with this feature is a little less thought and a little more get-up-and-go, otherwise the danger is that opportunities in life will be missed.

Figure 67 illustrates a variety of thumbtip shapes.

Subtlety is the name of the game with a thumb that has a nicely tapered top phalange.

But a spade is a spade for those whose top phalanges are thickly developed. There seems to be a lack of finesse here – 'what you

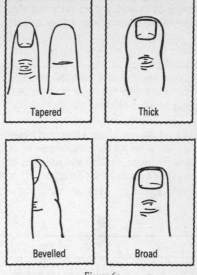

Figure 67

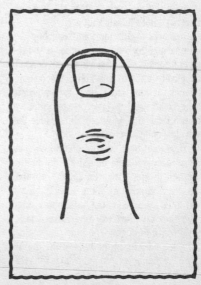

Figure 68

see is what you get' is very much an axiom associated with these types. Life can be rather hard for them because things don't simply fall in their laps; everything they possess and achieve has been worked hard for – every inch of the way.

Life is much easier, however, for those whose thumbs, when viewed from the side, appear bevelled off as if chiselled into the nail. This is because such a thumb shows a strong psychological insight into what makes other people tick so that their owners know just how to handle people and situations in order to get what they want out of life.

A very broad top phalange is a sign of a fiercely assertive individual with an aggressive manner and disposition.

Discretion is not a quality that accompanies a thick second phalange for, with this formation, there's no beating about the bush. What has to be said is said without too much careful choosing of the words. But there is honesty here, albeit somewhat blunt, and a rather   unfortunate   foot-in-the-mouth tendency.

Traditionally, a narrow middle section, which gives the thumb an hour-glass appearance, is known as 'waisted' and is illustrated in Figure 68. When present it reveals a tactful and diplomatic approach.

JOINTS

In some hands the joint between the first and second phalanges may be noticeably pronounced. This formation acts like a blockage between will and reason and as such usually proclaims loudly and clearly that its owner is obstinate and pigheaded. Once she has dug in her heels not a lot will shift her.

Suppleness at this top joint, enabling the nail phalange to bend backwards, is indicative of flexibility. This flexible thumb denotes adaptability and an easygoing disposition, although at the same time it represents changeability and a lack of concentrative ability in the nature which can render the individual quite unreliable.

A rigid joint here, so that the thumb is as stiff as a poker, tells of inflexibility in the approach to life. However, on the positive side, these people are more reliable by far than their supple-jointed colleagues and, when they say they will undertake a task, they do see it through to the end.

The second joint at the base of the thumb where the digit joins into the palm is interesting because when large, so that it protrudes noticeably, it is known as the **angle of manual**

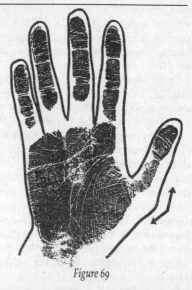

Figure 69

dexterity and as such denotes that the individual is skilled in the use of her hands (Figure 69). Very often there is a love of tactile pursuits when this formation is present: handicrafts, cookery, DIY – anything, in fact, that involves using the hands.

With a square-shaped tip, the character is practical, level-headed and extremely fair-minded. Organizing ability predominates.

A thumb that tapers up to a conic tip denotes a graceful nature and bearing.

The spatulate tip on a thumb is interesting for it is not as common as the other formations and when present denotes an active and energetic individual.

A pointed thumb shows an inability to concentrate for any length of time. Thus persistence and staying power are lacking with this formation.

Just as with the finger tips, short horizontal lines across the tip of the thumb are also a sign that the individual is under emotional pressure.

DIFFERENCES BETWEEN THE PASSIVE AND DOMINANT HANDS

When the thumb in the dominant hand is weaker than its passive counterpart it is a sign that the individual has difficulty in motivating herself to confront the challenges of life. Rather than initiate action, people with this formation tend to wait for others to take the lead, or for circumstances to dictate the direction. Their basic urge is to be closeted, safe and secure, depending on others and happy to toe the line in the background.

Differences in the angle of opening may occur between the dominant and passive hands which, interestingly, will reveal progress in the development of the individual. For example, a thumb that forms a wider angle in the dominant hand to that in the passive hand indicates a broadening of one's attitudes and perspectives in life.

The tighter angle in the passive hand would suggest that the individual had a tendency to be more introverted, more uptight, when younger (and perhaps may still be inclined to be so at times in her private life). But the widening out of the dominant thumb points to greater relaxation of mind and to a widening vision which, in turn, suggests a mellowing and an easier attitude all round.

When the reverse is the case, such that the dominant thumb forms a tighter angle to the hand than its passive counterpart, it suggests that the individual is undergoing a period of learning, of self-discipline. It does suggest that times are leaner and harder, coming from a broader, more relaxed and expansive attitude of mind to a more reserved and introverted state of being. Such might be the case if, perhaps, one falls on financial hardships, or if poor health should constrict an erstwhile active individual. On the positive side, it may be said that such an experience will teach its owner restraint and self-control and that, though frustrating, the fact that only one of the digits is thus affected suggests that the situation may well be a temporary state of affairs. With the coming to terms of the situation, it is possible for the dominant thumb to open out again and match its passive colleague.

CHAPTER NINE

INTERPRETING THE LINES

THE MAP OF LIFE

Imagine that the hand is like a road map so that the lines in the palm represent highways and byways, motorways, avenues and streets. Here one will find junctions and roundabouts, one-way systems and dead-end roads.

When a close look is taken at this road map, it will be possible to see all sorts of pointers and directions. There will be built-up areas, crossroads, shortcuts, bends, railway-cuttings, rivers and bridges. Here one will come across the high spots, the industrial zones, the 'red light' districts, the power stations, the development sites, the landscaped parks.

In fact, just as a map charts one's neighbourhood, so the hand charts all sorts of personal details about one's character and potential. It highlights how the individual works and how she loves, it shows influences that she's likely to bump into and events that could happen to her in her journey through life.

With just a little knowledge of the basic signs, then, it will be possible to negotiate the bends better, to distinguish between a rocky path and a scenic route. It will enable the individual to find out how to avoid the road-works or understand when one simply has to sit in the traffic and bide one's time. Just a little knowledge, then, could make each individual 'streetwise' in the management of her life.

FLEXURE, TENSION AND PAPILLARY LINES

When talking about the lines in the hand there are three separate categories to consider: **flexure**, **tension** and **papillary** lines. The papillary lines, or skin ridges, have already been discussed in Chapter 3 on fingerprints. Tension lines are those creases that allow the skin its elasticity and enable us to flex and clench our hands and fingers and have been dealt with in Chapter 4.

But when any mention is made of lines in chirology it is usually the flexure creases in the palms that are referred to. These are the ones upon which hand analysts base their findings regarding the mental and emotional disposition, the events and directions in the individual's life.

Anatomists call these lines creases or folds because, they tell us, these are the paths along which we fold and bend our palms. Furthermore, they act as anchors, pinning down the top skin to the fascia below – a concept which never fails to bring to mind a spot-welding job.

It has been suggested that lines develop according to occupation so that seamstresses, let's say, who bend and flex their hands constantly in the course of their work not only should all share similar markings but that those markings should be notably distinguishable from the lines in the hands of doctors, for example, or actors or secretaries.

Moreover, it is also supposed that an individual in manual work, such as a labourer or bricklayer, would have many more flexure lines in his or her hands than someone in a non-manual occupation – a lawyer or a politician.

These arguments are simply old chestnuts. Whilst it's true that certain shapes of hands lend themselves more to particular types of jobs – the Earth hand to outdoor employment, the Water hand to artistic occupations – there are no hard and fast rules. It is quite possible to find an Earth hand as a brilliant concert pianist or a Water hand running a market garden.

But research and experience have proved over the centuries that manual work *does not* lay down more lines in the palm than non-manual work. Callouses, yes; more lines, no! Indeed, in most cases the reverse is true so that one is likely to find more lines in the hands of someone in an intellectual profession than in the hands of someone in a manual job.

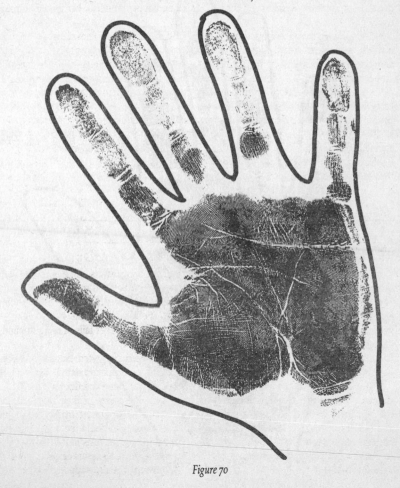

Figure 70

Figures 70 and 71 illustrate this very point, where 70 is a print belonging to a manual worker and 71 to a designer of turbo-jet engines. Notice how few lines exist in the hands of the manual worker, a man who spent all his life working with his hands, in comparison to the designer, a great deal of whose working life has been spent in front of a draughtsman's board and who, incidentally, is also quietly making a name for himself as a fine watercolourist.

And if, because of the nature of the job and the similarity of its repetitive hand movements, each occupation were to lay down a similar pattern of lines amongst its operatives, how easy it would be to recognize the mechanic, the lawyer, the butcher, the engineer.

But it simply isn't like that! As someone who has analysed the hands of thousands of people and given career advice to a good many of them, I wish it were that easy.

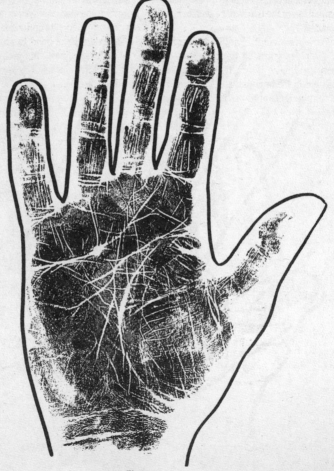

Figure 71

THE 'FULL' AND 'EMPTY' HAND

Although there are five major lines (and several more secondary ones) not all hands necessarily contain all five. Some hands might only have three whilst others have so many that they look as if a spider has laid a web over the palm.

The hand with very few lines is known as an 'empty' hand, whilst one covered with an entanglement of lines is called a 'full' hand. A comparison of the two may be seen in Figures 72 and 73.

People with 'empty' hands are regarded as rather blithe spirits in the sense that they seem to breeze through life completely oblivious of their nervous systems (and of the nervous systems of others!). They're the sort of stout fellows who don't miss a day's work through ill health in their entire careers, and can't understand why their colleagues might buckle under nervous strain or fall down with exhaustion. It is said that perhaps they do tend to lack a bit of sensitivity.

The 'full'-handed person, conversely, is probably too sensitive for his or her own good. The more lines in the hand, the more sensitive the nervous system and the more anxious and nervy the individual.

The best type of hand to possess, then, is one with clear lines – not too many and not too few. Such a hand represents a well-balanced disposition.

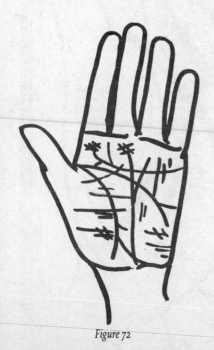

Figure 72

Figure 73

THE FIVE MAIN LINES

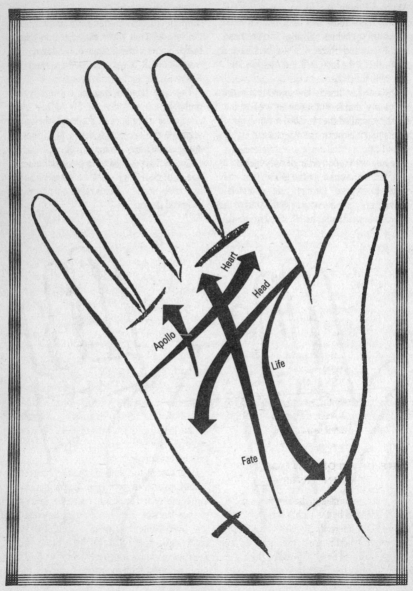

Figure 74

Of all the lines, the five major ones have been known throughout the centuries as the **Life**, **Heart**, **Head**, **Fate** and **Apollo** lines (Figure 74). Anatomically, these lines are divided up into two sets – those that lie across the palm (or transverse), which comprise the Heart and Head lines; and those that are vertical (or longitudinal), the Life, Fate and Apollo lines.

To distinguish between the two horizontal lines, the Heart line is known as the **distal transverse** – that is, furthest away – whilst the Head line is called the **proximal transverse**, or the line that is closer to the main body.

The three vertical lines are differentiated one from the other according to whether they are closer to the thumb side, or radial line as in the case of the Life line, found in the middle of the palm or medial, such as the Fate line, or towards the percussion or ulnar edge, as with the Apollo line.

So, scientifically, the major lines are referred to thus:

Transverse Set:
HEART LINE – Distal Transverse Line
HEAD LINE – Proximal Transverse Line

Longitudinal Set:
LIFE LINE – Radial Longitudinal Line
FATE LINE – Medial Longitudinal Line
APOLLO LINE – Ulnar Longitudinal Line

In comparison to the anatomical names the traditional names seem far simpler and perhaps easier to commit to memory!

THE DEVELOPMENT OF THE MAIN LINES

These lines are formed in the embryo and can be distinguished by the eighth week of foetal development. Interestingly, it has been documented in medical research that it is the Life line that is formed first, followed by the Heart line and then by the Head line.

They are formed at the same time as the papillary ridges so it would be logical to say

that as genetic influences play a part in the formation of the dermal ridges, so that any chromosomal aberrations produce specific markings, then the same genetic problems wil stamp in peculiarities into the very lines themselves. The most widely recognized example of this is the Simian line which is associated with Down's Syndrome, although it must hastily be added that this particular line can also occur in a small percentage of normal hands.

Figure 75 is a print of a subject with Down's Syndrome, more commonly known as Mongolism. Notice the strong horizontal crease, or Simian line, which is one of the main features of this condition.

CHANGE AND FREE WILL

Although the lines are fully developed in a baby's hand at birth, it must be remembered that they can and do change throughout life. Some lines may grow longer, stronger or thicker; may break, form into islands, become intercepted by other minor lines. Alternatively, they may disintegrate, fray, grow fainter and even disappear altogether.

Major changes of environment or diet may produce any of the above-mentioned transformations in the lines, as might changes of attitude, emotional upheavals or any number of life-threatening events. On the medical side, doctors recognize that dramatic changes in the lines on the hand can take place in some dieases of the nervous system and in certain cases of paralysis.

I have seen the lines in a hand ravaged within a matter of months by the trauma of a rather messy and unpleasant divorce. And on the positive side, I've also come across a hand that over a couple of years of careful treatment and sensible diet, rid itself of several negative markings which were representing a serious illness. With the return to health, the lines in the patient's hands returned to normal.

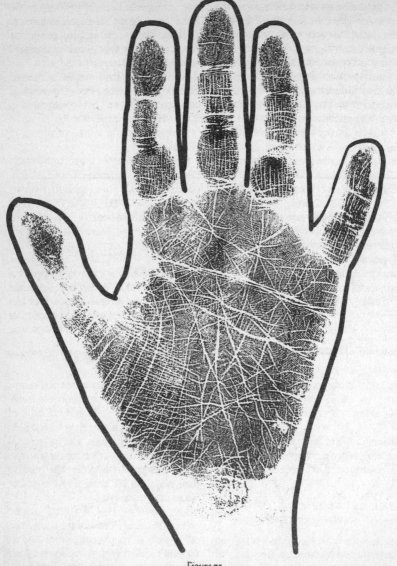

Figure 75

What must always be borne in mind is that we each have *free will*. We each, to a greater or lesser degree, have control over our own lives. What this means is that if, for example, we were to detect some future negative trend in our lines, we might well have time to do something about it.

Perhaps, having been alerted to the danger,

we could devise some form of evasive action so as to avoid the event altogether. This could apply, say, to the warning of an impending illness which, with prompt and early diagnosis, could be successfully treated before it ever had the chance of developing into a full-blown clinical disease.

Alternatively, by being made aware of future complications, we would be in a position to meet the needs of that situation. The idea of possible financial problems in the future, for example, might make an individual lay down a nest-egg and review her insurance policies so as to be in a position to weather the storm.

Or, if an event were completely unavoidable, at the very least we could be psychologically prepared for it: forewarned is forearmed, the saying goes.

CHANNELS OF ENERGY

The lines in our hands represent not only our physical, mental and emotional states of being, but act as a record of influences and events that occur in our lives.

Some hand analysts think of the lines as channels of energy, rather like electrical current running through a flex. A vivid analogy might be that of a river carrying a torrent of energy along its course. The deeper the river bed, the greater the volume, and the faster the water will flow. A wide, shallow bed will produce sluggish energy. A dam across it will stop the flow. Little tributaries or rivulets will take some of the energy from the main source and channel it to other regions. Huge rocks and boulders will impede the flow and, if a small island is present, the river is split into two.

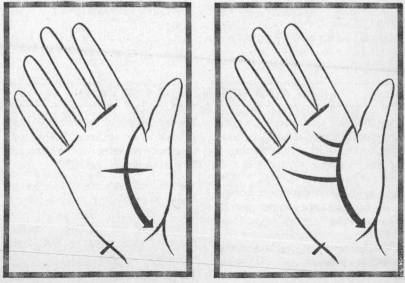

Figure 76   Figure 77

Just like rivers, the lines in our hands act as conduits of energy. Deep, clear lines denote solid strength and energy, while more shallow lines suggest that the energy is more brittle and superficial. Any bar line cutting across a main line (Figure 76) represents an obstacle in real life, just as the boulders or the dam would obstruct the river in its flow.

Branches radiating out from a main line (Figure 77) may be considered as positive or negative depending on their position. In some cases they are negative because they may rob the main stream of some of its power, whereas in other cases they would positively energize a particular area in the same way that tributaries of a river would irrigate the surrounding land. Islands (Figure 78), wherever they are found, however, are always considered a negative sign because they weaken the energy by dividing up the flow, so that the current is no longer running at its full potential.

So, imagine the lines as vital energy carriers – the Head line carrying mental energy, the Life line physical energy, the Heart line emotional energy. If a nice healthy colour runs through the lines, the current is flowing well. But if the lines run pale, are heavily inter-

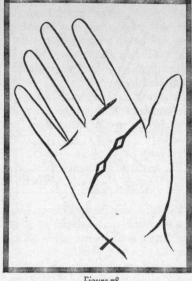

Figure 78

cepted, chained or islanded, it's a sure bet that that energy, whether physically or psychologically, is somehow being impeded. The job of the hand analyst, then, is to find out why.

LINES ACCORDING TO HAND TYPES

In any analysis it must be remembered that the quality and quantity of lines differ in each of the hand types. It's not only the shape of the hand but also the system of lines in the palm that characterizes the type. A Water hand, for example, is noted for its profusion of fine lines which is completely characteristic of the nature of a Water-type person. To find a Water hand with just the barest of lines, then, would be so unusual as to merit close investigation in order to determine precisely why it is an exception to the rule.

The Earth hand is recognized by its square palm, topped by short fingers. This type commonly has only a few essential lines, although these are usually well defined (Figure 79).

The Air hand has a square palm but the fingers are notably long. As a rule, the Air hand contains very clear, uncomplicated lines. Although they might appear thin they are, nevertheless, strong and well formed (Figure 80).

The Fire hand is characterized by an oblong palm, but the fingers are markedly short. Like

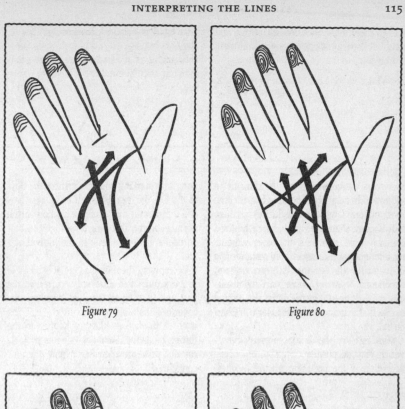

Figure 79

Figure 80

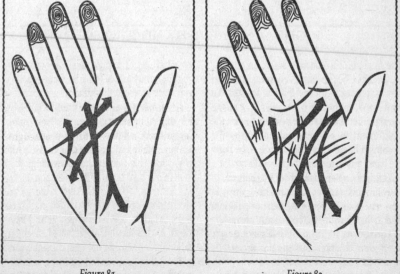

Figure 81

Figure 82

the Air hand these lines, too, are strong and clear but there are a good deal more of them (Figure 81).

The Water hand is easy to spot as it is made up of a rectangular palm with long fingers.

This hand is unmistakable not only for its elegance but also because it contains a veritable jumble of lines which are, more often than not, thin, fine and brittle-looking (Figure 82).

TIMING THE LINES

Precise, accurate timing can be difficult to achieve in hand analysis because hands come in all different lengths and widths. Any gauge that is used, therefore, has to be customized for each hand, stretching the measurements for a longer palm or necessarily compressing them for the smaller one. With practice and experience, however, some startling results can be obtained. Instructions for timing events on the individual lines follows in Chapter 10.

Markings on the lines represent events which may be positive, negative or neutral according to the particular feature in ques-

tion. Any marking which interrupts the flow of the line, be it an island, a break or a bar, will temporarily act as an obstruction to the normal current, throwing a spotlight on that particular period in time in the individual's life.

By applying the timing gauge, it is possible to work out when an event occurred in the past and, putting all the clues together, discover *why* it should have occurred. Or, if the event is marked as likely to happen in the future, by dating it and analysing its possible causes, preventive measures may then be considered.

RIGHT- AND LEFT-HANDEDNESS

The final point to consider before an analysis of the lines begins is the question of lateral dominance, or right- and left-handedness. To avoid any confusion it is better to call the hands either **dominant** or **passive**, so that the right hand in a right-hander becomes the dominant hand whilst the left one is the passive hand. Reverse that for left-handers.

Left-handers are, and always have been, in the minority. Latest statistics puts them at beween 12 to 13 per cent of the population, and of that percentage the majority are male.

Throughout the centuries left-handers have been viewed with suspicion and shamefully censured because of it. Left in Latin is **sinister**, so it doesn't take a massive imagination to

see what sort of imputations were put upon any poor unfortunates who happened to have been born amongst this minority group.

Yet history has given us a pretty impressive list of left-handers, amongst them Julius Caesar and Leonardo da Vinci. In fact, it was da Vinci's left-handedness that enabled him to produce his famous mirror writing. And even in our own times Charlie Chaplin, Harry S. Truman, Judy Garland and Paul McCartney may be numbered amongst their ranks. Martina Navratilova and John McEnroe, both left-handers, dominated the international tennis scene for a good many years, whilst other left-handed sporting notables include Gary Sobers, David Gower and

Jimmy White.

Although left-handedness has been a vexed issue throughout history, this century has seen a flurry of research into the whole area with an ingenious variety of tests carried out to show its causes and functioning, papers in learned journals carrying articles on direction and degree of handedness, on proficiency and preference measures.

This research has thrown a good deal of light onto the whole subject. We now understand that the right and left sides of our bodies are each governed by one of the two hemispheres that make up the cerebral cortex of our brains. Each hemisphere, it has been revealed, is responsible for different functions. Put very simplistically, one specializes in the rational, analytical, verbal, mathematical and organizational processes: any function, in fact, which might be described as linear or sequential in its operation. These processes have been described as logical, masculine, dominant.

The other, however, processes information in quite a different, more diffuse manner. This hemisphere deals with such functions as the appreciation of art and music; with our responses to the world in which we live; with any process, in fact, which might be described as creative, emotional or intuitive. These processes have been described as passive or feminine.

Confusingly, however, messages from each hemisphere cross over as they pass to the body so that an instruction from the left side of the brain will pass to the right side of the body and vice versa.

When considering the 'logical' hemisphere, one normally refers to the left side of the brain so that, in the cross-over, it is the right side of the body (and therefore the right hand) that becomes the dominant side. The 'emotional' responses are said to come from the right hemisphere and therefore control the left side of the body, together with the right, or passive, hand.

In a left-hander the functions of the hemispheres are completely reversed so that it is the right side of the brain that controls logical function and governs the left side of the body. Thus, it is the left hand that becomes the dominant hand.

Interestingly, too, lateral dominance swings from right to left throughout the first few years of a child's life before dominance becomes fixed at around the age of eight, either to one side or the other. Moreover, tests have shown that in cases where damage to the dominant side of the brain occurs before laterality has become fixed, the 'other' side can take over the hard-core logical processes, making up for the loss, as it were. Unfortunately, this does not apply in adults once lateralization has taken place.

But whether right- or left-handed, chirologically it is the dominant hand that reveals all sorts of information about how an individual appears and behaves *in the outside world*. It presents a picture of his or her persona – the public face, if you like. It also records actual events in the individual's life and tells how he or she publicly responds and reacts to each situation in turn.

Moreover, this hand can give valuable hints as to possible future trends, delineating potential likelihoods and outcomes of decisions and actions taken in the present.

The passive hand describes the *inner self*, the inherent side of the nature, the anima or more private self. It reveals the inner depths of the personality, how an individual thinks, feels and behaves in his or her private surroundings. Inherited physical characteristics, potential gifts and talents are all outlined here, but whether or not these manifest themselves in reality depends largely on the overall character and personality of the individual in question. If the inherent talents are developed they will be reflected in the dominant hand. And if they're not, there will be major differences between them.

Any discrepancy between the two hands,

then, will highlight a complex personality, one where the persona may be at variance with the anima. A Heart line denoting a romantic nature on a dominant hand, for instance, might well belie hidden calculating emotions as displayed in the passive hand.

Differences between the hands may also be highlighting important changes that take place in the development from child to adult. A case in point might occur when the passive Head line is straight whilst the dominant hand contains a much more curved Head line (Figure 83). Here it would show that if the child chose to follow a rigid scientific curriculum at school, as the straight Head line might suggest, she would become rather frustrated and hemmed-in in later life when her mind developed a need for expansion and diversification as indicated by the more creative and artistic curved Head line.

To advise a youngster of this need for diversification and thus persuade her not to embark on too rigid a career path which would restrict unnecessarily her choices in future life would, to my mind, certainly justify the existence of hand analysis.

Although in the majority of cases deciding which is the dominant hand and which the passive is relatively simple, in the few cases where true ambidexterity occurs it does present a problem. But even here there are a few tricks which may be employed to help make the decision.

Consider first which hand is most used to hold a pen, which would automatically reach for a comb, or a toothbrush, or upon which arm is the wrist-watch worn. These simple expedients usually give a fair idea as to which is the dominant hand in any cases of doubt.

Figure 83A

Figure 83B

IN THE FINAL ANALYSIS

So, when it comes to analysing lines there are many aspects which the analyst has to take into consideration.

First, there is the suitability of lines to the type of hand, whether it belongs to the Earth, Air, Fire or Water categories.

Secondly, the course and direction of the lines as additional information about the individual's character and personality.

Thirdly, the actual quality of the lines, whether they are clear, strong, shallow or weak.

And then the lines must be minutely analysed for any details, such as islands, breaks or branches, that will give data about events, situations and circumstances, past, present and possible for the future.

Finally, the dominant and passive hands must be mapped one on top of the other to take account of any discrepancies that might occur between them and that would highlight a mismatch between the private and public sides of the individual's life.

A hefty bill to keep in mind but one that has to be meticulously applied to each line in turn.

CHAPTER TEN

THE PSYCHOLOGY OF THE MAIN LINES

THE LIFE LINE

The Life line represents the quality of life. The length of it *does not*, contrary to some popular opnion, reflect longevity or duration of life. What it reveals is information about the physical strength – the stamina, robustness, energy and vitality – of the individual.

This is the first line to be formed within the early months of foetal development, that critical time when our genetic inheritance is being stamped in. This line, then, as well as reflecting our own individual pattern of health and well-being, will also be a record of any medical history that we may be inheriting from our parents.

Often, health markings on the Life line, particularly in the passive hand, will merely highlight our *predisposition* or *tendency*, to a certain condition. This does not necessarily mean that we are 100 per cent on target to developing that illness into full-blown clinical disease.

Recently, attention in the media has been given to a piece of research carried out by a team of doctors at the Bristol Royal Infirmary in which a significant correlation was found to occur between the length of the Life line and the length of life.

The findings were based on the measurements of the Life line in the hands of 100 corpses. The Life lines were each measured and statistically expressed as a ratio of the maximum potential of the line, from the radial edge of the palm, right round to the wrist beneath the thenar eminence or mount of Venus. Age at death was taken from the hospital records and the two measurements

were compared.

The results seemed to show that a correlation between the length of the Life line and the span of the life does exist. Interestingly, the results were impressively significant for the right hand but not so for the left which, to any chirologist worth his or her salt, leaves behind a rather big question mark.

If it is the case, as chirology states, that the dominant hand more accurately charts times and events in the individual's life, then at first sight one would indeed expect the more significant findings to occur on the right hand. A short Life line on the left would simply hint there was a chance of an early demise, whereas a short line on the right hand would be a much stronger warning that the odds against it happening were considerably shortened.

That is, if the subject were right handed! However, we know that on average 13 per cent of the British population is left handed, a factor which, on reading the research methodology, the team did not seem to take into consideration. How different, one may ask, might the results have been, had the left-handed element been taken into account? – Either truly unassailable, or not very significant at all?

Nevertheless, although the findings are certainly interesting, they do go contrary to the principle of chirology which teaches that the Life line is **not** indicative of longevity but describes the quality of the life, the health and vitality of the individual. Many examples in the annals of the subject are quoted of octogenerians with a short Life line, equally of those who die prematurely sporting an impressively long line.

Very often, too, Life lines are mistakenly pronounced as short when in fact they are joined to a newer section of line further out into the centre of the palm. In that case, it would be indicative of a major change in the individual's life. And then it must not be forgotten that lines can and do change throughout one's life. They can grow and strengthen or weaken and fade, break, develop islands or fray away. It is these negative markings on the line that are more likely to warn of serious, life-threatening disease than the actual length of the line itself.

In view of this, it is possible to accept that findings would indeed be significant in such a retrospective study using corpses where perhaps it could be said that Life lines would not change once death had taken place; but whilst the lines in the living hand are still subject to change it is perhaps less valid to make sweeping predictions regarding longevity from the length of the Life line alone.

Though the research was scientifically tight and rigorous there is, however, another criticism that could be levelled at the statistics. In comparison to the millions of hands that have been studied over the centuries by sincere and dedicated individuals, a sample of 100 would seem to be a mere drop in the ocean. Statisticians themselves would agree that significant results over a small number of trials may often pale into insignificance when a much larger sample is employed.

In order, then, to substantiate the findings, further trials would have to be undertaken and the research replicated using a much greater number of subjects. And, as the team themselves acknowledge, it would be of great benefit to the NHS, to individuals with short Life lines and to medicine in general if it were truly proven that Life line length corresponds to length of life. It would certainly be of great value also to Hand Analysis scientifically to

have this old chestnut once and for all proven one way or the other.

GEOGRAPHY

Figure 84

The Life line begins on the edge of the palm somewhere between the thumb and index finger (Figure 84). It encircles the ball of the thumb, sweeping a course out into the centre of the palm and may end at a number of different locations towards the wrist. In some hands it tucks itself back around to end beneath the thumb. In others it continues its sweep out into the centre of the palm. Sometimes it may end in a fork, it may thin out and fray or simply peter out altogether. Figure 85 illustrates some of the possible variations of the course of the Life line.

PSYCHOLOGICAL CHARACTERISTICS

The actual quality of the Life line gives many clues about the character of the individual.

A strong line, that is, a well-formed, uninterrupted channel of good colour, denotes plenty of vitality and energy. This would reveal someone who is physically robust, who can shake off illness, has plenty of energy and endurance and masses of get-up-and-go.

If, on looking at a hand, it is the Life line that has the greatest impact – that appears to stand out strongly in comparison to the rest,

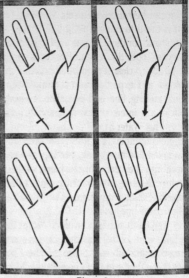

Figure 85

as in Figure 86 – then it's a sure bet that it's the physical qualities above all others in life that are the most important to that individual. Such a dominant Life line, for example, might be found in the hands of sportsmen and women for whom physical strength and stamina are of the essence.

A weak line, one that is thin, chained or pale in colour, reveals poor physical resistance. It tells of someone who is prey to all the illnesses that may be doing the rounds, and who, having succumbed to ill health, then takes a long time to recuperate afterwards. These people suffer from a lack of energy and

Figure 86 is a signed photocopy of the olympic athlete DALEY THOMPSON. Note the strength of his LIFE LINE, denoting stamina and power of sheer physical dynamism.

vitality. Physical strength and robustness are not really their strongest assets.

It is usual to find a strong Life line on an Earth hand for these people tend to be physical types. Both the Air and Fire types should have good, clear Life lines that are well formed. But expect to find a thinner, more brittle-looking line and one that is heavily crossed and intercepted by anomalous markings on the Water hand.

As the examples in Figure 85 show, in some hands the line may sweep out in a generous curve into the centre of the hand whilst in others it hugs the thumb tightly, almost afraid to venture out into the palm.

A wide arc reinforces the idea of energy and vitality. It denotes an open, generous, carefree type of personality, someone who enjoys the adventure of life to the full. These people tend to be outgoing, extroverted individuals. Because this line allows for a wide expanse of the mount of Venus within its arc, it therefore also reveals a good deal about the individual's attitude to love. The bigger the mount of Venus, the more warm, loving and passionate the individual. In addition, it confirms good recuperative and regenerative powers.

When the line sits tightly close to the thumb it reveals a cooler, more critical personality. They are introverted individuals, the sort who tend to play their cards close to their chests. People with this type of line lack warmth and understanding for their fellow man. They can be mean in their attitude and rather self-centred, especially so if the mount of Venus is small, which inevitably it would be with this cramping type of Life line.

If, in its course, the Life line swings out towards the centre of the palm and either ends or puts out a branch towards the Luna mount, it generally means that the individual has 'itchy feet', loves travelling, and may even put down roots abroad.

The person who prefers to stay put, however, who is quite contented with the security

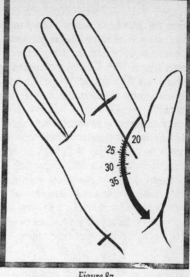

Figure 87

of her own home is likely to have a Life line which tucks its end in neatly below the thumb at the wrist.

Figure 87 illustrates how the timing gauge is applied to the Life line.

TIMING THE LIFE LINE

The line is read from the top downwards towards the wrist. If a vertical line is dropped from the inside edge of the index finger it should strike the line at approximately twenty years of age. With a sharp-pointed pencil each year, backwards and forwards, can be marked off from that point against the line. Depending on the length of the palm, one millimetre is roughly equivalent to one year. So twenty millimetres back from that mark should reach the beginning of the line at the edge of the palm and would represent the first twenty years of life. Each millimetre forwards from this point adds on one more year.

NEGATIVE INDICATORS

Some Life lines begin with a chained formation, or else there may be one single island in
the line directly beneath the root of the index
finger (Figure 88a). This type of beginning
usually denotes early childhood illnesses,
especially those of a bronchial or respiratory
nature.

Any horizontal lines that cut right across
the Life line are known as crossbars and
usually indicate a time of difficulty or emotional upheaval (Figure 88b). Depending on
the length, depth and strength of these lines,
it is possible to estimate the cause as well as
the severity of the impact such an event will
have on the individual's life. The stronger
and longer the line, the more serious the
problem.

Sometimes a horizontal bar, or a series of
bars, may be seen crossing the mount of

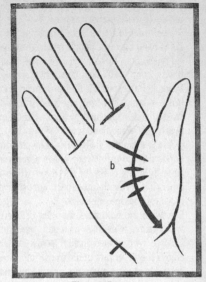

Figure 88B

Figure 88A

Figure 88C

Figure 89A

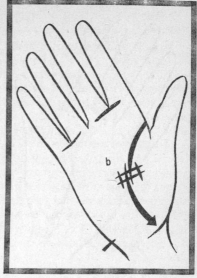

Figure 89B

Venus and reaching out towards the Life line but not actually crossing over it (Figure 88c). Here it implies a time of worry, of decision-making, when the subject is torn between two options and is confused and uncertain as to which one to take.

A break in the line shows that temporarily the current has been turned off (Figure 89A). This might apply if the individual, for instance, decides to make a complete break with the past, to 'up sticks' and change the whole course of her life. In this case a completely new section of Life line will come into play, either sweeping down from the Head line or merely overlapping ends, thus denoting the new way of life ahead.

Sometimes a clean break might suggest a health problem at that time indicated in the subject's Life line. In this case all other clues would have to be minutely investigated in order to discover the cause. But, if the break is joined by a fine thread of a line, or is surrounded by a protective square formation, and the Life line continues strongly after-

wards, it's highly likely that the subject will recover completely (Figure 89B).

Islands in the line imply ill health. The analogy here is of the current being split and therefore weakened so that the energy and resistance of the subject are running at a low ebb during that period of time. The body's natural immune system is therefore not strong enough to fend off disease, or unable to bolster up the individual, resulting in temporary ill health or a feeling of malaise.

The position of the island in the line will throw light as to the cause of the ill health. High up at the beginning of the Life line, an island suggests a predisposition to bronchial or respiratory problems (Figure 90a). A third of the way down might indicate a proclivity to back or spinal conditions (Figure 90b). And further down still may be suggesting problems connected with age, such as a lack of vitality, or diminishing strength (Figure 90c).

A Life line that is noticeably fraying or thinning out is another sign of the ebbing of energy or vitality (Figure 91). This is often

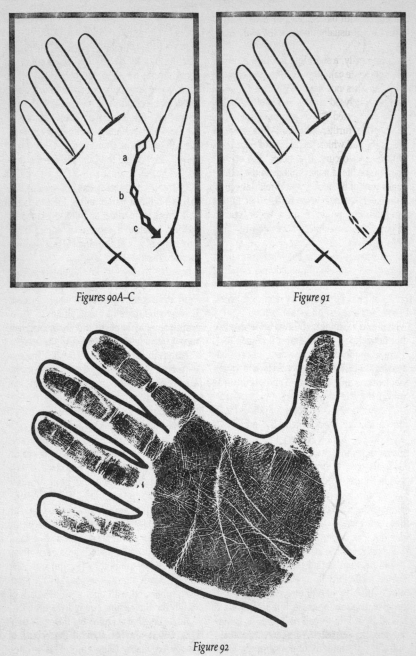

Figures 90A–C   *Figure 91*

Figure 92

associated with old age and so when seen it occurs more usually towards the end of the line.

Occasionally, a short Life line may occur in a hand (Figure 92). It can't be stressed enough that this does not imply a short life. When carefully analysed such a line is often found to be connected by a hair-line thread to another line, further out towards the centre of the palm, and which then takes over from it. Whenever it occurs, it denotes that at that point in the life, a major change in the individual's way of life took place. Should the new line that takes over start further out in the hand, the change will bring a wider type of lifestyle, more people, more activity, and wider horizons.

If, however, the new line that takes over begins on the inside of the old line, closer to the thumb, it would indicate that the individual's life has become more restricted, more introverted and less open than before.

Figure 93 highlights the two variations on this theme.

POSITIVE INDICATORS

Sometimes a line may be seen on the inside running parallel to the Life line, either in short sections for just a part of the way or, in some cases, running along the whole length, rather like a shadow of the main line itself (Figure 94). This secondary line is known as the Line of Mars and whenever it appears, even if only in a short burst, it acts as a bolster, supporting the Life line for the duration of its run.

This is a very useful line, especially if it covers a difficult period in the Life line such as a break or a time of intense emotional activity, because it represents added inner strength which will help the subject through the difficulties.

Branches that spring out and upwards from the main body of the Life line denote times of effort and achievement, times when personal ambitions are striven for and fulfilled.

The nature of the effort and attainment may be deduced from the direction of the branch.

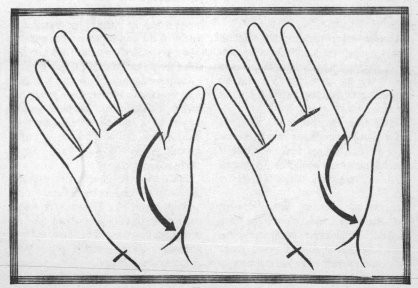

Figure 93

Figure 94

Figures 95A–D

Working for a scholarship, passing exams, graduating from university or any academic triumph may be implied by a branch that shoots out towards the index finger (Figure 95a).

A branch sent off in the direction of Saturn implies commitment, responsibility or some sort of achievement on the home front (Figure 95b). Buying the house of one's dreams, for instance, may well be recorded by this feature.

As the Apollo mount deals with happiness and creative fulfillment, any branch shooting off in this direction will represent a time of personal success and satisfaction. This branch acts as an alternative to the Sun line (Figure 95c).

Business achievements, financial rewards and successes in connection with the scientific field, communications or any commercial venture are highlighted by a branch (Figure 95d) which leaves the Life line and rises up towards the Mercury mount.

Any obstructions or impediments, such as

islands or stars, in these branches warn of adverse conditions in connection with the events implied. For instance, an island in a branch rising up to Saturn might suggest that, having found the house of her dreams and putting all the legal paperwork into motion, the subject suddenly wakes up one morning to find she's been 'gazumped' (Figure 96a).

Another example might be that a branch rising up towards Mercury has a strong bar through it (Figure 96b). This feature might suggest that a business venture could well attract a good deal of opposition or that a scientific project will suffer from complications and set-backs.

Minute wispy branches that peel off the Life line on the inside of the line denote relationships (Figure 96c). These may represent any new responsibilities that we take on throughout the course of our lives, children perhaps, or lovers, a faithful pet or even granny moving in to stay.

As opposed to the rising branches of effort and success, the downswept branches have a

Figures 96A–B

Figure 97A–B

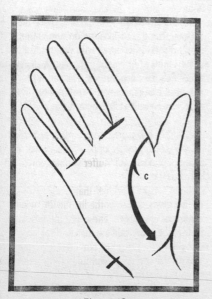

Figure 96C

different meaning altogether. These are known as movement lines and may denote anything from a change of residence to an important journey overseas. The longer and stronger the line the further the journey and the more important its impact on the subject (Figure 97a).

Another indication of movement may be represented by a strong line that enters from the percussion edge of the palm and travels horizontally towards the Life line. A series of these may occur in the hand, let's say, of someone whose work takes him abroad a lot (97b). Or else it might be found in the hand of someone who deals with overseas countries in the general course of his work, someone in the import/export business, for instance.

DIFFERENCES BETWEEN THE DOMINANT AND PASSIVE HANDS

Sometimes it might occur that one of the hands has a short Life line whilst the other is long. If in this case it is the passive hand that is the shorter it suggests that the individual, disenchanted by her early beginnings, environment, or influences, pulled herself out from those early roots in order to seek a broader way of life. The longer line on the dominant hand would confirm that the change was successful and that the individul smoothly sailed from one lifestyle to the other.

But if the reverse occurs – that is, the shorter line is on the dominant hand – the outcome is not so happy. In this case it would suggest that the individual was somehow forced to make that change against her wishes. The change here, then, would be resented.

It might occur with some people that the passive hand contains a Life line that lies tightly hugging the thumb whilst the one in the dominant hand forms a much wider arc. Here it would suggest that the individual has, with maturity, outgrown health weaknesses that she may have suffered as a child. It also implies that the early influences, background and environment were restrictive but that the subject has been able, in adult life, to find a much more expansive and outgoing way of life.

When the reverse occurs, so that the wider line is on the passive hand, it tells that the individual has met with certain problems in life that have meant a reduction in her circumstances. The type of situation this might be representing, for example, might be where the health of the individual somehow became impaired as she grew older, or where emotional or financial problems have had a deleterious effect on that person's life.

If the endings of the line differ between the passive and dominant hands it usually highlights a discrepancy to do with travelling and settling abroad. If the line, or a strong branch, should sweep out to Luna only in the dominant hand, it indicates a love of travelling but also an enjoyment, after the adventures, of getting home again. Alternatively, this feature can sometimes mean that the individual could well run two homes, one here and one abroad, and divides up her time between them.

If the features are reversed so that the swing to Luna is on the passive hand whilst the right ends beneath the thumb, it is a sign of the armchair traveller, the person who loves to think and dream of adventures overseas but only from the comfort of her own home.

In any situation where the cross bars appear strong and deeper on the passive hand, it reveals a person who doesn't like to show emotion in public. The shock of the upset may go deep but she will put a brave face on it and others won't realize quite how much she is really suffering inside.

THE HEART LINE

The Heart line represents our emotions: how we feel; how we love; how we interact with other people. It highlights our attitude to love, to sex, to relationships and to marriage in general, and reveals how we behave towards others and how we would like others to behave towards us.

The other important side to this line is that it also gives clues about the health of our cardiovascular system and about the physical state of the heart itself.

GEOGRAPHY

This is the first horizontal line that lies across the palm beneath the fingers (Figure 98).

Figure 98

Opinion as to the starting point of the Heart line is divided. Some believe that the line springs from below the index finger, sweeps its way across the palm towards the percussion and ends somewhere below the little finger. The more modern theory is that the line takes root from the edge of the percussion below the little finger and then travels out in the opposite direction towards the thumb side of the hand.

Looking at the line and comparing it to the other main lines of Life and Head it would seem that the latter point of view holds more validity. The other two lines both begin at their thickest end, sometimes feathered, islanded or chained, and thin or fade out as they reach their end.

Furthermore, both Head and Life lines begin from roughly the same point in all hands, give or take a few millimetres here or there. But in both cases, they may vary widely in their termination points. Some Life lines sweep out towards Luna, some reach the centre of the palm and some tuck themselves back around to end beneath the thumb. In the case of the Head line, some end on the mount of Mars, some further down and some bury themselves deeply into the base of the Luna area. And both the Head and Life lines can equally split into forked endings.

Similarly, then, for the Heart line. Some stretch right across the palm to end almost at the other edge above the thumb. Some may end below the index whilst others curve right up to touch the base of that finger.

In some hands the line sweeps up to end in the web between the first two fingers, and some Heart lines are so short that they barely reach to below the Saturn finger at all.

And just like the others, the end of the Heart line, too, may grow or it may thin or fade out; it may stop abruptly or, there again, split into branches, sometimes two and sometimes even three.

But though the course and direction of the line may differ from hand to hand, the fact of the matter remains that there is very little variation, give or take the odd millimetre up or down the palm, at the percussion edge, or what must be concluded as its root.

The final argument for the modernist thinking is that the percussion or Mercury side of the hand deals with the subconscious side of the nature. A beginning here, then, would take the expression of the emotions from the subconscious through to the conscious awareness and realisation of our feelings. Pretty well matching, it seems to me, the process by which we feel love or sexual impulses, instinctively at first, before they register consciously in our minds.

PSYCHOLOGICAL CHARACTERISTICS

If the Heart line is clear and deeply etched it shows self-confidence in relationships together with a warm and loving nature. But if the line is weak it is a sign of insecurity and

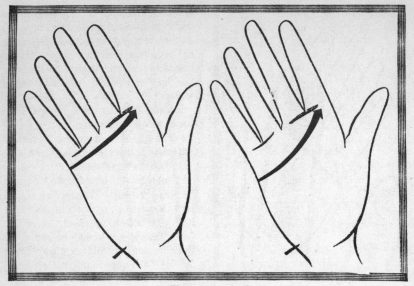

Figures 99A and 99B

personal uncertainty when it comes to relating to others.

The higher up in the palm the Heart line is located, so that it looks as if it's crowding the fingers, the cooler the emotions and the more distant and calculative the individual (Figure 99a).

Lower down in the palm, closer to the Head line and effectively encroaching into the mental area of the hand, is always a sign that the emotions take precedence and dominate the personality (Figure 99b). This reveals a more passionate individual.

Similarly, if the Heart line is the most dominant line in the hand it would suggest that affairs of the heart are the driving passion of the individual (Figure 100). In short, the heart rules the head.

A curved heart line denotes warmth and passion (Figure 101). It shows a physical response to emotion. People with curved lines take a dominant role in relationships and in lovemaking. There is a strong sexuality about them and they are often described as sexy or as having that elusive quality of sex-appeal that has so often been associated with personalities like Robert Redford and Marilyn Monroe.

In contrast, a straight Heart line is more cerebral in its expression of love (Figure 102). They can love just as warmly as those with a curved line but they tend to be more cautious, more analytical. They are not quite so sexually impulsive but tend to quietly work out the consequences of their interactions and the implications of their relationships. People with this formation, then, are receptive types who prefer the more passive role.

If the gap between the Heart and Head lines is wide it reveals a warm, generous and giving nature. But if it is very narrow it has been said to denote that there is a certain self-centredness in that kindness and generosity. Figure 103 illustrates the two variations.

When the line ends high on the webbing between the first two fingers it denotes someone who is very sensible in all emotional matters (Figure 104). Such people are realistic

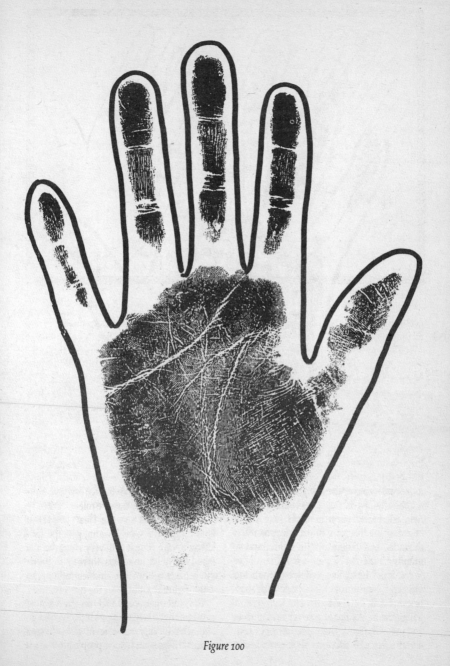

Figure 100

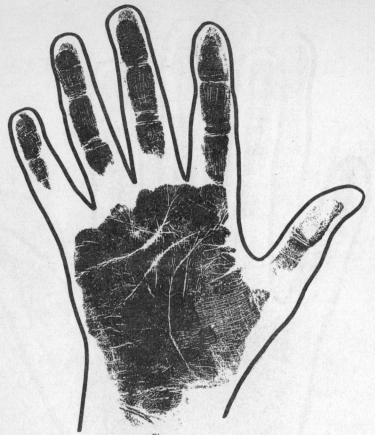

Figure 101

in their relationships and expectations of love but their failing is that they cannot express their innermost feelings in words.

Sometimes (Figure 105) the line may reach as far as the centre of the index mount, ending on the fleshy pad below the Jupiter finger. This highlights the idealist, the person who sees love through rose-coloured spectacles who, in fact, is in love with love itself.

In some hands the line sweeps right up to the base of the index finger (Figure 106) which shows a fierce loyalty towards the loved ones

but also possessiveness too. A mother with this marking may, for example, aggressively oppose her son's choice of partner unless she herself approves wholeheartedly of the girl. Alternatively, a man with this type of line would marry for love, yes, but only to someone he deems is worthy of his position and station in life.

Now and again a Heart line is found that travels straight across the palm from edge to edge. This formation **should not be confused with the Simian Line** because, although it

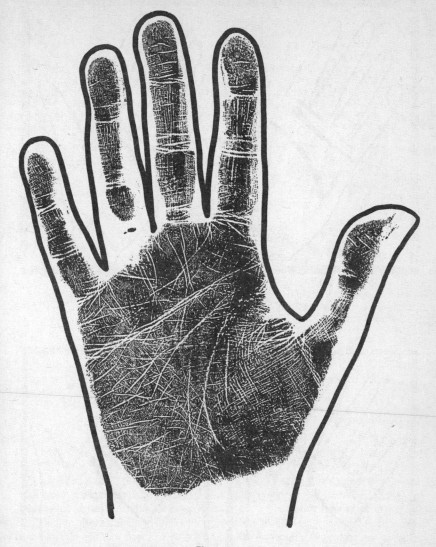

Figure 102

does lie straight across the hand, the Head line is nevertheless present in its normal position. With this formation it denotes the workaholics, people who devote their lives to a cause, to helping humanity (Figure 107). For these, work and career always come first and love must necessarily be fitted into second place.

The Simian Line, a straight, horizontal crease incorporating both the Head and Heart

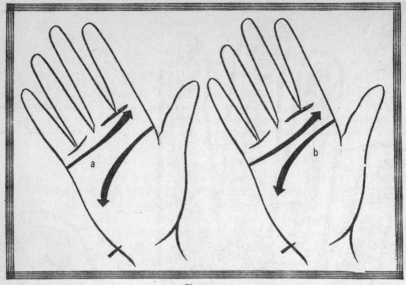

Figure 103

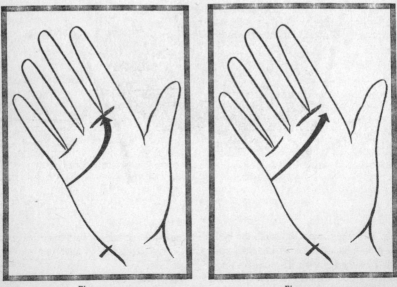

Figure 104   Figure 105

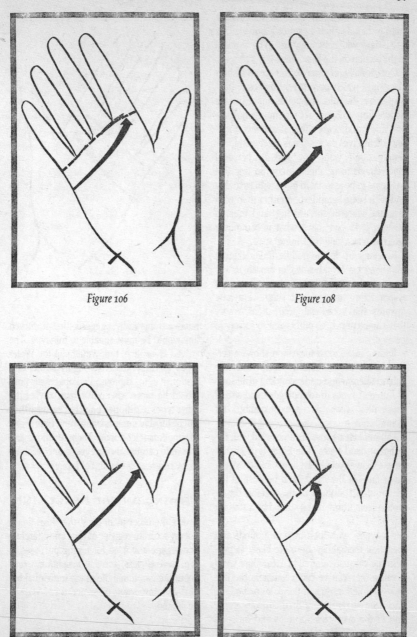

Figure 106

Figure 108

Figure 107

Figure 109

lines in one and which looks as if it cuts the palm in half, is often a sign of jealousy. This line is dealt with separately and in more detail in the section on the Head line.

Occasionally, one may come across a short Heart line which only barely makes it half-way across the palm and peters out below the middle finger (Figure 108). People who possess this marking are either afraid of committing themselves to a serious relationship or simply don't want any sort of personal involvement to tie them down. So this line has come to be associated more with sexuality and with sexual gratification rather than with love and warmth and sharing, and thus its owners, it is said, have what is commonly referred to as a 'one-track mind'.

Reaching up to the middle finger (Figure 109) shows a level-headed approach to the emotions. Such people have a strong sense of responsibility in life and might gravitate towards the vocational occupations where they can be of help to others and to society in general.

Ending in a forked formation shows a certain emotional adaptability which makes the subject tolerant and understanding of all sorts of different types of relationships and sexual proclivities such as homosexuality, for example (Figure 110).

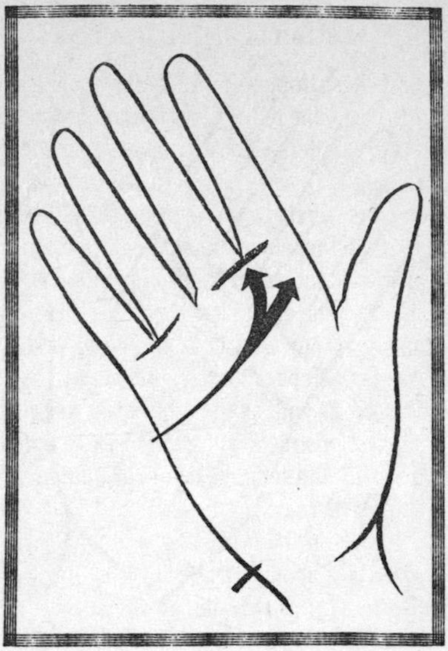

Different Heart lines are associated with the different hand types. The **Earth** type should have a clear strong Heart line to match all the other lines in the hand. And because of the matter-of-fact attitude of this personality, it would seem fitting that it should be a straight line.

Air types, with their inquiring minds and analytical mentalities are more likely to possess the calculative straight Heart line. And because they can be cool customers the line may well lie high up in the palm or be long and clear, suggestive of their curiosity in life and of the many relationships and interests that seem to attract them.

The exuberance and enthusiasm of the **Fire**

Figure 110

hand automatically suggests that a curved line would be most suitable to this type. The curved Heart line, too, would suit the **Water** types for they are often highly sexual and responsive to stimulii. Perhaps their lines would be more susceptible than any of the other types to dropped branches because they can be terribly impressionable and thus prone to emotional let-down. Their idealistic and romantic natures also suggest a line reaching to the centre of the mount of Jupiter.

TIMING ON THE HEART LINE

Unlike the other main lines, the Heart line is not an accurate register of time and therefore is not generally used for timing purposes. It can, nevertheless, provide insights not only about the emotional life of the individual but also give important clues about her state of health too.

NEGATIVE INDICATORS

Branches dropped from the Heart line onto the Head line tell of disappointments in emotional matters and in affairs of the heart (Figure 111).

When a relationship goes seriously wrong so that the subject is left with bitter disappointment and disillusionment, she may find that the end of her Heart line dips down and joins up with both the Head and Life lines at their beginning (Figure 112 p.140).

Here, as with all the other main lines, bars suggest obstructions and worries in connection with the subject's emotions and relationships (Figure 113).

Islands in the Heart line are more likely to give clues about the health of the individual (Figure 114). Depending on where they occur in the line they can denote a predisposition to problems with sight and hearing.

A heavily chained Heart line can indicate that the body's chemistry is out of balance

Figure 113

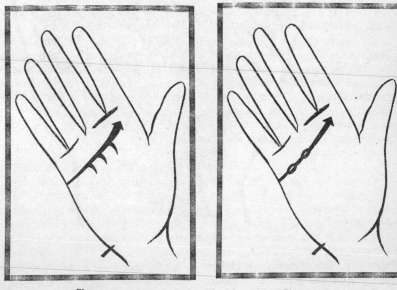

Figure 111   *Figure 114*

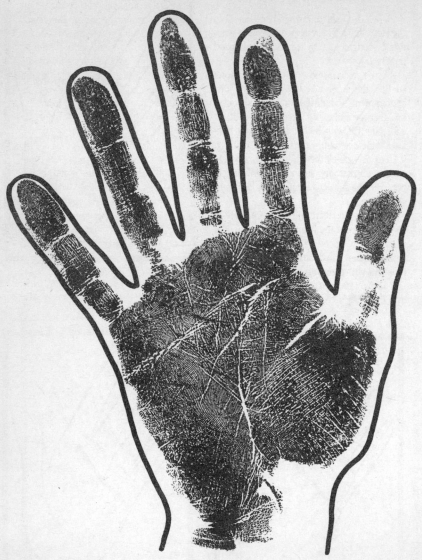

Figure 112

(Figure 115). This formation may also be alluding to a susceptibility to circulatory problems.

Another indicator of a tendency to cardio-vascular conditions might be suggested by a break in the line (Figure 116).

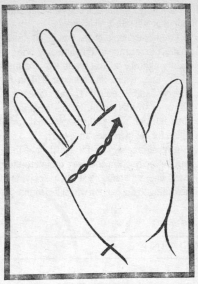

Figure 115

It must be stressed, however, that all indications to health problems must be backed up by other corroborating signs in the hand, such as the condition of the nails, for example, and no diagnosis should ever be attempted simply on the strength of one indicator alone. More information on the diagnostic value of the Heart line will be found in the section on Health.

POSITIVE INDICATORS

Traditionally, a Heart line that ends in a triple fork is said to show a sympathetic and understanding nature, which certainly would be of great benefit in all the subject's relationships (Figure 117). As long as none of the forks bend downwards to touch the Head line, this formation is held to bring good fortune and happiness to its owner.

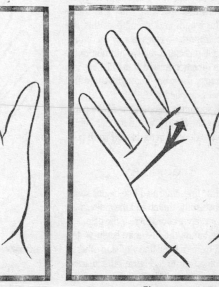

Figure 116   *Figure 117*

DIFFERENCES BETWEEN THE DOMINANT AND PASSIVE HANDS

Any differences in the Heart lines between the dominant and passive hands will highlight a complex emotional nature.

If, for example, a man posseses a very short line in his dominant hand whilst the passive line is much longer, it would show that he presents a picture, let's say, of the office wolf. He is sexually highly charged and motivated to have as many partners as he can, but inside he justifies this to himself with the belief that he is simply seeking that one perfect relationship that will satisfy all his needs.

Another example of the emotional duality that a discrepancy in this line may bring to light might be a deeply curved dominant Heart line, whilst its correspondent in the passive hand is straight. This example would show an overtly warm, loving, sexy individual but one who perhaps uses that sexual allure for her own calculative ends.

Any discrepancy in the Heart line, then, can be analysed in this way by interpreting each line separately and then applying it according to the hand in which it is found.

THE HEAD LINE

The Head line represents the intellect and mentality, the reasoning powers and logical capacity of the individual. In short, it reveals how a person thinks and what she thinks about. The length and strength of this line will give important clues about an individual's intelligence and mental attitude to life whilst the direction in which the line lies and travels across the palm highlights how that intelligence is applied.

It is the second horizontal line in the palm, lying below the Heart line and the third of the major lines to develop in the hand (Figure 118).

GEOGRAPHY

Like the Life line, the Head line begins somewhere between the thumb and the index finger and then sweeps a course across the palm.

In some hands the line may begin widely separated from the Life line whilst in others it may be joined up to it. Figure 119 illustrates the two variations. Whether the Head line then springs free early on or whether it remains intermeshed with the Life line for some considerable distance will have an important bearing on the individual's attitude to life.

Figure 118

Several variations exist in the course of the Head line from hand to hand. Sometimes it may lie horizontally across the palm, almost as if drawn with a ruler. In other hands it may

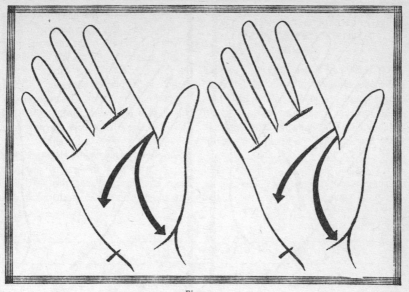

Figure 119

sweep downwards, in a shallow curve perhaps or alternatively trace a steep descent right down to touch the wrist.

The line may fork in a variety of places along its course so that the lines shoot off in different directions or it may even grow a parallel line to form a double Head line.

PSYCHOLOGICAL CHARACTERISTICS

The straighter the Head line, the more rational and logical the approach (Figure 120a). This type of line is associated with practical, analytical and calculative subjects. Owners of the straight Head line don't like to deal with airy-fairy notions. They like to work with solid facts connected to material matters. So the sort of areas they're likely to find themselves in are science, business, technology, the world of finance or mathematics or anything of a practical, down-to-earth nature that requires basic common sense.

When the Head line has a gentle, springy

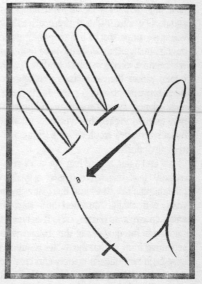

Figure 120A

curve to it, it adds imagination to the mentality (Figure 120b). Whereas the straight

Figure 120B

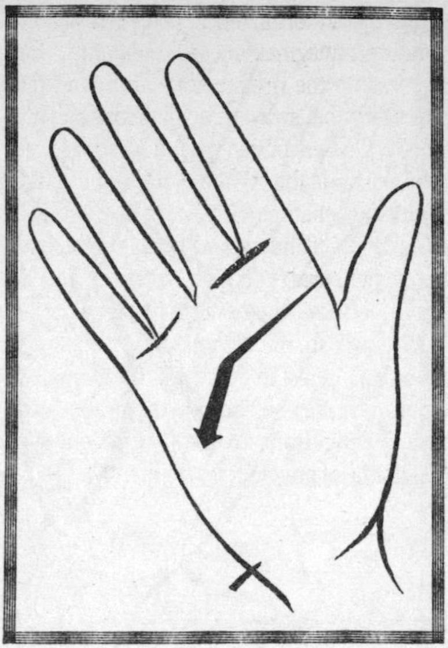

Figure 121

Head line denotes a factual mentality, this one tells of a more instinctive approach to life. People with this sort of line may react more spontaneously. They are likely to be found in the creative fields, often working with people, rather than with facts and figures. The Humanities, languages, the media or the softer sciences such as sociology and psychology, tend to attract this type and so, too, does any creative employment such as hairdressing or floristry.

Now and again a hand may contain a combination Head line which follows a straight course across the hand and then, at a given point, will change direction and start to sweep downwards (Figure 121). This type of line blends the qualities of the straight with the curved lines so that the owner is quite at home both with factual matters and creative ideas and will be happiest in any employment that combines the two.

A very steeply curved line is almost the opposite to the straight Head line (Figure 122). Rather than dealing in facts, this one

Figure 122

works mainly on instinct. It reveals an outstanding imagination, a mentality that responds to the rhythms of Nature and that can easily be swayed by atmosphere and moods. Owners of this type of Head line gravitate towards the Arts and are found in any occupation that requires a high degree of imagination. Painters and poets might have the steep Head line, for instance, and so would mystics. And because this line reaches right down to the mount of Luna, it also shows an interest in history, in traditions and racial memories so that anything about the past ranging from archaeology to antiques will also be of great interest to them.

There is a very unusual Head line that combines into one single channel both the Head and Heart lines and looks like a thick horizontal crease that divides the palm almost into two. This is a special form of the line which is known as the Simian line and is dealt with separately below.

A strong Head line will show a positive attitude to life, denoting a strong-minded individual with an ability to make decisions that are clear and sound.

Weak Head lines tell of an inability to make up one's mind, and highlight a rather weak and vacillating mentality.

The longer the Head line, the more the thirst for knowledge. A long Head line, especially if it has a springy curve to it, is associated with the type of mind that is flexible and enjoys a wide range of subjects and interests. Anyone who thoroughly relishes digging out facts and researching material is likely to possess a long Head line.

Conversely, a short Head line, that is, one

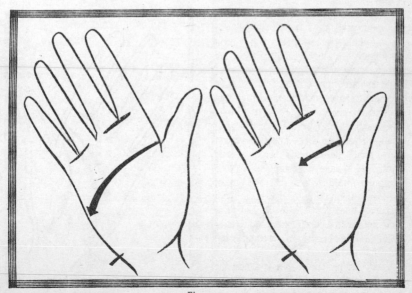

Figure 123

that ends below the middle finger, belongs to the specialist, the sort of person who might make one subject into a lifelong interest. Owners of short Head lines are more narrow-minded than those of long ones. However, they are more able to apply themselves to the tasks in front of them for their powers of concentration are by far greater than that of their longer-lined colleagues.

Figure 123 illustrates the comparison.

Perhaps one of the best forms of the Head line is one which is just slightly separated from the Life line as this tells of a good blend of independence and self-confidence in life. But one that is widely separated at the beginning shows masses of independence together with a rather unconventional attitude to life (Figure 124 A–B). It does, though, also suggest impulsiveness, sometimes to the point of foolishness. Owners of this type of line have a tendency to make decisions without first having worked out the full implications of their actions. For example, one of the types of

mistakes that tends to recur, until they learn that valuable lesson, is that they find themselves falling in love with the wrong people for totally the wrong reasons, especially so during their teens and twenties.

Some Head lines begin at the edge of the palm joined to the Life line. The interpretation of this line very much depends on how long the two remain interlocked. If the Head line springs away quite early on, say beneath the outer edge of the index finger, it denotes that the individual has a good mixture of caution and daring. They can be independent without necessarily being reckless, courageous without being foolhardy.

But if the line continues to be joined to the Life line for a considerable distance it will show someone who is perhaps a late developer (Figure 125). It is the sign of an individual who tends to be over cautious in life, sensitive and dependent on family and background. Such people are often afraid to leave the security of the nest in order to make

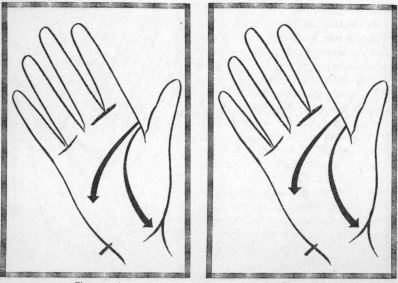

Figure 124A   Figure 124B

Figure 125   Figure 126

their own way in life. Often, the point at which the two lines finally separate is when the individual gets married, exchanging one secure nest for another.

The Head line may, in some hands, take its beginning from inside the Life line (Figure 126). Whenever this occurs it shows a highly apprehensive mentality, almost a fear of life that makes the subject want to shy away, to hide away from the world. Should this formation be seen in the hand of a youngster, there is a great deal the parent could do, firstly to recognize and understand the child's natural timidity, and secondly to help him strengthen his self-confidence and encourage him to stand on his own two feet.

The Head line may split into branches directly below the second, third or fourth fingers. The branching must be a clear splitting of the line and not be confused with the Fate or Sun lines which may cut their way through the line of Head.

Should the Head line split into two below the second finger it reveals a talent for any-

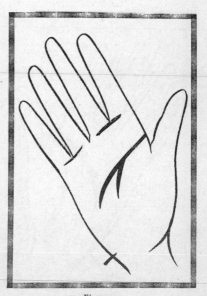

Figure 127

thing to do with property or real estate (Figure 127). Connections with the land, interior design, or a love of buying up old houses and doing them up may all be denoted by this formation.

The split Head line below the ring finger is rather special and known as the writer's fork (Figure 128). It is always a sign of a very creative mentality although not all who possess it do go on to become writers. However, when pressed, they will admit to having been 'good at English or languages' or admit that 'English was their best subject' at school. If not published writers, they will at least enjoy writing, especially letters, in which they take great pride and send in large numbers to their friends and loved ones.

When split below the little finger it is a sign of business acumen (Figure 129). Owners of this feature are adept at handling money and should seriously consider running a business of their own if circumstances permit.

Very rarely one comes across a double

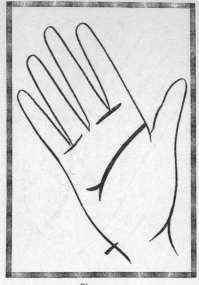

Figure 129

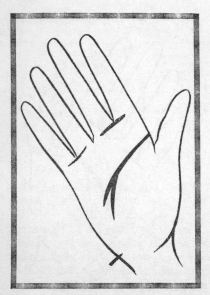

Figure 128

Figure 130

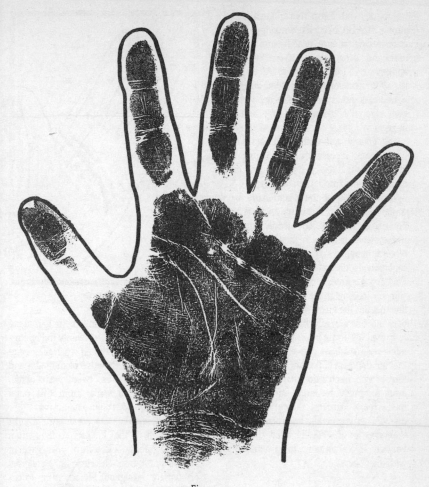

Figure 131

Head line (Figure 130). This is not a function of the forking but a true independent second line of Head. It may follow the main line through its course or it may shadow just a section of it. When it exists, whether as a complete line or merely as part of a line, it bolsters up the intellect, adding an extra dimension to the thinking. In some cases this denotes a dualistic way of looking at life, per-haps being able to see things through both the 'masculine' and 'feminine' angle. Whatever, it is special and a rare find.

Particular Head lines are to be expected with the different hand types. Anything not conforming to type would merit closer investigation as the unusual nature of the feature would add special interest to that individual.

Typically, the **Earth** hand should have a strong, straight Head line to complement its concrete, logical, level-headedness.

The **Air** hand should have a long, clear, springy curve to its Head line. As they revel in communications and media matters, it would be logical to expect this line to be forked especially below the ring and little fingers.

The energy and enthusiasm of the **Fire** hand is best represented by a strong Head line but one that has, perhaps, several anomalous markings throughout its course.

Without a doubt the **Water** hand would contain a fine, long Head line that has a very noticeable curve to it. The steeply curved line is associated more with this type than any other as it reflects the imagination and susceptibility to different moods for which the Water type is known.

If, on looking at the hand, it is the Head line that has the greatest impact, that appears to stand out strongly in comparison to the rest, then it's a sure bet that it's the mental or intellectual qualities above all others in life that are the most important to that individual (Figure 131). Such a dominant Head line, for example, might be found in the hands of intellectuals, logicians, theoreticians or anyone who may generally be described as cerebral types, or of a 'cold-blooded' disposition, who are able at all times to rule their hearts with their heads.

TIMING THE HEAD LINE

Figure 132 illustrates the timing gauge applied to the Head line. The line is read across the palm from the thumb side towards the percussion edge. As with the Life line, if a vertical line is dropped from the inside edge of the index finger it should strike the line at approximately twenty years of age. With a sharp-pointed pencil each year, backwards and forwards, can be marked off from that point against the line. Depending on the

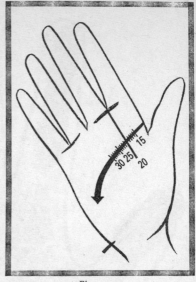

Figure 132

length of the palm, one millimetre is roughly equivalent to one year. So twenty millimetres back from that mark should reach the beginning of the line at the edge of the palm and would represent the first twenty years of life. Each millimetre forwards from this point across the palm adds on one more year.

A short Head line *does not* indicate a short life, nor that the intellect suffers from dementia, stops, falls asleep, goes gaga or any such nonsense. The Head line may grow or contract throughout life according to circumstances and in no way reflects on the longevity of the individual.

The Head line deserves the most minute and thorough analysis. Precise and detailed inspection of this line will yield an outstanding amount of information about its owner.

NEGATIVE INDICATORS

Islands in the line split and thus weaken the flow of energy (Figure 133). They indicate a time of worry and anxiety, a period when the

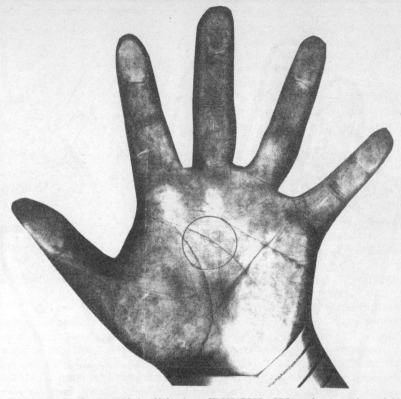

Figure 133 is a photocopy of the hand belonging to SIM HARRIS, a BBC sound engineer who was held hostage in the Iranian Embassy seige in 1980. Note the islands in his head line beginning at the time of his capture and illustrating the enduring effects of such a mentally and emotionally traumatic ordeal.

subject is unable to think clearly, but is confused and befuddled.

A chained Head line or one that is furry or fuzzy denotes a lack of concentration and a sense of 'woolly-mindedness' (Figure 134). It is possible that these markings suggest a mineral imbalance which could be affecting the smooth running of the organism.

Spots puncturing the line, either individually or in a series, focus the spotlight on specific worries (Figure 135). An investigation of the other lines and markings occurring at the same time should throw light on the cause of the problem.

A star on the Head line may be rare to find but when it exists it could imply a shock to the system – either physically or psychologically (Figure 136). For instance, it may represent a knock or bang on the head, the sort that might occur in a car accident or a fall from a ladder. Alternatively, it could denote an emotional shock, the sort that comes on receipt of sudden bad news, for example, although on the positive side it is just as feasible that the

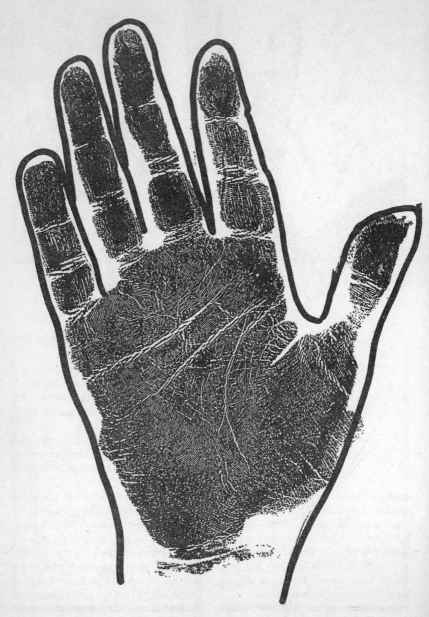

Figure 134

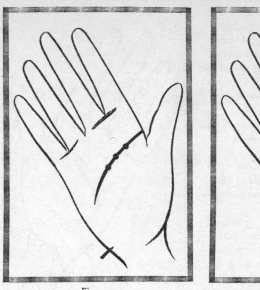

Figure 135

Figure 137

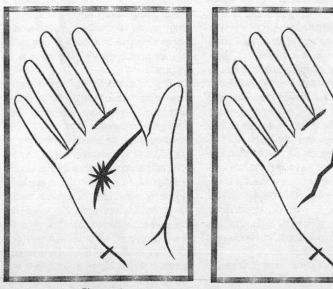

Figure 136

Figure 138

sudden surprise of good news might well produce exactly the same effect on the line.

Bar lines are always a sign of impediments and obstruction (Figure 137). They may be considered as blockages across the road or as dams stemming the flow. Either way they are obstacles which somehow need to be negotiated.

Now and again one comes across a Head line that visibly zig-zags up and down throughout its course across the palm (Figure 138). This is a 'moody' line and invariably tells of someone whose mental attitude and thinking processes run in discrete phases throughout life.

When the section of line rises upwards it suggests a time of good progress; of positive, channelled work that builds up to a crescendo of achievement. When the line is on the descent it reveals a 'looser' period, possibly giving more time for relaxation, but perhaps less productive – a temperamental period which can lead to sudden changes of mood. Each section can be timed so that perhaps plans can be put into motion in an attempt to evenly balance out the phases and at least offset the vacillating moods.

Occasionally one may come across a Head line that has a break in it (Figure 139). There are two possible interpretations of a broken Head line. The first is that it is indicative of a physical cause. This, like the star, could well be a warning of danger, suggesting perhaps an injury to the head. If so, there will undoubtedly be other markings to substantiate this, possibly an island in the Life line, or a corresponding break in the Fate line.

The second interpretation is that the break denotes a psychological development. This might occur if an individual suddenly changes attitude, philosophy and orientation in his or her life, for example; leaves the past behind and starts afresh.

I have seen this in the hand of someone who described it as 'suddenly seeing the light', in another who was 'born again' and in

Figure 139

a third who turned his back on drugs and alcohol to lead a more spiritual life. The break that denotes the mental or psychological growth usually has overlapping ends and the whole process of change and development may be measured for it takes as long as the lines are overlapped for the process to be completed.

A tiny dip in the line is a sign of unhappiness, a time when mentally things are not going well and the individual feels thoroughly depressed (Figure 140). This period can easily be timed, problems beginning to occur as the line starts to dip, the worst of it happening when the line is at its lowest point, followed by a slow resolution and the redressing of the situation as the line rises up and levels out again. People with this formation in their hands have described the period corresponding to the dip as a time when they felt they had reached rock bottom, and then slowly, slowly clawed their way back up again.

The dip in the line may sometimes be

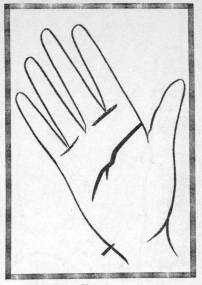

Figure 140

Figure 141A–D

accompanied by a thin, wispy downswept branch, not to be confused with one of the three important forks in the Head line. The short wispy branch is another sign of depression and unhappiness.

POSITIVE INDICATORS

Branches rising upwards from the Head line are very encouraging signs and show achievement and advancement as a result of one's intellectual efforts.

A branch that beats a course up towards the index finger would indicate academic success (Figure 141a). A branch to the middle finger represents an achievement connected with property or the home (Figure 141b). One that shoots up to the ring finger implies creative fulfilment, possibly connected to the Arts, or more generally personal effort that brings contentment and satisfaction in life (Figure 141c). A branch that rises up in the direction of the little finger may indicate financial rewards or recognition (Figure 141d). Alter-

natively, this feature can also represent success in the scientific or business fields as well as in the 'Mercurial' world of the media.

THE SIMIAN LINE

The Simian line is a very distinctive marking. It looks like a strong, fairly thick crease that cuts right across the hand almost dividing the palm in two. This line, illustrated in Figure 142, is made up of a combination of both Head and Heart lines rolled into one. In some cases the Simian line may have two branches shooting out of it, one up in the direction of the index finger, which is in fact the tail of the Heart line, and the other sweeping downwards as part of the tail end of the Head line. This line occurs quite naturally in a small percentage of normal hands but it is more generally associated with Down's Syndrome.

When the line does occur in the hand of a Down's Syndrome subject there will be other skin markings that confirm the condition. One clue might be found in an above average

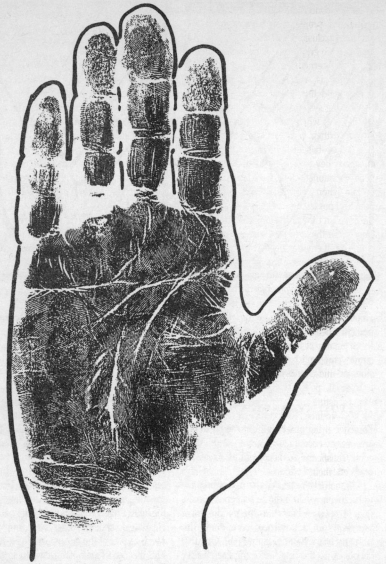

Figure 142

number of arches in the fingerprints. Another could be a horizontal skin loop in the Luna area, or a triradius pattern high up on the percussion edge of the palm.

But when the line occurs in a normal hand, it represents very particular mental characteristics. The Simian line always denotes intensity. People who possess it are capable of complete concentration: their minds focus on whatever project they have in front of them to the exclusion of all else.

There are no grey areas where Simian-lined folks are concerned; for them right is right and wrong is wrong, with nothing in between. And they seem to operate on an all-or-nothing system: when they work, they work flat out; when they enjoy themselves, they give it their very best shot; when they believe, they believe with total conviction; and when they love, they love exclusively. Indeed, emotionally they are so intense that, especially when young, they can be extremely jealous and possessive.

But love isn't the only emotion they feel so intensely, for they can hate with just as much fervour too. If emotionally thwarted they can behave rather immaturely, sulking and smouldering with fury and, like the proverbial elephant, they never forget!

The inner tension that these people suffer is lessened if the two ends of the Head and Heart lines peep out from the main crease. And in many cases, it appears that the extreme emotions start to mellow from around the mid-thirties onwards.

In general, people with Simian lines are clever and astute and, similar to all those with straight Head lines, they can be practical and factual in their approach to life. But it is their very intensity or inner tension that can make them dissatisfied with their work, their marriages and their lives in general. Children with this feature in their hands, then, should be shown from an early age how to appreciate simple pleasures and, if they display any creative talent, should be encouraged to develop it and especially so if it teaches them to relax.

DIFFERENCES BETWEEN THE DOMINANT AND PASSIVE HANDS

It is very interesting when there is a discrepancy in the length of the Head line between the two hands. If the line is longer in the passive hand it shows that there is a lot more inherent power than the individual has as yet developed. Perhaps this is because of a lack of opportunity, or laziness, or maybe the individual in adult life needs, for whatever reason, to constrict her thinking. If the latent powers are developed, though, the line in the dominant hand will grow in length to match its passive counterpart.

Alternatively, if it is the line in the dominant hand that is longer than the other, it tells that the individual has intellectually developed beyond the mental inherited 'lot' and progressed further than the early background might have allowed.

If a straight line exists in the passive hand whilst the dominant hand sports a curved one it is a sure sign that the subject's imaginative powers will grow and expand in adulthood. This is an important discrepancy to note in a child's hand, especially when thinking of career guidance. Should the youngster choose too narrow or too rigidly scientific an academic course, he or she may regret it in later life, when the dominant Head line will demand expansion and creativity.

When the reverse occurs – that is, the curved line is in the passive hand and the straight one is the dominant line – it tells that the creative, imaginative child will need a more rigid intellectual structure in adult life. An out-and-out artistic career will not suffice, for order, method and pragmatism will be the requirements of the day.

If there are more anomalous markings crossing the passive Head line than are seen in the dominant hand, it reveals a subject who is a quiet internal worrier, someone for whom problems and hurts go deep but who doesn't show it on the outside.

THE FATE LINE

The Fate line is perhaps the most complex line in the hand for it not only has a variety of beginnings and a diversity of endings but it can also represent several different aspects. In general, however, it can be said to represent the course of our lives. It maps our career and public life, charts our ambitions and successes, showing by every twist and turn the many changes that we put into motion throughout our lives.

The construction and appearance of the line will throw a good deal of light on the sort of grasp and control we have over our own lives and our destinies. And it tells, too, about our sense of duty and commitment, our feelings of responsibility as well as our attitudes to work and the general way we want to live our lives.

Lying in the centre of the hand as it does (Figure 143), it cuts a dividing line between the conscious and subconscious sides of the palm and interestingly reveals how we manage to balance those two sides of our nature.

GEOGRAPHY

The Fate line is the long vertical crease that rises from the wrist through the centre of the hand to end just below the fingers.

There are several different starting and ending points for this line. Some may take root from the Mount of Luna or from the Mount of Venus; others spring out from the Life line or start at some indeterminate point in the middle of the hand and a few follow the classical route from the centre of the palm at the wrist, shooting straight up the middle to end beneath the Saturn finger.

The most usual ending for this line is just beneath the middle finger, although some may swing over to the bases of either the index or ring fingers. Some Fate lines don't make it as far as the fingers at all but might terminate abruptly as they hit the Head line or, further up, when they meet the Heart line.

PSYCHOLOGICAL CHARACTERISTICS

The structure and composition of the Fate line is critical in order to ascertain the psychological characteristics associated with this marking.

A strong line, deeply etched and clear, reveals good control over one's life, together with a fundamental sense of responsibility. It also shows that the individual knows what she wants out of life and moreover knows how to go about getting it.

A weak line, faint or thin, shows a lack of control; the individual isn't fully in the driving seat of life, if you like. The same holds true when the line is chained, because the

Figure 143

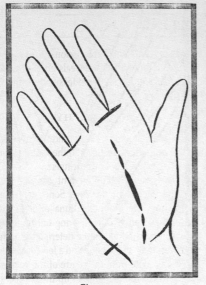

Figure 144

Figure 145

actual chaining effect weakens the line con-siderably.

A fragmented Fate line reveals a 'stop-start' type of life, each short section of line depic-ting a burst of activity which is sustained only for a short duration at a time. Indecision, vacillation and constant drifting in and out of jobs might be represented in this way. Figure 144 represents the fragmented Fate line.

A Fate line that runs straight up the middle of the palm from the wrist to the base of the middle finger, as in Figure 143, is the classic textbook formation that highlights a some-what set pattern of life and career. Such people may automatically follow in father's or mother's footsteps, or make up their minds from a very early age where they want to go in life and never deviate from that idea. This particular formation may be described as a rather conservative line which points to a settled, conventional way of life.

Springing up from the very line of life itself is rather a special feature of this line as it shows close family associations (Figure 145).

In some cases this Fate line may reveal that the career is somehow tied up with the family, either that the individual has been considerably helped or is in the family firm. Alternatively, this marking shows early family duties and responsibilities, the sort that might occur if the father dies or the mother is an invalid so that the youngster has to take the burden of looking after, or of pro-viding for, the rest of the family.

Similarly, when the Fate line begins from the Mount of Venus, inside the Life line (Figure 146) it also reveals family obligations. Here, it shows that the youngster has felt duty bound to follow the dictates of the parents, to pursue a particular career or way of life simply to please the mother or father. Once the Fate line leaves the mount and the area governed by the Life line, it is interesting to see whether any changes take place in the Fate line itself. If they do, it reveals that the individual has finally shaken off the strong family influences.

Those who possess a Fate line that takes

Figure 146

Figure 147

root from the Mount of Luna generally prefer to work with people in creative and imaginative fields (Figure 147). These are invariably independent types and success for them depends to a great extent on how they are accepted in their work by the general public.

Starting higher up in the palm it shows that the individual doesn't quite 'get her act together' until a bit later on in life (Figure 148). The actual beginning of self-determination, of a feeling of control over one's life and a sense of direction, takes shape from the point at which the line begins; this can easily be measured by applying the timing gauge.

If the line has a forked beginning it suggests that the individual is being pulled in two directions. Should one fork start on the Luna mount, for instance, whilst the other takes root from the Life line, it shows a conflict between family dictates and the need to follow an independent career and way of life (Figure 149). Whichever fork is the strongest wins through in the end so that if, say, the

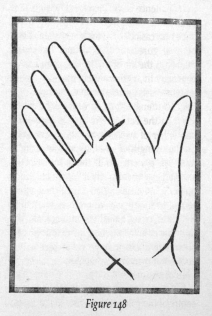

Figure 148

Figure 149

Figure 150

branch joined to the Life line is more dominant than the other, it would seem likely that
independence is sacrificed for the needs of the
family.

Very occasionally a double line of Fate may
occur (Figure 150). This invariably tells of a
duality in the life or career. Two jobs running
concurrently, perhaps, as in the case of a busy
and successful mother and business woman,
might be denoted by this formation.

When the Fate line is absent altogether it
has either of two interpretations depending
on the strength or weakness of the rest of the
hand. In a weak hand, the lack of Fate line
will indicate an unsettled individual, someone who might be called a misfit, who drops
out of ordinary society or conventional life.
But in a strong hand, the absence of a Fate
line can denote a freeing of restrictions and
such individuals may go on to become very
successful men and women, often in unusual
lines of business.

Just as the classical beginning is from the
centre of the palm at the wrist, so the classical

Figure 151

ending of the Fate line is just below the middle finger.

In some hands the line, instead of ending below the middle finger, swerves sharply in the direction of the finger of Jupiter to end just beneath the index (Figure 151). This is a fairly unusual ending and when seen it suggests a self-motivated individual. Often celebrities, politicians, well-known personalities and those whose work takes them into the public eye may possess this type of marking.

Should the line swerve towards the ring finger it is a happy sign of creative fulfilment and satisfaction (Figure 152). Often a career in the Arts is indicated by this formation.

Ending in a triple fork is perhaps the happiest feature to possess as it incorporates all the elements associated with the Jupiter, Saturn and Apollo influences and thus is very fortunate indeed (Figure 153).

The Fate and Apollo lines act as a back-up to one another so, if there are any weaknesses in either, one may bolster up the other or take

over altogether. Consequently, it is always important that these two lines be considered together.

Just as with the other major lines the quality of the Fate line should be consistent with the type of hand in which it is found. For example, by its very nature an **Earth** hand should contain a strong Fate line, for these positive, hard-boiled people have a strong sense of duty and commitment in life and always seem to know where they're going. Either the classic 'straight up the middle' line, or alternatively the 'early responsibility' line that stems from the Life line would suit this type.

The **Air** hand should have a clear line and, true to its love of imagination, people and communications, perhaps starting from the Mount of Luna; whilst the **Fire** hand, although also strong, would perhaps contain several breaks and branches to reflect its enthusiasm for new projects.

The **Water** hand is the most likely to con-

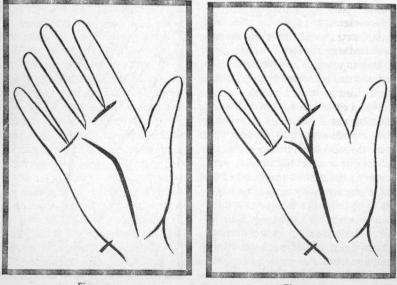

Figure 152   Figure 153

tain a Fate line that is fine, as consistent with all its other lines, but perhaps one that twists, turns and changes direction as it echoes the impressionability and changeability of this elemental type.

TIMING THE FATE LINE

The line is read from the wrist up towards the fingers. There are several different systems which may be used. One of the most popular is to say that the point at which the Fate line intercepts the Head line is the thirty-five-year mark. Given that the location of the Head line can vary markedly from hand to hand, in some, lying higher and in others lower, this system seems arbitrary.

A far more reliable method, to my mind, is to fix the thirty-five-year marker exactly in the centre of the palm. This can be worked out by measuring the hand from the topmost rascette, or bracelet, at the wrist right up to the bottom line that joins the middle finger to the palm. If a vertical line is drawn to connect these two points and divided into two, that half-way point, then, becomes the thirty-five-year marker.

Figure 154 illustrates how the timing gauge is applied to the Fate line.

Only in very few hands will the Fate line actually match this vertical line. On some hands the Fate line will lie obliquely across the palm either from the Mount of Luna or from the area of the Life line. In others, the Fate line might not even begin until further up in the palm. But regardless of the location of the Fate line, the measurements are still made on the drawn vertical line and then transferred across onto the the main Fate line itself.

Just as with the other lines of Life and Head, each millimetre marked off with a sharp-pointed pencil is roughly equivalent to one year. On the Fate line the counting starts from the top rascette, adding one year for each millimetre to coincide with the thirty-

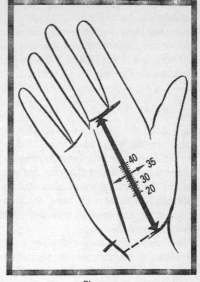

Figure 154

five-year mark. Alternatively, one could start the counting from the midway line and subtract downwards to the wrist. Then, from the half-way point each millimetre adds on one more year upwards towards the fingers.

By placing thirty-five in the centre of the palm it would seem to predispose everyone to an allotted three-score years and ten. But of course not all people reach the grand age of seventy and then again, many others happily live on to grander ages still.

In order to compensate for this, and also to take into account the fact that one year in the early formative period of a youngster's life feels, to the child, a good deal longer than the same year does to an adult of say fifty, the timing gauge has to be expanded to fit between zero and thirty-five and compressed thereafter towards the fingers. The millimetre-a-year rule still holds good in principle when it comes to the Fate line, but it is simply that the millimetres are stretched a little more generously up to the thirty-five-year mark than beyond it.

A methodical inspection of this line will highlight changes in the individual's way of life. It will show direction in life, successes and failures, difficulties and frustrations, ambitions that may be fulfilled or that simply evaporate into thin air.

NEGATIVE INDICATORS

As with all the other lines an island here reduces the energy and power represented by the Fate line (Figure 155). Generally, this formation points to a time of difficulties. In some hands it describes a period of dissatisfaction, especially connected with work. In other hands it suggests financial restrictions and anxieties over money.

Bars cutting across the line invariably point to obstacles, interference or obstruction around which the individual somehow has to negotiate (Figure 156).

A clean break in the Fate line (Figure 157) warns of a sudden change in the career, the

Figure 156

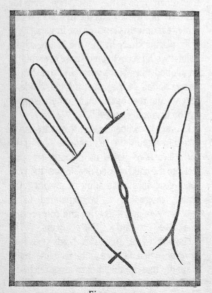

Figure 155

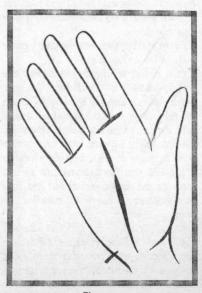

Figure 157

sort that might occur, for example, if an individual were to be made redundant out of the blue.

Stars can imply a shock or a major surprise to the system (Figure 158).

If a Fate line should end on the Head line it often implies that wrong decisions are made which are likely to have an adverse effect on the career (Figure 159).

Many Fate lines tend to end on the Heart line although branches or new sections of the line often sprout up and take over from it. In the cases where the Fate line stops dead on the Heart line it suggests that emotional influences or decisions have blighted the career (Figure 160).

POSITIVE INDICATORS

When a section of the Fate line comes to an end and is overlapped by a new piece, the interpretation is somewhat different to that of the clean break (Figure 161). Here, it is a posi-

Figure 159

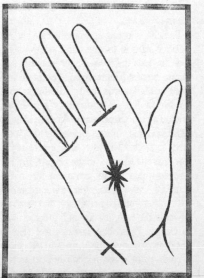

Figure 158

Figure 160

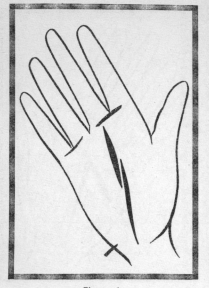

Figure 161

Figure 162

tive indication in as much as the change has been thought about and put into motion by the subject's own volition. Applying for a new job, moving to another part of the country and deciding to change career in midstream may all be denoted in this way.

Now and again a square may be seen on the line (Figure 162). A square is usually considered a sign of protection or of preservation. If the formation occurs over a break or an island, or over any of the negative markings, it shows that somehow the individual won't feel the effects quite so dramatically but will find a way of overcoming any of the adversity implied.

But sometimes the square, rather than sitting over the line, is attached to it by one of its sides. In this case, the square suggests a period of hard work, a time when the subject may feel almost as if trapped in a box. That period does indeed denote a time when the only thing to do is grit one's teeth and get the shoulder to the grind. And if the individual doesn't buck against it, but simply gets on

with the work before her, then she will find that it is a time of personal growth, a period of positive constructive progress when she is laying down very firm foundations for the future.

Branches shooting up from the Fate line are positive signs of progress and achievement. One towards the index finger suggests academic success (Figure 163a). The main line itself heads towards the middle finger so a branch in this direction does not apply. Should a branch reach out to the ring finger it tells of personal success and satisfaction, possibly connected with the Arts (Figure 163b). Towards the Mercury finger (Figure 163c), a branch would signify advancement in the financial, business, scientific or literary fields.

Branches from the percussion that reach up towards the Fate line are indicators of relationships. Those that fail to meet (Figure 164a) or cross over the main line altogether (Figure 164b) show relationships that fail. Branches that reach as far as the Fate line and merge into it are signs of relationships that do

Figure 163A–C   Figure 164A–C

work and indicate marriage. The whole question of relationships, including further information about this particular feature, will be
found in Chapter 12.

DIFFERENCES BETWEEN THE
DOMINANT AND PASSIVE
HANDS

The starting point of the Fate line may differ
between dominant and passive hands.
Remembering that, in brief, the passive hand
deals with the inner nature and the dominant
hand concerns the public side of the individual, any discrepancies will highlight conflict
according to in which hand the feature
occurs.

For example, a passive hand might contain
a Fate line that starts on the Mount of Luna,
whilst its correspondent in the dominant
hand ploughs a straight route from wrist right
up the centre to the middle finger. This would
reveal an individual who yearns to break out,

to be independent; perhaps to work in a field
that is rather different and has a bit of pizzazz
to it. In reality, she finds it safer to follow a
traditional trade and live a conventional life.
Ah, but she can still dream . . .

Just as with beginnings so, too, the endings
of the line may differ widely. Supposing the
Fate line in the dominant hand is much shorter than its passive partner ending on the
Head line, for example. This would illustrate
that the individual has made some unfortunate intellectual errors, perhaps was ill-
advised and made the wrong decisions thus
putting her job on the line. The shorter line
shows that as a result her career was prematurely jeopardized.

Any anomalous markings, such as bars or
islands, which appear only on the passive
Fate line will indicate internal doubts and
misgivings about work and about one's
private life. But the individual, however,
would not necessarily show any signs of such
problems on the outside.

THE APOLLO LINE

This line is variously known as the Apollo line, the Sun line, the line of success or even the line of fame (Figure 165).

It is usually considered to denote a deep, inner sense of fulfilment. Creative talents, artistic sensibility, luck, optimism, contentment and even financial rewards are each associated with this line depending upon the rest of the indications in the hand. But whatever it represents, from the very point it makes its appearance in the hand, the Apollo line signifies an awareness of contentment and satisfaction in one's life or work.

People find fulfilment in many different ways. For some it might come through success in business. For others it may be through creative work. For a man who has spent his working life in an unrewarding job, retirement may bring the opportunity of diversification and the time to pursue a creative hobby. For a woman, the birth of a much-loved and long-awaited baby may bring her the completeness she desires.

The Apollo line in its variety of forms, then, can represent that unique expression of satisfaction, that emotional fulfilment that comes with the recognition of one's talents. And it brings with it greater optimism, a sunnier outlook, affords a smoother ride and promotes an overall improvement in the general lot of one's life.

Figure 165

closer to the Head line. For many people it is seen only from above the Heart line whilst for others it may swerve in from the percussion edge, or even from the Life line on the opposite side of the palm. Now and again it springs from the Fate line itself, seemingly appearing like one of its branches rising up in the direction of the Apollo mount.

GEOGRAPHY

Like the Fate line, the line of Apollo lies vertically in the palm and may have several alternative beginnings. But, unlike the Fate line, this one always ends on the Mount of Apollo beneath the ring finger.

In a few rare instances it may be seen rising from the wrist and shooting its way up towards the third finger, paralleling the Fate line. More usually it may begin higher up,

PSYCHOLOGICAL CHARACTERISTICS

A strong Apollo line ensures its owner will enjoy a sense of self-fulfilment and satisfaction in her life and work. Creative talent will be prominent and if long and strong may even denote that the career will take the individual into the public eye.

A weak, thin or fine line shows untapped talent – it's certainly there but not developed to the best of the subject's potential.

Figure 166

Figure 167

Very occasionally, the Apollo line is seen to rise from the base of the Luna mount and to forge its way right up to the ring finger (Figure 166). This is the sign of exceptional talent which is spotted early on in the career and is sustained by the approval of the general public. A popular actress, a politician or a pop star might possess this sort of line.

If it should start a little higher up, taking root from the top of the mount of Luna, it has been referred to as the line of inheritance (Figure 167).

Shooting out from inside the Life line or from the Life line itself and then up towards the middle finger, tells that the individual has started off her career with a lot of help and possibly even financial backing from her parents (Figure 168).

When the Apollo line springs from the Fate line it tells that goals and ambitions in life are likely to be reached (Figure 169).

When the line sweeps in from high up on the percussion edge it is entering the hand from the mount of Mars (Figure 170). This

Figure 168

Figure 169

Figure 171

Figure 170

shows a true fighting spirit in life, a belief in one's talents and a determination to win through despite the odds and find fulfilment and success in work and in life in general.

Beginning from the centre of the palm, the Apollo tells of an awareness of happiness and satisfaction which only comes a little later on in life and which is achieved after much effort and persistent hard work (Figure 171).

Similar to the above, if the Apollo line takes root from either the Head or Heart lines it, too, shows that the awareness of satisfaction begins much later on in life and success in one's work is also due to the individual's own determined efforts and hard work (Figure 172). Beginning from the Heart line, at least, one is assured of an enjoyable retirement and an old age filled with love and warmth. This is the most common form of the Apollo line.

Traditionally, when three parallel Apollo lines are seen to rise above the Heart line (Figure 173) it is considered a most fortunate sign because, it is said, those possessing this marking will never be poor. However, it may

Figure 172

Figure 174

Figure 173

not mean that the subject will become filthy rich either, simply that money comes in when it's needed – sometimes just in the nick of time! Whether it is that such people are prudent and always have a little tucked away for a rainy day, or whether indeed they are 'born lucky' is a debatable point. Suffice it to say that even if they haven't a penny in their purses something always seems to turn up to save the day.

There are people who possess a whole bundle of Apollo lines on the Apollo mount, some may be thick or thin, some fragmented and some more prominent than others (Figure 174). Here, the formation denotes versatility, for these people are blessed with a host of different talents. They need and enjoy variety, turning their attention easily from one task to another. It is sometimes considered, however, that, despite their prodigious talents, by thus scattering their efforts across the board they may fail to achieve success in any specific area. Better perhaps to concentrate their attention in one direction and bring that to success.

The Apollo line acts as a back-up to the Fate line, so that if any adverse markings should exist on that line, a strong Apollo will compensate and even take over altogether. In exchange, the Fate line will bolster up the Apollo line in just the same way.

If the Apollo line throws out a branch to the Saturn mount or ends itself in that direction it indicates a serious, weighty approach to life; perhaps the career will be more vocational and carry a great deal of responsibility (Figure 175a). But if it should end further towards the Mercury area, it suggests a more social and extroverted personality which would reflect not only in her choice of career, but also in the way she conducts herself through the course of her work (Figure 175b).

Indeed, it would be wrong to conclude that the mere presence of the Apollo line signifies success and creative talent. Some people who are highly creative and very successful have a hand which is conspicuous for its absence of

Figure 175A–B

the line. But although they may have made it to the top of their profession, or have the approval and adulation of the public, the lack of the line shows that they themselves do not feel any satisfaction in what they do. The Apollo line does not simply represent creative talent, riches and success for the owners of the hands in which the line occurs, but what it *does* mean is that they will appreciate the inner contentment that their talents bring them.

As with all the other lines, the effectiveness of the qualities represented by the Apollo line varies according to the type of hand in which it occurs. Its impact is best felt on a hand with fewer lines so that if it should be strongly present in the **Earth** hand it would show that the creative talent in that person really stands out. More often than not, it is the Earth hand that lacks the line, or that has a shortened form if it starting high up, as this would reflect the dogged persistence and inclination to hard work that eventually brings its own rewards.

The multitalented **Air** type would probably have several lines of Apollo. A clear line is frequently found in this hand.

Fire types, with their enthusiasm and exuberance in life, are likely to have long, strong Apollo lines. And because they, like the Air types, are social personalities, a line taking root from the Luna mount and ending towards the Mercury area would not be out of place here.

Although the Apollo line is frequently found in the **Water** type, the fact that it contains such a jumble of fine lines anyway seems, in the normal course of things, to detract from the strength and power of this line.

TIMING THE APOLLO LINE

Similar to the Fate line, the line of Apollo is read from the wrist up towards the fingers. Here, too, the palm is measured from the top

Figure 176

rascette to the palmar join of the middle finger and the half-way mark established as thirty-five years of age.

Figure 176 illustrates the timing gauge for the Apollo line.

Very few hands will contain a line of Apollo that stretches all the way from top to bottom; more usually the line begins much higher up towards the upper third of the palm. Nevertheless, if a vertical line is drawn between the two points of the upper rascette and the palmar join of the middle finger and the thirty-five-year marker is fixed, it is possible to measure along that continuum and then transfer the dates across to wherever the Apollo line is found.

Following the rules for measuring the Fate line, roughly each millimetre equals one year. Starting from the mid-point, the scale may be marked off on the drawn vertical line with a sharp-pointed pencil, slightly expanding the gauge from thirty-five to zero and compressing it from thirty-five upwards. Once the drawn line has been marked off, the measure-

ments are transferred across to meet the line of Apollo.

An analysis of this line will show the growing sense of satisfaction, of contentment and self-fulfilment that an individual feels in life.

NEGATIVE INDICATORS

As with all the lines, a break denotes a change of direction or an interruption in the course of the working life of the individual (Figure 177).

Islands in the Apollo line have always traditionally been associated with scandal, malicious gossip, bad press or infamous behaviour of some kind (Figure 178).

Chaining weakens the line, showing that the creative talent is obstructed and frustrated in some way, possibly through external interference, at least for as long as the chained effect continues (Figure 179a).

Any bars that cut across the line denote obstructions, either in the form of severe crea-

Figure 177

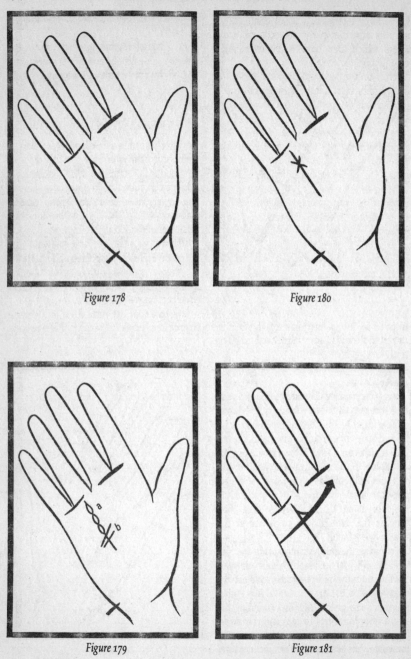

Figure 178

Figure 180

Figure 179

Figure 181

tive blocks or in terms of a negative influence that puts obstacles in the subject's path to success which then have to be overcome (Figure 179b).

A cross on the line has a similar meaning – that progress is hampered through obstruction and interference from outside (Figure 180).

Any little lines springing out of the Heart line and striking the line of Apollo, as in Figure 181, signify opposition in the path of success. This can come in the form of enemies scheming and plotting against the individual so that the subject's career is blighted.

A bar from the Head line that hits the Apollo line has much the same sort of significance, except that it is the individual who is responsible for destroying her own career through misjudgement and personal blunders (Figure 182).

Figure 183

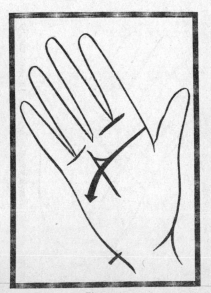

Figure 182

Figure 184

POSITIVE INDICATORS

A star on the line can indicate a major breakthrough in the career (Figure 183). Being 'discovered' as an entertainer, for example, or scooping the first prize in a major sweepstake, or pulling off the biggest deal in a businessman's life; these might all be represented by this feature in the hand.

A square formation on the line denotes a sense of protection, especially it if occurs over an adverse marking, in which case the difficulties implied will be mitigated (Figure 184).

DIFFERENCES BETWEEN THE DOMINANT AND PASSIVE HANDS

If the Apollo line is stronger in the passive than the dominant hand it suggests that talent is inherent but perhaps not as developed as it might be.

Should negative markings be seen only in the dominant hand, this suggests that forces and influences are responsible for creating adverse conditions in the subject's life which stand in the way of progress. However, as the passive line is stronger, it shows that the individual will not allow that interference to defeat her but will have enough inner strength to battle through.

CHAPTER ELEVEN

THE PSYCHOLOGY OF THE SUBSIDIARY LINES

Some hands are noticeable for the fact that they contain only a few bare lines. Others are more liberally covered, giving colour and interest to their owner's character and personality. And then, the nightmare of every hand analyst, there are those hands that are conspicuous for the very plethora of lines that cover the palm, that need time and patience to tease out each marking, to decide which line is essential and which might simply be irrelevant.

The difference between these hands lies in the subsidiary lines which are illustrated in Figure 185. **Earth** hands, for example, characteristically only possess the main lines. Subsidiary lines in these hands would not only stand out more markedly but, because uncharacteristic, would also be more significant.

Both **Air** and **Fire** hands are equally balanced in main and subsidiary lines. A complete lack of secondary lines here would be worthy of note.

Water hands, conversely, are known for the wealth of lines they possess. Subsidiary lines abound together with a variety of extraneous markings which simply represent the anxious, sensitive disposition of this type.

Attempting to classify as subsidiary lines these complex patterns of extraneous markings is a futile exercise, unnecessary and often a waste of time. For it is important to emphasize that, whatever its type, if a hand appears to be completely covered in a verit-

Figure 185

able mesh of lines, it is often an indication that the nervous system is badly stressed and possibly in need of medical treatment.

All other significant lines, other than the main ones, may be grouped together under the heading of **subsidiary lines**. These include the Mercury, Business and Health lines, the two curves of Intuition and Girdle of Venus, the two rings of Solomon and Saturn, as well as a variety of other markings, all of which help to add psychological insight to the jigsaw puzzle that makes up the individual.

THE MERCURY LINE

It is difficult to give a clear interpretation of this line because, although recognized since the birth of chirology, it has never really been satisfactorily pinned down, so to speak. It has been given various names and its significance, too, varies depending on whom one consults.

Some say it is better not to have the line at all. Others, that the line is best if solid and in one piece. There are those who believe it refers to health and those who see it as representing one's progress and acumen in the field of commerce.

Historically, the Mercury line has been known as the Hepatica, the Liver line, the Health line and the Business line.

It is certainly high time that some serious research was carried out on this line so as to clarify its significance once and for all.

When present, it is found towards the percussion side of the palm, or in the ulna area. Sometimes it may rise from the Life line, or from inside that line, from the mount of Venus (Figure 186). In other hands it may be completely independent and take root from the centre of the hand or even from the Mount of Luna.

Wherever it starts, its destination is the Mercury mount, hence its name; and hereby, perhaps, lies the clue to the essence of its meaning. The ulna side represents the subconscious part of the individual; the instinctive, intuitive, imaginative side of the nature. The area of Mercury deals with anything to do with literature; with relationships and communications; with the media; with business, science and medicine, and even with sexual matters. A wide brief, so it is not surprising then that the line should have so many alternative nuances.

In essence, though, the different facets of meaning to this mount all condense down to relationships and communications – how we

Figure 186

communicate through our writing, through our dealings with others; how we relate and express ourselves sexually, how we transmit news to one another and how our bodies state our health.

In addition to this the line, in the main, lies in the ulna area of the hand, its roots in the shade, its head in the light, thus linking our subconscious to our awareness. Communication, then, may be seen as a conscious expression of our instinctive and intuitive thoughts and feelings.

So, when we write or when we speak, it is a conscious manifestation of our inner thoughts. When we deal with others, we are opening ourselves to the outside world. When we're ill, it's our bodies' way of telling us that all is not well organically inside us. And when we use our sexuality, it is a means of relating, a way of expressing and releasing, our innermost, intimate thoughts to others.

Essentially, then, the Mercury line represents the bringing to light of our hidden or subconscious beings. It shows how we give vent to our imagination, how we communicate our inner thoughts, our dreams, and our intuitive instincts to the outside world.

And because communication takes different forms, so this line too may appear in different guises in the hand. Hence the historical confusion. But modern hand analysts nowadays agree on the multifaceted aspect of this line and readily distinguish between its variety of forms.

Consensus of opinion now confirms three distinct lines under this heading: the **Health** or **Hepatica line**, the **Business** or **Money line** and the **Bow of Intuition**, the line that measures our insight and powers of perspicacity.

THE HEALTH LINE

This is the line that is most commonly recognized as the Mercury line. It lies obliquely in the palm, either shooting up from the Life line or crossing it and taking root from the Mount of Venus. In some hands it is completely free of the Life line and begins just outside it on the Mount of Neptune.

Traditionally, the Health line has also been known as the Hepatica or Liver line because it was thought that the liver was synonomous with health – an unhealthy liver was believed to lead to a sick body and to a sluggish mind.

We no longer believe that the liver is at the root cause of all health, good or bad, but the line does, nevertheless, give a pretty fair idea about the individual's attitude to health.

When present, it denotes an awareness of one's nervous system. People with the line are responsive to each ache and pain in their bodies, can feel the slightest change in their autonomic systems and may somehow be physiologically vulnerable. They are, in general, simply in tune with their health.

People without this line are probably better off for its absence. Indeed, it has always been recognized that, unlike most of the other lines, no line of Mercury at all is better than possessing it in a strong, solid form. When missing, it implies that the individual is not plagued by the vagaries of ill health, is almost totally unconcerned by her nervous system and, on the whole (and assuming the Life line is strong), enjoys good physical health.

It is noteworthy that this line can come and go, strengthen, weaken, break, split into islands or develop all sorts of changes quite rapidly at times.

Although it is better that no health line should exist, if one does occur it is best when clear and strongly marked, either rising out from the Life line, or standing independent of it, and then running straight up to the Mercury mount. This shows an awareness of one's health on a general level; perhaps there's a keen interest in nutrition, in health care and also in keeping fit as a regular way of life.

Figure 187A–B

If the health line begins inside the Life line on the mount of Venus it denotes an individual who is sensitive to every slight change in her health. It can also suggest someone who suffered with more than average ill health as a child.

When the line is twisted, thins out and frays, or is formed of broken segments, it may be suggesting gastric or digestive problems (Figure 187a).

Islands in this line (Figure 187b), like those found at the beginning of the Life line, can denote bronchial or respiratory problems.

THE BUSINESS LINE

The second form of Mercury line is the Business line. This often begins higher up in the palm, sometimes independent and sometimes springing from the Fate line. Like the Health line this, too, ends on the Mercury mount (Figure 188).

Whenever it occurs, this line highlights an intuitive understanding of business matters, of the world of commerce and of money. People who possess such a line often make excellent businessmen and women. They have a gift for running organizations, a flair for generating money, are instinctive wheelers and dealers and somehow always seem to come out on top in the money markets.

THE BOW OF INTUITION

Although not usually classified as such, the Bow of Intuition is the third line which comes under the category of Mercury lines.

At its best, it is a semicircular line which begins on the Mount of Luna and sweeps its way up and round to the Mercury area (Figure 189). To find it perfectly formed in this way is unusual. More often than not it may appear in fragments, or be made up of tiny

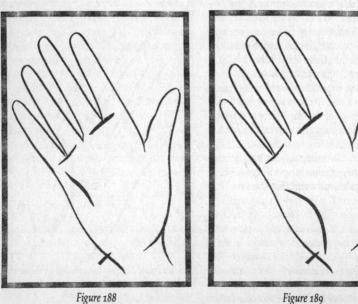

Figure 188   Figure 189

sections; it may only exist in part or, as in the majority of hands, be absent altogether.

When found it denotes strong powers of intuition. Such people have the power of pre-cognition; they are sensitive to natural rhythms, can read between the lines and sense what is going on – almost read other peoples' minds.

When the line is strongly formed in both hands it points to individuals who must be sensitively wired. These are the psychics and clairvoyants amongst us; they are telepathic, able to pick things up and uncannily predict future events. The stronger the line, the stronger the intuitive powers. When the line is weaker, broken or fragmented it reduces the power but still highlights a keen empath-etic understanding of others and a positive sixth sense which, nonetheless, should not be dismissed.

Figure 190

THE GIRDLE OF VENUS

The Girdle of Venus is another semicircular line, as illustrated in Figure 190. As with the Bow of Intuition, it is unusual to find it in its complete form. More often it exists as barely a fragment, perhaps a small section composed of little dashes. Like the Health line, it is perhaps best when missing altogether.

The line is located in the space between the Heart line and the root of the fingers, begin-ning on the web between the first and second fingers and sweeping round in a crescent to end between the ring and little fingers. Occa-sionally, it may take the form of a straight line, confusing the inexperienced eye by looking for all the world like a second bit of Heart line.

When present as a complete line, it reveals extreme emotional sensitivity. People with this formation may have difficulty rationalizing their emotions and as a con-sequence can suffer from nervous excitability, often working themselves up into an emo-tional lather of nervous tension. They seem to have little control over their passions, their hearts completely overruling their heads.

The more fragmented the line, the better the control over the emotions. Though sensi-tive, heightened emotion and nervous excite-ment can be restrained and kept within the bounds of reason.

THE VIA LASCIVIA

Historically, the Via Lascivia has, as its name implies, been mistakenly associated with lascivious and debauched behaviour. Modern research into the line has cleared its name and now is better referred to as the **Allergy** line or the **Poison** line.

As illustrated in Figure 191, it is found lying horizontally across the Mount of Luna, sometimes in the form of a short straight line and, at other times, extended into a rather ragged line that stretches to the Life line.

When present in the short horizontal form, it denotes a sensitivity to certain allergens. People with this line may be allergic to drugs, alcohol, tobacco, chemicals, pollens, fumes and a whole host of foods which produce an unpleasant physiological reaction in them. Allergy testing or controlled elimination programmes, under medical supervision, can often produce excellent results, pinpointing the irritant in question.

Such people are perhaps happier following a more natural way of life, steering away from modern chemicals and carefully watching their diets.

But when the line is extended to reach the Life line it can suggest a propensity to take drugs. When troubled, people with this formation may tend to run away from their problems, think they can resolve them by hitting the bottle or by using drugs to help them forget. It is for this reason that the line was

Figure 191

also called the 'Escapist' line. Those who possess this feature, then, must be aware of the dangers of drug, alcohol or solvent abuse to which they could easily succumb.

THE MEDICAL STIGMATA

The marking known as the Medical Stigmata, or Samaritan lines as they are sometimes called, is found on the fleshy pad beneath the inside edge of the little finger (Figure 192). It is composed of three short parallel lines, either placed vertically or slightly obliquely, and one horizontal line cutting across them.

The Medical Stigmata denotes an innate instinct for healing. People who possess this formation have strong therapeutic potential and tend to be drawn towards any of the branches of the medical profession, including alternative or complementary medicine and therapy and counselling of every description.

Though not all doctors, nurses, or vets necessarily have the Medical Stigmata, possession of the mark distinguishes those who, apart from the ability to heal, have those extra special qualities of empathy, caring and understanding that are recognized in a 'good bedside manner'.

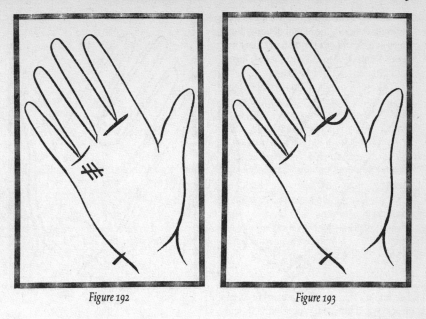

Figure 192   *Figure 193*

RING OF SOLOMON

The Ring of Solomon takes the form of either a diagonal line or a curve encircling the base of the index, or Jupiter, finger (Figure 193). Occasionally, it may consist of two parallel lines whilst in some hands only a fraction of the line may appear.

This marking is the sign of wisdom. Those who possess it seem to have an innate understanding of life. They make good psychologists, whether professionally or simply on a day-to-day basis, for they have excellent powers of insight and penetration. These people are often referred to as 'having old heads on young shoulders'.

THE TEACHER'S SQUARE

Also on the Mount of Jupiter beneath the index finger might be found the Teacher's Square, a set of four tiny lines that arrange themselves into a square formation (Figure 194).

When present, the marking denotes a special gift for imparting information. Teaching for such people is like second nature. Not only do they seem to have an innate appreciation of the difficulties and complexities of learning, but they are also able to put across their material in a natural and fluid manner.

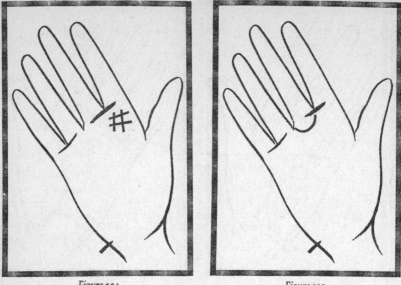

Figure 194   Figure 195

RING OF SATURN

This marking consists of a semicircular line lying like a collar beneath the middle, or Saturn, finger (Figure 195).

Fortunately, the Ring of Saturn is not so commonly found but when it does make its rare appearance it acts almost as a dampener, as a wet blanket. The ring looks like a barrier, hemming in the spontaneous common sense and equilibrium of the personality that the middle finger represents. The result is someone who finds it hard to muster any feelings of *joie de vivre*, who is considered a bit of a misery or an old Jonah, as the saying goes.

TRAVEL LINES

Travel and movement may be represented in the hand in several different ways.

An important journey or a move may be indicated by a downswept branch that springs out of the Life line and shoots towards the centre of the hand. The more important the move, or the longer the journey, the stronger and longer the travel line (Figure 196a).

A change of address or a removal might be indicated in this way and sometimes, when property is implicated (the purchase of a much-wanted home, for example), the movement branch may be accompanied by a rising

Figure 196A–B

Figure 197

line, springing out from the same point in the Life line and shooting up in the direction of the middle finger.

Important journeys or holidays are also marked with a strong branch and, when travelling takes the individual overseas, the branch may extend right over to the Luna mount.

Any problems, difficulties in the buying and selling of property, for example, or possibly disruptions during a trip, could well show up in the form of an island (Figure 196b), a star, a break in the line or a bar across it. The stronger and clearer the line, the better the auguries of a successful journey or move of house.

A Life line that forks towards the base of the palm so that one line shoots off towards the Luna area is another indication of a love of travelling. Those who possess this line may be confronted with the choice of living abroad.

A third way that travel may be represented in the hand is by actual Travel lines. These lie horizontally across the Luna area, entering the palm from the percussion edge and stretching out towards the Life line (Figure 197). Representatives, businessmen and women, seasoned travellers and anyone whose work regularly takes them overseas may possess a series of these lines.

Occasionally, a series of cross-lines may occur a little higher up on the percussion just below the Heart line. Rather than actual travel lines these represent a form of restlessness and denote the individual who simply can't keep still but must be constantly on the go. It may be the sign of the compulsive traveller, the person with itchy feet, but more usually the feature points to someone with a low boredom threshold, who simply has to keep compulsively busy (Figure 198).

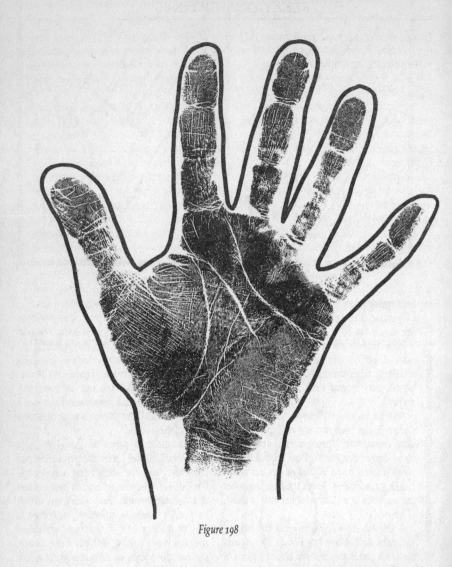

Figure 198

RELATIONSHIP LINES

Like movement and travel, relationships may be represented in a variety of ways according to the type of relationship in question.

It used to be thought that children were represented in the hand by tiny vertical lines on the top edge of the palm just below the little finger. Years of observation, however, seem to have disproved these markings as reliable indicators, although a few palmists do still appear to give them some credence.

Evidence, though, has shown that they do not correspond to one's own natural offspring, as they have been found in the hands of people who have not borne any children of their own at all but who have admitted to being close to nieces, nephews, foster children or pupils.

An alternative indication of relationships, which can include the birth of a child, may be seen as tiny branches peeling off the inside of the Life line (Figure 199). This is better described as denoting a new responsibility, whether it is the development of a new romantic attachment, the birth of a baby or even granny moving into stay.

Matters concerning parents and the family may be reflected in the **Family Ring**. This formation is usually a chained line marking the base of the second phalanx of the thumb as it meets the palm (Figure 200a). Good parental links and strong family bonds are denoted by a strong Family Ring whilst a weak one would suggest little or no feeling for one's family at all.

Horizontal lines emanating from the Family Ring and stretching out towards the Life line show parental influence and sometimes pressure exerted by members of the family (Figure 200b). When one of these influence lines actually touches the Life line it denotes a con-

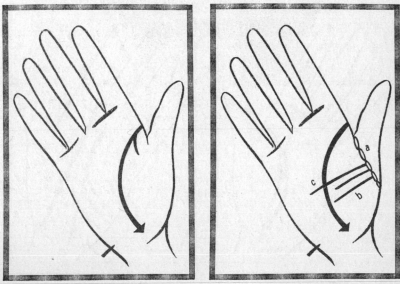

Figure 199   Figure 200A–C

flict of interests, a time of decision, of divided loyalties. The eternal problem of duty versus desire may be highlighted by such a line as this.

But when the influence line cuts right across the Life line and beyond (Figure 200c) it then becomes a trauma line, implying that the problem concerns stress or opposition stemming directly from the family.

MARRIAGE LINES

As with the children lines, it used to be thought that the number of marriages one was likely to have corresponded to the number of tiny horizontal lines that cut the edge of the percussion just beneath the little finger. Again, as with the children lines, this is a controversial point: some practitioners maintain that they do emphatically represent marriages, whilst others flatly refute it.

Because this is the subconscious side of the hand, these lines can only symbolize the attitude or feelings one has towards one's marriage and partner in life, rather than denoting the actual union itself.

New relationships, which may or may not ultimately lead to marriage, may be denoted, similar to the indications of children, by the tiny branches that peel off the inside of the Life line. If the branch strengthens and then continues parallel to the line of Life, it shows that the relationship will develop into a very strong influence in the individual's life (Figure 201).

But a still more reliable guide to marriage is seen in the branches which stem from the Luna area and sweep in from the percussion

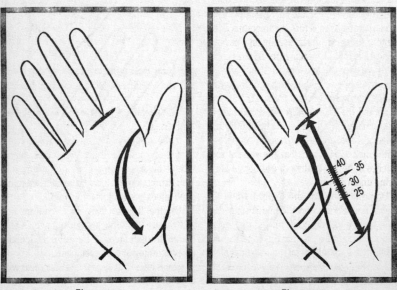

Figure 201　　　　　　　　　　Figure 202

edge towards the Fate line. If the branch doesn't quite meet, or if it crosses right over the Fate line, the relationship is likely to break up. But if one should run towards, and actually merge in with the Fate line itself, it is classically a sign of marriage. Using the timing gauge against the Fate line will give a good indication of when the marriage is likely to take place (Figure 202).

LINES ON THE FINGERS

Some fingers are noticeable for their smoothness whilst others have marked creases running either diagonally or horizontally along the phalanges (Figure 203).

As a general rule, lines on the fingers are a sign of tiredness and stress whether on a physical or psychological level. Remembering that each digit represents a different aspect, it is often possible, then, to identify and isolate the source of the problem.

Small horizontal lines across the basal phalanges highlight frustration whilst stronger vertical creases show strain. These are often the two signs of tiredness, warning that the individual needs time to rest and to rebuild her physical reserves and energies.

Horizontal lines across the fingertips again denote stress but this is usually on a psychological level. Such markings reveal stress from personal worries and anxieties and identify the areas in one's life which are giving the subject cause for concern.

Should the lines, which are also known as stress marks, occur across the tip of the index finger, they denote worries in connection with one's work, and that the general confidence in one's standing or position in life is being undermined.

Domestic concerns are implied when the cross-lines are seen on the middle fingertip. And if they should occur on the ring finger one's whole area of happiness and self-fulfilment is brought into question. Often, these two together are especially marked with stress lines which focus the problem area as one connected with relationships and the

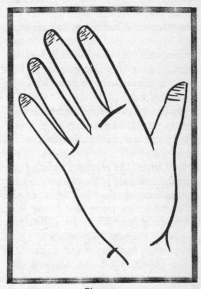

Figure 203

general feeling of stability and security of the individual.

If the majority of these lines are concentrated on the little finger it may be a sign of either business worries or a problem with self-expression – which may also encompass difficulties in sexual relations.

On the thumb, these lines confirm and emphasize that the pressures have filtered through to all areas of the subject's life and are beginning to overwhelm him.

Stress lines may appear and disappear with some frequency. Pressures at home or at work can produce these markings almost overnight, but with the proper rest and relaxation, and often with a change of attitude and a new perspective on life, the markings can disappear just as quickly as they appeared.

Vertical lines on the top phalanges of the fingers, however, are another matter. It is believed that they again highlight stress, but this time it is purely of a physiological nature and represents stress on the endocrine system. Such marking will be discussed more fully in Chapter 21.

THE RASCETTES

The rascettes, or bracelets as they are otherwise known, are those lines right at the base of the hand which act as the divider between palm and wrist. They may occur singly or in a set up to four in number and usually take the form of a chain.

Historically, claims have been made about the rascettes as indicators of longevity but there seems to be no substantive evidence to corroborate this.

But there is one important indicator concerning these lines which has some bearing on health matters. Normally, the rascettes lie in a straight line at the base of the palm. Occasionally, however, the top rascette may be seen to curve markedly up into the palm thus forming itself into an arch (Figure 204). When this occurs it is often a sign of some gynaecological weakness – menstrual irregularities, for example, or difficulties in childbirth. All such problems with the reproductive system may come under this category.

Figure 204

PART FIVE

THE EMOTIONS

CHAPTER TWELVE

RELATIONSHIPS AND COMPATIBILITY

Holding hands is often the first sign of love. Tender caresses, gentle fingers outstretched touching, intertwining. Palms hot, electric on the lover's skin, conveying urgent messages of passion and desire. Thus, two people express their feelings for one another, show they're in love. **With** our hands we show emotion, feelings and affection. With our hands we show others we care. But **in** our hands lie our innermost thoughts and desires, deepest secrets of hate and love.

Indeed, emotions, relationships, how we interact with others, the kind of lovers we are and our attitudes to sex and marriage are all reflected in our hands. By understanding the patterns we are able to gain a better insight into our psychological processes: how we tick, the sort of signals we give out, how we think we present ourselves to others and how others actually perceive us.

Very often when we make mistakes in our relationships. When we choose the wrong partners, it could be because we simply don't understand ourselves well enough; we haven't fully worked out the sort of partner we want, or need, to share our lives with. Hand analysis, then, may hold some of the answers.

Simply looking at the shape of a hand will be enough to give some general pointers and directions about an individual's motivations, ambitions and drives. The shape will give broad clues about the sort of lover a subject will make, the type of partner she is likely to be, what she will bring to a marriage and expect out of it. The shape, then, is the first line of approach when considering the whole question of emotions.

THE EARTH TYPE LOVER

Earth types are just as sensible when it comes to matters of the heart as they are in all other aspects of their lives. Solid, even stolid individuals, they make reliable partners, practical and with their feet firmly planted on the ground.

As lovers, these will woo with logic and common sense. There will be little flowery prose for they are not the most romantic and definitely not the most imaginative of people. But, when they think they have found the mate with whom they want to spend the rest of their lives, they will pursue that person with vigour and determination, not giving up until they have won the affection of the object of their desire.

And because they are staunch traditionlists, Earth types are more likely than any of the other groups to fall into conventional, stereotype roles within marriage – the male is the leader, the provider, whilst the female's place is in the home.

Not great talkers about their inner emotions, they love with no pretensions, and often with no frills or furbelows either. But on the whole they are sincere individuals, honest and level-headed, and what they lack in romance they more than make up for in the security they give and the practical support they bring to their partners.

THE AIR TYPE LOVER

Whizz kids who are something in the City – she with her crisp, tailored suit, he with the double-breasted and silk shirt – are likely to belong to this category.

Air types are intelligent people, gifted with sparkling conversation and ready wit. Those who cannot match their intellect or quick repartee may indeed feel intimidated by these seemingly formidable types. Hardly surprising as they are masters and mistresses of the verbal put-down. One crosses their path at one's own peril!

When looking for a suitable mate people of this group will be very fussy in their choice. They have high standards of excellence and anyone they choose will have to pass muster. Intellectually and financially they will expect a good match and they will go for the best they can find; anything less simply will not do.

As partners, however, they can seem cool and remote, sometimes blowing hot and then, when least expected, blowing cold again. Indeed, their love tends to be more intellectual than emotional, yet they are emotionally fairly stable types, knowing what they want out of life and out of their relationships and, furthermore, knowing just how to go about getting it.

In marriage they can be enormously stimulating, for their Mercurial mentality means they have wide-ranging interests with which to engage their vast curiosity. But they do enjoy pitting their wits against fresh challenges and if their relationships cannot provide this piquancy for them, their whole interest in the marriage could well be put in the balance.

THE FIRE TYPE LOVER

Just as fire can hold a thrill and fascination, so too, can Fire types when in love.

People of the Fire category have masses of vitality and tend to live life in the fast lane. They are excitable and emotional, easily prone to tears of sadness and equally of joy.

Of all the types, these can be the most ardent, the most exciting and enthusiastic of lovers. Passionate individuals, they will pursue their beloved with energy and fervour, using all the powers of persuasion they possess until they get what they want.

But as with fire too, there is a danger that they may sometimes come on too strong, burning too fiercely with their passion, falling out of love just as quickly as they fell in.

But, once they think they have found their true mate, they will make constant and faithful companions. And what makes them truly happy is to have their egos boosted every now and again. A husband or wife, then, who knows how to respond to this need, and is able to make their fiery partners feel ten feet tall, will be going a long way towards preserving a happy marriage.

As partners, the Fire types are warm and caring, ready to comfort and support, to cheer and spread happiness with their natural extroversion and effervescence, which seems to rub off on anyone with whom they come into contact. Whatever difficulties life has in store, their natural buoyancy and optimism carry them through – along with anyone fortunate enough to be in their wake.

THE WATER TYPE LOVER

Water types are in love with love. Romantic and idealistic, they see relationships and marriage through rose-coloured spectacles.

They live very much on their emotions, more so than any of the other three categories, and some have even been described as verging on emotional instability. Their notorious sensitivity means they can be easily hurt, with every minor slight cutting them to the very quick.

People belonging to this category are characteristically impressionable. Indeed, they are easily influenced, often falling for rogues with a hard luck story, or simply marrying for all the wrong reasons. All too often, then, Water types attach themselves to quite unsuitable partners, forming unsatisfactory and unhappy marriages. In extreme cases, because of their gentleness and peace-loving nature they may find themselves victims not only of unscrupulous but also of aggressive partners.

Because they are unworldly, living with their heads in the clouds, Water types do well to marry someone who can deal with the nitty-gritty of everyday life – taking charge of the finances, for example, paying the bills on time – all the basic mundane necessities that modern life requires.

And when they do make suitable matches, they bring wonderful qualities of gentleness and understanding to their marriages. As partners, they can be loving and tender, instilling a sense of peace and filling the house with music and beautiful artefacts, very often of their own creation.

GETTING ON TOGETHER

Earth types get on very well together but to others they could seem somewhat dull and lacking in inspiration. They may not get on so terribly well with Air types as these are rather too volatile for them. Fire hands would do because they are as energetic as Earth is hardworking and they could add that sparkle of inspiration that Earth sometimes lacks. Water types are far too wet for positive, determined Earth.

Air types go well together, they would enjoy each other's enthusiasm for communication and gas their way into the early hours of the morning! Earth types wouldn't be stimulating enough and would probably fall asleep just when Air was thinking she was getting to the good bit in her story. Fire would be stimulating and both could get a charge out of being together. Water and Air could muddle along together, living off each other's dreams.

Fire types would make passionate lovers together but equally their passions can lead to a very stormy relationship. Earth may dampen their ardour at times but they could still get on well enough together. Air and Fire make a good combination. With Water partners Fire people could find their enthusiasm fizzles out.

Water types would make sweet music together but, as they're both so dreamy, who would deal with the nitty-gritty tasks in life or, for that matter, remember to pay the gas bill on time? Earthy types wouldn't normally make good partners for them, they're too basic for lovely, gentle, ethereal Water-handed folk. Air would make good companions. Fire would evaporate them!

The compatibility chart opposite shows at a glance who gets on with whom; which general types make viable companions with each other and which would be simply explosive in the others' company.

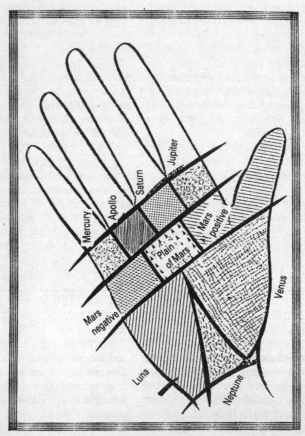

Figure 205

COMPATIBILITY CHART

	EARTH	AIR	FIRE	WATER
E A R T H	Sensible relationship. Hard-working. Solid. Conventional. Perhaps lacking a certain 'je ne sais quoi' that adds a touch of spice to life.	Could have its difficulties. Air may appear too breezy or superficial for sensible Earth. Earth needs too much routine for buzzy Air.	This might work. Fire provides stimulation that Earth lacks and Earth can provide stability with which to channel Fire's energies. But with these two there could be fireworks!	These two live in different worlds. Not an auspicious match as neither would understand the passions of the other.
A I R		Both Mercurial types who would breeze through life together. Creative partnership full of ideas but perhaps a little shallow at times.	Good potential here. Both lively and spirited making a stimulating partnership. Only small snag is Air might be too cool for Fire whilst Fire too ardent for Air.	Good partnership. Each appreciative of the other's creative sensitivities. Water could rely on Air's worldliness to deal with day-to-day business. Air would be inspired by Water's vision.
F I R E			Active and adaptable. Full of ideas. Partnership could be steamy and sultry one minute, then stormy the next.	Could work. Fire would benefit from Water's culture and refinement, as long as Fire's energy doesn't burn out delicate nature of Water.
W A T E R				Gentle understanding relationship full of meaning and beauty. But as neither very worldly may have trouble dealing with the realities of everyday life.

THE MOUNTS

The shape of the palm, then, will outline the general characteristics – how particular types of people are likely to love and interact with each other, and what sort of partners they are likely to make. But the mounts, the digits and the line formations will focus in from the general to specific qualities, according to the hand in which they occur. Any mount that is especially pronounced, or that stands out in any way, will home in on distinctive characteristics and tendencies that give strong clues about its owner's romantic inclination and chances of making a happy marriage (Figure 205).

JUPITER

With a prevalent Jupiter mount the disposition is a happy, jovial one. Jupiterians are particularly noted for their generosity and largesse. And because they like to share their luck and good fortune with others, so they like to share their lives, too, and as such they do tend not only to marry but to marry well. Jupiterians make solid, traditional matches, enjoying fairly conventional relationships and marriages.

SATURN

People whose Saturn mounts are over-developed are characterized by their parsimony and lugubriousness. Often described as miserable types, fairly depressive and with a tendency towards a wet-blanket approach to life, they tend to be loners, preferring a solitary existence, and thus tend not to marry at all. But if they do fall in love, however, and decide to get hitched, it is more likely to be much later on in life or to marry someone much older than themselves.

APOLLO

Those with a very well-developed Apollo mount are happy, creative types, often finding a rich, spiritual meaning to life. As partners they are great fun to be with, full of enthusiasm and optimism for the future. Life with this type is never dull. Marriage for them is a form of enrichment, of extending one's personal creativity. On the whole, then, Apollonians do like to get married, very often making successful and rewarding matches.

MERCURY

People whose Mercury mounts stand out generally marry well. Their partnerships tend to be lively and full of activity. There's always plenty going on in a Mercurial relationship, which will be seen by outsiders as rather dynamic. Intellectual, scientific, financial or business interests will be shared and form a central core of interest within the partnership. But the most important aspect of the Mercurial individual is a need for freedom. If they feel themselves too heavily tied down, they will rebel with a vengeance. So marriage with this type, though lively and fun has to be somewhat open-ended, with not too many strings or conditions imposed.

MARS

With Mars most pronounced, the relationship may be powerful and steamy. If the lower Mars area is large there could well be physical aggression, whilst fortitude and persistence may characterize a relationship where the upper Mars area stands out. One way or another, there will be a lot of energy in the Martian household and the partnership could well share several sporty interests. Those with this feature often make faithful lovers and lifelong partners.

LUNA

When the Luna mount is highly developed and also the largest mount in the hand it tells of a cold and distant nature. Owners of this formation possess somewhat intangible emotions – that is to say, it is difficult to pin them down when it comes to their feelings. There is a general tendency for this type to lack affection and any marriage they make tends to be unviable and possibly even unconventional.

VENUS

Contrary to the Luna mount, the fuller the Venus mount the more outgoing, exuberant and happy-go-lucky the individual. People with this formation are warm and friendly and make lusty lovers. The bigger the mount, the bigger the libido. Full of the joys of spring, Venusians make loving partners and, in general, happy marriages.

THE DIGITS

A comparison of the digits will yield a great deal of information about the way two people are likely to interact. A partner with long fingers, for example, takes a completely different approach from one with short digits.

Long-fingered individuals are patient and love detail. They enjoy fine, intricate work and have a meticulous character which can make them fussy and finicky or plain pernickety at times. They hate cutting corners and tend to go strictly by the book.

Shorter fingers show a tendency to impatience, especially when it comes to pedantic or nit-picking behaviour. They are quick, sharp on the uptake and often inspirational. Excellent planners, they make good organizers as long as they can leave the detailed stuff to their longer-fingered friends.

Obviously, here, there are some fundamental behavioural differences which, on the surface, are likely to conflict one with the other. Couples with discrepant finger lengths may indeed come to loggerheads, each insisting that his or her way is the best. Learning to combine their efforts, however, each concentrating on the tasks best suited to his or her nature, would be far more conducive to a successful relationship together.

People don't all hold their fingers in the same way, and how the digits are actually held in relation to each other will also reveal behavioural tendencies which have to be taken into account when considering compatibility. Of particular interest here is how the two middle fingers are held, whether close together or wide apart.

Held close indicates a strong need for security, a need to touch, to cuddle up. Such people are sociable and enjoy the company of others around them (Figure 206).

Apart, is the sign of the loner (Figure 207). These people may be described as shy or even considered plain antisocial at times. They are self-reliant and resourceful but above all they need some time to themselves in the day, just a little space and silence in order to recharge their batteries and regain their mental and spiritual composure.

Thumbs are a big character giveaway. Both the structure and how far a thumb opens away from the palm are most revealing.

An acute angle of opening is usually the sign of a cautious, reserved nature (Figure 208). Life is considered fairly tough by this type. In some cases the restraint can extend to

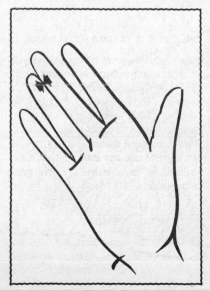

Figure 206

Figure 207

narrow-mindedness and even penny-pinching meanness. A partner possessing this feature is no sugar-daddy!

Contrary to this, a thumb that opens out more than ninety degrees denotes extravagance (Figure 209). Champagne and caviare will be produced at the drop of a hat by a partner with this thumb formation. Any excuse for a celebration will do.

The thicker and more bulbous the thumb, the stronger and more aggressive the individual. People with this type of thumb have a need to control, to dominate, to rule with a fist of iron. In any relationship they will want to be top dog: what they say goes – or else.

The longer and more elegant the thumb, the more refined and rational will be the intellectual processes. Such people will be fair-minded and tolerant, always ready to discuss matters with their partners and to share in making decisions.

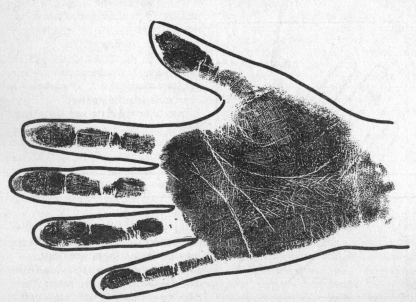

Figure 208

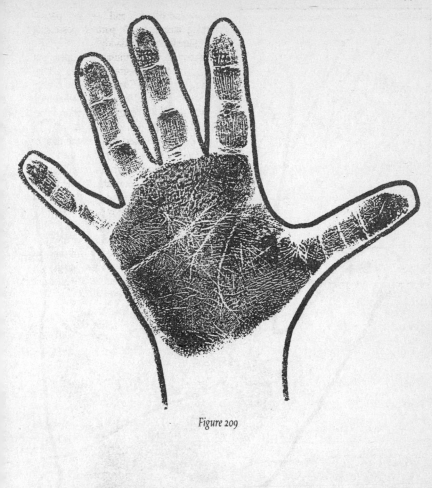

Figure 209

THE LINES

It is the Heart line which directly represents our emotions, what we expect from our partners and how we see love and marriage. But the Head line, too, will provide a good deal of information when considering how we express our feelings, how we interact with others, and how we might learn to coexist harmoniously within a partnership.

THE HEART LINE

A Heart line that curves right up to end between the first two fingers reveals a warmhearted and down-to-earth approach to love and relationships in general (Figure 210). The problem here is putting one's feelings into words. These people prefer to show their

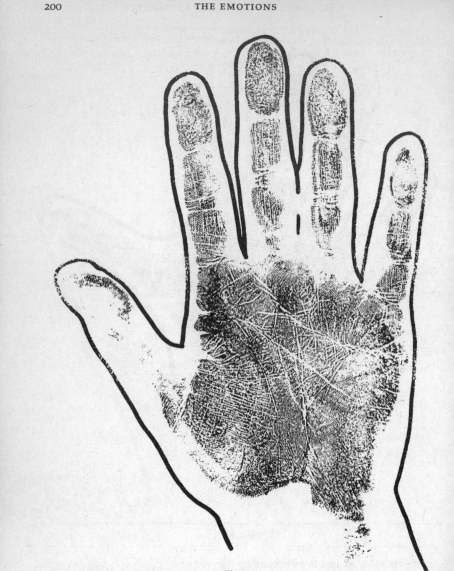

Figure 210

affection through their actions rather than talking about those deeper, inner emotions. Often, however, the inability to verbalize their innermost feelings means that they bottle them up inside, and if a release mech-

anism, (such as a friend who's a good listener, for example), can't be found, they can become, emotionally at least, potential volcanoes.

If a lady has a partner with this marking, it

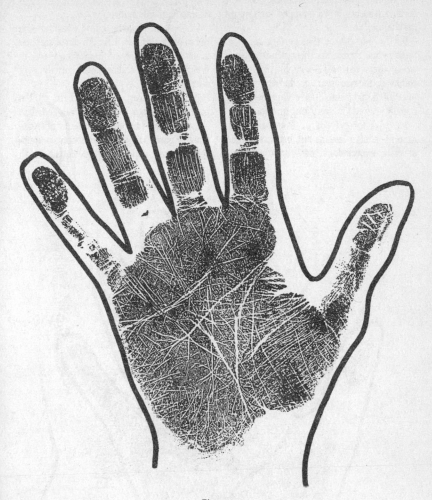

Figure 211

is useless to expect him to whisper sweet nothings – he's most definitely not that sort. However, he can be relied on for his genuine warmth and love, even if he doesn't say so. And if he does manage to utter those three little words, then it has taken a lot of guts for him to do so.

Romance with a capital R is essential to anyone whose Heart line ends in the centre of the index mount (Figure 211). These people are terrific idealists who tend to see things through rose-coloured spectacles. Their view of love and marriage is straight out of fairytales: they dream of knights on shining chargers, roses around the door, velvet-whispered words of love against a setting sun. And the lover has to be perfect, a hero or heroine who can be worshipped high up on the altar of love.

But no one can be that perfect, much to these people's chagrin. Their picture of love, when their partners inevitably show the chinks in their armour, or the rips in their tulle gown, fades into dust leaving them emotionally scarred for a very long time indeed.

Many of these types do eventually learn from life's bitter lessons but, because of their idealistic expectations these, in comparison with the other types, are more likely to suffer disappointments in love.

One answer could be to find a partner with the same marking so that both can share their fantasy world of illusion and romance and, in typical fairytale ending, live happily ever after!

When the Heart line ends right on the index finger it is a sign of the high achiever, someone who has high standards of excellence (Figure 212). Great perfectionists themselves, they expect to see equally high

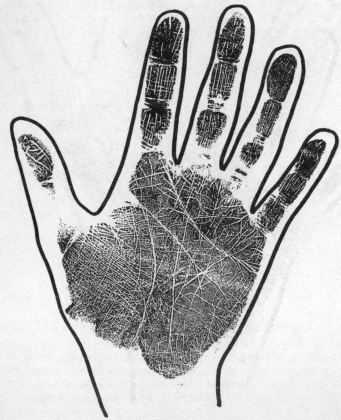

Figure 212

standards in others. Consequently their partners have to earn their stripes, have to work hard to win the affection of these types.

Unlike the former category, these are not at all idealistic. Rather, they may be described as very realistic. When it comes to marriageable partners, they aim high. But, to give them credit, once they have tracked down the right person for them these people will become loyal and devoted companions throughout life and do their utmost to make the relationship a good one.

With a long straight line that stretches across the palm almost to touch the other side, work is given priority over love (Figure 213). This line is not a common marking and when it does exist it is more likely to be found in a man's hand. It may well represent a workaholic, someone who takes his commitments and responsibilities seriously. There is no doubt that as partners they make responsible providers and that they are loving people. It's just that, when work calls, everything and everyone must take second place.

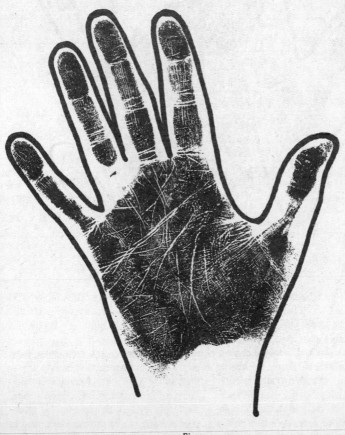

Figure 213

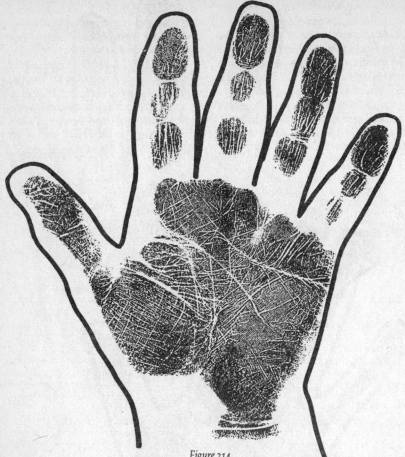

Figure 214

Another fairly uncommon Heart line is the short, straight one which barely manages to reach beneath the second finger (Figure 214). Again, this is more often considered to be a masculine line and is said to be the mark of egotism and selfishness. People possessing this feature are characteristically sexually aggressive and out purely for their own self-gratification. Thus the line classically high-lights the Casanova instinct. Perhaps this is simply a strategy for masking personal inade-

quacies; perhaps insecurity drives their need for sexual conquests. Whatever the spur, this line is not the best augury for a happy and fulfilling relationship.

The Simian line cuts a deep crease from edge to edge of the hand. (Figure 215). This is the marking of intensity; of emotional tunnel-vision; of downright jealousy. Such strong, passionate feelings, so prone to the green-eyed monster can, in extreme cases, lead to possessiveness which may ultimately stifle a

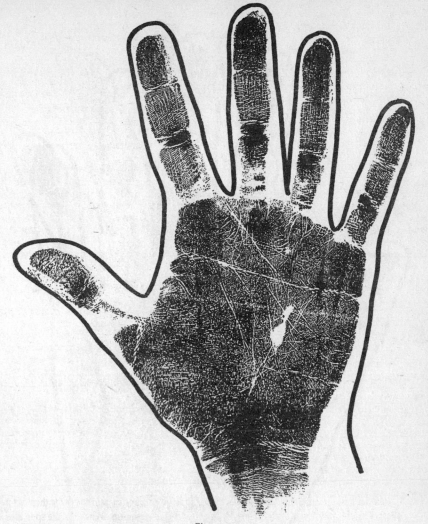

Figure 215

relationship if not destroy it altogether.

Sometimes, as in Figure 216, the Heart line has a forked ending. When it ends with two or, better still, three branches it is an excellent sign of a healthy and well-balanced attitude to love. These people are usually very happy types who make caring, loving and understanding partners in life.

The picture becomes complex but fascinating when discrepancies occur in this line between the left and right hands. The dominant hand represents the public persona whilst the passive hand reflects the **anima** – the inner, private self.

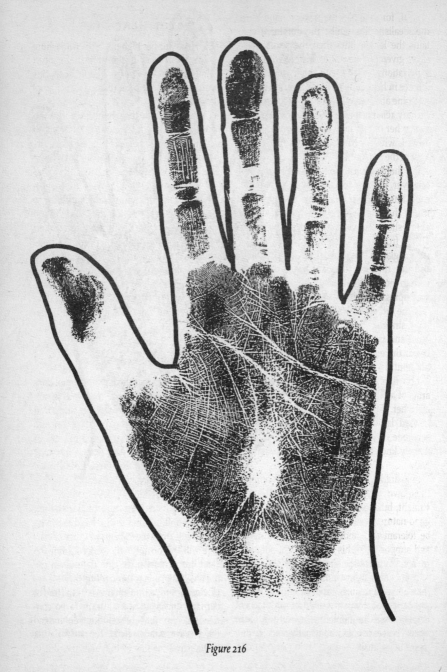

Figure 216

So if, for example, the passive hand bears the idealistic line whilst the dominant contains the longer line, then the sexual messages given out are not consistent with one's expectations. A lady with this particular difference in her hands would see herself as soft, feminine and romantic. She'd be looking for a dreamy relationship with a man who would sweep her off her feet, bring her roses by the armful, whisper words of love to her by the light of the moon.

But the messages she's actually giving out, however, is not of tulle and of starlight but of cool, business-like efficiency; and until she learns that her persona does not match her anima she will go on wondering why men are all so frosty and starchy towards her. A simple glance at her Heart lines would soon sort out the confusion and then she could start to modify her behaviour and, indirectly, the impression she gives out.

If the situation were reversed so that the long straight line occurred in the passive hand and the romantic one in the dominant hand, the emotional pattern would be quite different. Here, the message that's given out is of a romantic daydreamer who needs the arms of a big hunky man around her to look after her. In reality, this is one cool, level-headed lady, efficient and self-resourceful, someone who knows her own mind and equally knows how to get what she wants in life!

In a similar fashion, couples may compare their own Heart lines. If the man has the straight, business-like line and the lady's is a good-natured one ending in a fork, she will be tolerant and understanding of his needs and supportive in his work. But, if she possesses the idealistic line and he the short 'wham-bam-thank-you-mam' one, then she'll have to kiss romance goodbye. And if either possesses the Simian line their early years together will undoubtedly be riddled with sexual possessiveness and tormented by the pangs of jealousy.

THE HEAD LINE

If the Head line lies high up, as if encroaching on the Heart line, it shows that the head definitely rules the heart. People with this formation may be described as cool customers.

The reverse is the case, however, when the Heart line is low, dropping into the territory of the Head line. Here it suggests that the individual can be over-emotional, that it is the heart that rules the head.

A straight Head line reveals a straightforward, practical, no-nonsense attitude to affairs of the heart (Figure 217). In terms of love, these people tend to control their emotions and make rather conventional lovers. A curved Head line is quite different. These people are far more broad-minded (Figure 218). They are prepared to take risks, to experiment, and are more understanding and accepting of unconventional relationships.

MARRIAGE LINES

It used to be held that the tiny horizontal lines entering the palm from the percussion directly beneath the little finger, as illustrated in Figure 219, were signs of marriage. Indeed, these have even been labelled the Lines of Union. It was, and indeed still is by some chirologists, believed that these lines predict the number of marriages or serious relationships that an individual is likely to have.

Moreover, it has been stated that from their condition and position in the hand it is possible to tell from these lines whether a marriage will last or not and, working from the Heart line upwards, roughly date when the union will take or has taken place.

Evidence for their reliability as predictors of marriage, however, would seem to be controversial. In some hands they do indeed reflect partnerships, even accurately dating the time and the fate of the marriage. But in

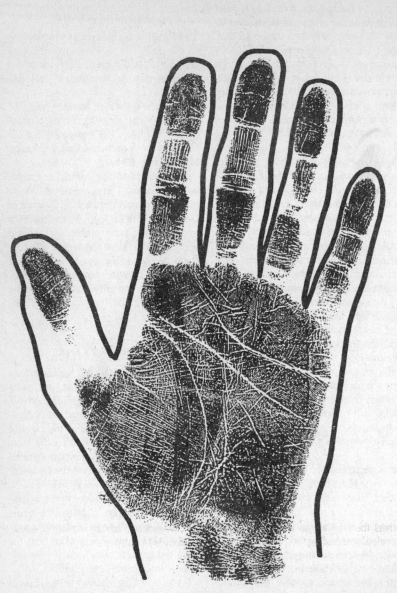

Figure 217

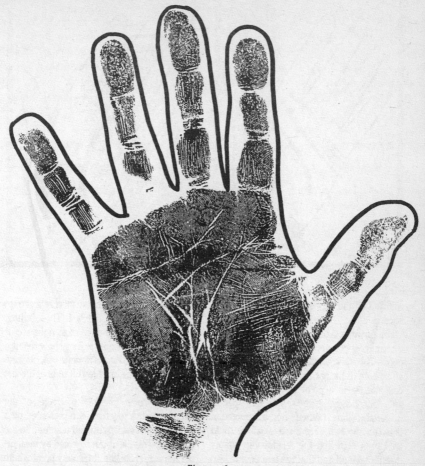

Figure 218

others the lines are so inaccurate as to be hopelessly misleading.

More reliable markings regarding relationships do exist elsewhere in the hand and principally so in connection with the Fate line. Indeed, to some hand analysts it is this line which is one of the most important indicators of compatibility. In addition, it is the Fate line which can accurately pinpoint a relationship and forecast whether a marriage is likely to be viable or not.

THE FATE LINE

It would be expected that, if two people are to share their lives together (taking into consideration, of course, any discrepancies in age), similar parallel markings should

Figure 219

Figure 220

coincide all the way along each of their Fate lines.

For example, a break in the line suggesting a change of job should be marked on both people's hands, as this would undoubtedly affect both of the partners' lifestyles. If events coincide up to a point and then mismatch after that, it suggests the couple split up after a certain time. When no corroboration between the two lines exists at all, it could well be a sign that the relationship simply doesn't take off and that the two people lead lives completely independent of one another.

Relationships are often represented by branches sweeping in from the percussion edge of the palm towards the main Fate line. The stronger the line, the more important the relationship (Figure 220). Markings on these branches describe the nature and progress of the relationship represented. For example, islands, dashes or crossbars would suggest a stormy, problematic association, causing anxiety and frustration to the subject (Figure 220a).

Branches which just fail to meet reflect relationships which will not last. Those which reach the Fate line but then cross right over it are also unhappy signs for they show that the relationship involved is serious but, for one reason or another, is called off right at the last minute.

But the commitment of marriage, or the decision to live together, is represented by a branch which sweeps up and merges into the Fate line. This event can be timed by measuring the main Fate line at the very point where the two lines meet.

The quality of the Fate line itself after the merger with the relationship branch will reveal the sort of influence the union will have upon its owner. If the line is islanded, for example, there are likely to be difficulties, financial problems or that the marriage will generally have a detrimental effect. Breaks or short cutting lines will highlight frustrations and setbacks (Figure 221).

And if the main line should strengthen in one person's hand and weaken in the other's,

Figure 221A–C

Figure 221D

it's a sure sign that one partner is happy with the union but that the other is dissatisfied.

A deep, channelled Fate line continuing strongly after the merger is an excellent augury of a solid, positive and healthy partnership.

Yet another, but much more uncommon, sign of a strong relationship is a branch which, having swept in from the percussion towards the Fate line, doesn't actually merge into it but turns and runs up the hand in a course parallel to the main Fate line (Figure 221a). Such a feature suggests not only a good relationship but a solid partnership too.

That kind of togetherness, that soul understanding, may also be represented in another way. It may be seen in a line running parallel to the Life line – the shadow line beginning at the time the relationship was struck. This feature, showing a kindred spirit or lifelong affinity to the partner is, however, an exceptionally rare marking (Figure 221b).

Still on the Life line, new responsibilities, new influences and new relationships are sometimes marked by tiny branches that peel away from inside the Life line (Figure 221c). However, care needs to be taken here in the interpretation because not all of these symbolize a sexual relationship entering the individual's life. In some cases this may represent the birth of a baby, a new and greatly-loved puppy dog or even granny moving in to stay.

One final marking which, happily, is not so rare is a bold cross on the index mount (Figure 221d). Those fortunate enough to possess such a feature may be glad to know that this is a wonderful augury of a happy marriage with a good deal of love and understanding from both partners.

MARITAL DISCORD

But, however happy a union might be, the mere fact that two egos have come together suggests that at some time or other there is likely be a clash of ideas, or conflicting opinions which will inevitably lead to discord.

Emotional problems may be registered in the hand in several ways. Adverse markings on the relationship branches or on the Fate line, which have just been described, are the first pointers that not all is well in the relationship. Trauma lines – those horizontal bars that cut right across the Life line – are often signs of emotional upsets. The longer and deeper the crossbar, the greater the anxiety felt. Islands in the Head line, or tiny dropped branches, denote firstly worry and secondly a period of depression.

Any one of these markings could well indicate a rough patch with one's partner, but several of the signs occurring simultaneously will show that the problem is much more serious with far-ranging consequences that affect many different areas of the individual's life.

When a grouping of these markings occurs it could be registering the build up of serious discord. By putting all the clues together it is possible to untangle the components that are leading to the breakdown, not only in communications but also of the relationship itself.

A fairly typical example might look like this: crossbars in the Fate line are accompanied by a series of trauma lines cutting across the Life line. These in turn are corroborated by a long island in the Head line. Following the trauma lines a strong branch peels away from the inside of the Life line and a travel line shoots out of the Life line and makes its way towards the Luna mount. At the same time a break occurs in the Fate line and a branch from the new section rises up towards the Apollo mount.

The picture here, as represented in Figure 222, reveals several years of attrition within an unhappy marriage due to the constant infidelity of the subject's partner. The period of opposition and friction (crossbars on Fate) in the subject's life leads to a series of emotional upheavals (trauma lines across Life). The worries these upsets cause the subject may be timed against the long island in the

Figure 222

Head line, representing the long years of worry and anxiety that the subject has had to endure.

The inner branch off the Life line suggests a new influence, a new relationship, entering the subject's life, and the travel branch and break in the Fate line represent both the final breakdown of the marriage and the new life the individual makes for herself with her new partner. Finally, the branch to Apollo confirms the happier times ahead that the new life has in store for her.

With statistics on divorce telling us that one in three marriages breaks down, markings such as these in the hand cannot be ignored. To the discerning eye, then, it is possible to piece together the clues in order to reveal the build-up of tension that, unchecked, could lead to an eventual breakdown. Invariably, when divorce is registered in the hand, the tell-tale indicators will be a series of trauma lines, closely packed together, in conjunction with signs representing some sort of a change, or move perhaps, depicting a new life.

And although the Lines of Union may be unreliable as indicators of permanent relationships they can, under certain conditions, throw some corroborating light on the fate of a union. In some hands a Line of Union may be seen either to extend its course across the top of the palm to meet and cross a strong trauma line from the Life line, or it may turn downwards and cut its way through the Heart line (Figure 223). Either of these markings may suggest a breakdown of the individual's marriage, or that its owner will outlive his or her partner.

These markings, as with all markings in the hands, reflect potential trends. With foresight and judicious action it may well be possible to circumvent or prevent certain situations from occurring altogether. A build-up of tension within a marriage, for example, may be allowed to escalate into confrontation. Or, it might be stopped – talked about, territory negotiated and agreement reached. Thus marital discord may progress unchecked to a complete breakdown or, if the partners feel the marriage is worth saving, a way may be found to cement over the rift and give their partnership a chance to survive.

And, if signs of incompatibility are found, it should not be assumed that the relationship is

Figure 223

doomed from the start. Attraction of opposites occurs time and again and can lead to a stimulating marriage. Moreover, differences can often strengthen a relationship and, if each is prepared to listen to the other's point of view, they can between them arrive at a richer, broader understanding of their life together.

CHAPTER THIRTEEN

SEX

For most people sex is an inextricable component of love, a deep and intimate expression of one person's feelings for another. And bound up with the sex act is sexuality – that certain allure, that inexplicable something that others find so irresistible. Undeniably, some people seem better able to use their sexual powers than others. They have a warmth, a personal magnetism about them that attracts others like iron filings to a magnet. People, it would seem, either have sex-appeal or they don't!

The whole question of sexiness, of libido – whether one makes a good lover or not – is reflected in the hand. Indeed, the elements that describe one's sexual expression, one's drives and desires may be unravelled from the shape of the hand, from the construction of its mounts and from the lines that are found in the palm.

But first and foremost it is in the initial feel of the hand that one can gauge the sexiness of an individual.

Soft, flabby hands that are doughy to the touch belong to sensual pleasure-seekers. These types enjoy sensual stimulation of all kinds but are essentially indolent in themselves so, whilst happy with personal gratification, may be too lazy to consider the needs of their partners. Such people are perhaps better at turning off than they are at turning on.

Hard hands have no time for soft frills. These people are difficult to excite and with them there will be little foreplay and even less tenderness.

Thin, hard, pale hands are too self-centred to give off any allure. Cold and selfish by nature, they attract like sirens for their own needs and, when satisfied, dump their suitors with scant regard to their feelings.

Sexy hands, however, are characteristically warm and springy to the touch. The mounts are full and vital, reflecting plenty of energy and generosity of feeling which will ensure pleasure for both the subject and his or her partner.

And, although the four categories of hands are very broad generalizations they do, nevertheless, give basic clues about attitudes to sex.

SEX AMONGST THE FOUR TYPES

Earth types, basic and solid in their approach to life, are just as pragmatic when it comes to making love. Air-handed types may be cool and aloof in bed, experiencing sexual encounters with intellectual curiosity. Those belonging to the Fire category positively steam and smoulder between the sheets, never averse to experimenting with new positions or techniques. And Water types, though preferring love and romance will, nevertheless, be warm and responsive to whatever fantasy role the situation demands.

MOUNTS OF PLEASURE

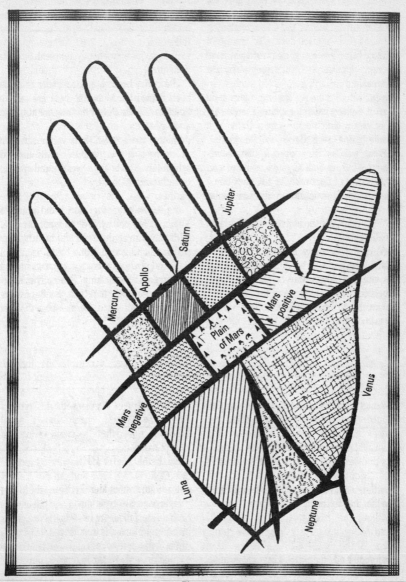

Figure 224

Sexual athleticism, too, is reflected in the condition and construction of the mounts, the most important of which in this respect is the Mount of Venus. Figure 224 highlights the location of the mounts in the hand.

Generosity of feeling and a love of sharing are associated with well-developed mounts of Jupiter. Those possessing this formation have strong appetites so will enjoy frequent lovemaking.

Saturnians, though, can be mean and moody. Solitary individuals, they are unlikely to be interested in sex – especially so if it means getting involved with another person!

Those with well-developed Apollo mounts are great fun in bed. Creative, sensual and appreciative of the beauty of sex, they enjoy the pleasure of eroticism and of sexual stimulation.

Mercurians are inventive in bed – and broad-minded.

When the Mars area is full it is a sign of a strong lover and a lusty sexual partner. But if the mount of lower Mars is too developed, especially when accompanied by a short, stocky thumb, the individual could well be sexually aggressive and the chances are that there could be some degree of sadism in the nature.

Like the Saturnians, those whose Luna mount is pronounced are not particularly affectionate lovers. They seem to possess unconventional sexual attitudes, able to tolerate a *menage à trois*, for example, or inclining, perhaps, to homosexual relationships.

The padded region around the thumb has been named the Mount of Venus, after the goddess of love. But, if this area is thin, pale and generally underdeveloped, the predominant characteristic here will not be love or sexiness; it will be pure, unadulterated selfishness. The libido is weak and there will be little warmth to attract one sexually to this partner.

But it is quite another story if the mount of Venus is full and well developed, because, with this formation, there will be a healthy sex drive and good, strong libido. Here will be found power and energy, enthusiasm and excitement in lovemaking. Generous and outgoing, those whose hands display this feature will enjoy with gusto the pleasures that sex can bring.

SEXY LINES

The lines in the hand add further information about one's sexual instincts, predilections and behaviour. And because the whole question of sexuality is as much mental as it is physical, it is the Head line that will yield the clues to an individual's psychology of sex. Figure 225 illustrates some of the variations of the Head line that may be found.

THE HEAD LINE

A curved Head line suggests that imagination and flexibility will be brought to the sexual encounter. Such people are open minded and sexually creative. People with this type of Head line possess charm and a social adeptness that reflects a certain sexiness in their personalities.

But if the line is too heavily curved the imagination is too vivid and can run riot and out of control. This line may be useful in that it reflects the ability to slip in and out of roles or to create a diversity of sexual fantasies. Its problem, however, is that its wild imaginings can bring a sense of unreality – imagined sexual slights, unfounded jealousies, unrealistic demands.

The straighter Head line belongs to those

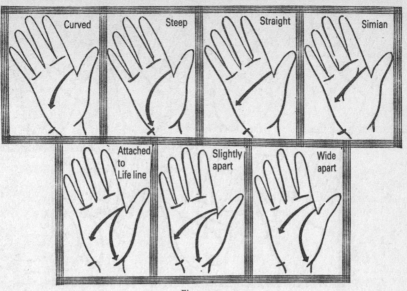

Figure 225

who are sexually pragmatic. These people usually take a conventional approach when it comes to sex. Perhaps they don't always say it with flowers, and don't necessarily ooze with sensuality, but there is a strength and depth to their sexual feelings behind their somewhat reserved façades.

In sexual terms the Simian line can prove a problem. People with this line have extremely intense feelings which they expect returned with equal vigour. And when their sexual advances are not accepted by their partners, for whatever reason, then jealousy will rear its ugly head. In sexual matters, those with the Simian line will expect total fidelity and total dedication. Moreover, they can become completely obsessed with, and just as completely possessive of, their sexual partners.

When the Head line begins attached to the Life line, there will be a cautious approach to sex and to sexual partners. If, however, the lines lie slightly apart, their owners are fairly self-confident and resourceful. They are independent and self-assertive, sure of their own sexuality, their needs and their expectations from a sexual relationship.

If widely separated, it is an indication that its owner will be adventurous, enjoy the thrill of taking risks, become excited at the thought of the odd dangerous liaison, perhaps jump in and out of bed without fully working out the implications, and then, when it's too late, find herself left to untangle the consequences of her precipitous actions.

THE HEART LINE

The Heart line, of course, reveals a great deal about our emotional feelings in our attitudes to sex. Figure 226 outlines the various types of Heart lines that may occur.

The more curved the Heart line, the more physical the sexuality and stronger the biological sex urge. A straighter line, however, suggests a more spiritual approach where the physical need for sex is by far outweighed by the need for love, comfort and support. Here, it is the spiritual instinct that is the stronger

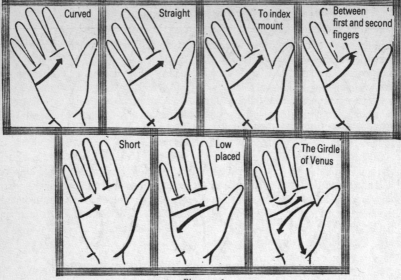

Figure 226

emotion than the fundamental sex need.

People whose Heart lines end on the index mount tend to be too idealistic about sex and are often let down because of it.

Curving up to between the first two fingers suggests practical and realistic expectations in sexual affairs.

A short Heart line, though, ending beneath the middle finger is the sign of promiscuity. Such people are sexually assertive both in their needs and in their behaviour. They, in particular, can enjoy sex for the sake of sex, with no love to complicate the issue.

The lower down the Heart line lies in a hand, the stronger the sexual tendencies; here the Heart line is encroaching into the territory of the Head line and dominating the intellect. With this hand, then, the heart tends to rule the head: the sex impulse is stronger than the reason.

In some hands, the curved line known as the **Girdle of Venus** may be seen above the Heart line (*see* p.181). Sometimes it is fragmented, existing only in short sections, whilst in other hands it may be seen in the form of a complete semicircle.

When present, this line represents emotional sensitivity, the stronger the degree of sensitivity according to the completeness of the curve. And because people with this formation have their emotions so close to the surface, as it were, they are easily aroused, responding keenly and quickly to erotic stimulation. Moreover, it is those whose hands contain the Girdle of Venus who possess a goodly bundle of sex-appeal.

POWER AND CONTROL

And finally, no discussion on sex would be complete without a word or two about power and control. Chirologically it is the thumb that will throw some light on this point.

It is the appearance and construction of the thumbs, in particular, that highlight the power and control one brings to the sexual relationship. An overly-flexible and weak-looking thumb tells of an impressionability and impulsiveness which may lead the individual into situations beyond her control. Weak thumbs always reveal a weak individual, and too much flexibility points to someone who can be easily influenced. In the sexual situation, then, such an individual can all too easily find herself completely out of her depth.

Thick, short, bulbous thumbs, though, are quite a different kettle of fish. Owners of such digits have an urgent need to be in charge and in control of any situation. Power excites them, drives them on, power over their environment and over other people. If an individual possesses such a thumb, in conjunction with other negative features in the hand, it will denote a brutal nature which needs to dominate and, in the sexual context, emphatically points out someone with strong sadistic tendencies.

CHAPTER FOURTEEN

CHILDREN

Many chirologists in the past would, on looking at a woman's hand, pronounce sententiously not only upon the number of children she was to bear but also on the sex those infants were to be.

The markings they scrutinized for such information may be found on the top edge of the palm just beneath the little finger (Figure 227). Here there are two sets of creases: horizontal ones, which some call the marriage

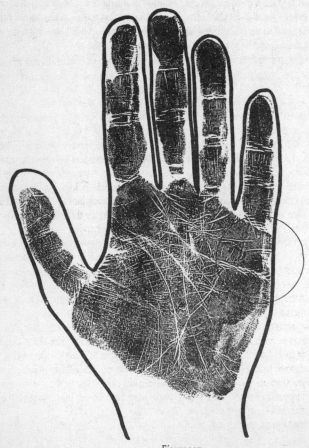

Figure 227

lines, and vertical ones that descend from the base of the little finger downwards to strike the marriage lines. It is these vertical lines that have been studied for centuries and believed to represent one's offspring.

Indeed, even today many hand analysts still take these markings into account in their assessments, although it is now widely recognized that neither the vertical nor the horizontal lines give a true picture either of children or of marriage partners.

Some practitioners, however, do seem to achieve startling results from their analyses of these lines. Others find the markings wholly misleading. Perhaps the conclusion one might draw here is that the success has more to do with the fact that some hands are clearer registers on these matters than others, rather than the fact that some practitioners are more able than others.

In fact, just as with the marriage lines, it is widely accepted that the children lines may not in all cases directly correspond to their owner's offspring, but may equally represent children of whom the individual has grown fond, or with whom a close bond or attachment has been formed.

And it is this argument that explains away the spinster aunt with no children of her own but who has several children lines on her percussion. Surely, then, they must represent her beloved nieces and nephews. Similarly for teachers with such markings who never married and never had children of their own. The lines here, some would argue, must surely indicate particularly favourite pupils.

But then, how would one explain the absence of these lines in the hand of a mother of three, or four, or five? Can it really be that she isn't fond or attached to any of them?

Another criticism that might be levelled here concerns the appearance of the lines. It is maintained that the stronger vertical lines represent boys whilst the fainter lines denote

girls. Another rule states the straighter lines refer to boys and the crooked ones to girls. Odd how the default always seems to fall on the females! In fact, the strength of the line represents the child's physical power, or strength of character, or intelligence, or determination, or persistence, or fighting spirit in life, rather than simply reflecting its gender. Not all boys are tough and some girls are tougher than boys!

Human nature being what it is, what if a mother enjoys a closer bond to her daughter than to her son, would the line denoting the son still be the strongest and straightest? And what of cases where the children are of mixed sex yet the mother's children lines are all of the same strength and equally parallel to one another? And the converse, where the children are of the same sex, yet the lines vary in their impact?

Perhaps, then, the best way to interpret these lines is to apply the same principles to them that one might to any other line in the hand, and that is as representing potential, possibilities, likelihood. So the unmarried teacher or the spinster aunt might have liked to have had children had the circumstances been different and biologically might have been able to produce the number of offspring indicated in their hands.

And perhaps the strength or verticality of the line corresponds more to the bonding or differing rapport the mother feels for each of her offspring than to its sex. Or else it might reflect the different strength of character that each child possesses.

Whichever, merely to accept these lines as reliable indicators of the number and gender of one's children is perhaps somewhat simplistic. However, other fairly reliable clues to children do exist elsewhere in the hand and these may be seen on the inside of the Life line.

CHILDREN INDICATOR LINES

Tiny, hair-like branches that peel off from the inside of the Life line denote new responsibilities, new influences, new relationships entering the subject's life (Figure 228). Sometimes these markings may represent the growth of a new romantic affair, its duration suggested by the length of the branch. In the cases where the branch grows longer, parallel to the Life line itself, it illustrates the development of that relationship into a strong and lasting partnership.

In other cases, the branch denotes a new responsibility: an ailing granny moving in to stay, perhaps, might be accounted for in this way.

Alternatively, these branches have been shown to denote the birth of one's children and each may be timed by applying the timing gauge to the Life line at the very point when the branch springs away from the main line.

The difficulty, of course, lies in distinguishing which branch indicates sexual relationships, and which responsibilities or children. But, because hand analysis is based on deductive reasoning, there will always be other clues in the hand which will be found to either support or reject any inferences that are made.

Sexual relationships, for example, may be confirmed by influence lines reaching up from the percussion towards the Fate line. The responsibility of looking after a sick or elderly relative might be accompanied by a horizontal line stretching across the Venus mount to link the tiny branch with the family ring. And anyway, bearing in mind the odd exception, one would logically expect this sort of event to occur more normally later on in one's life.

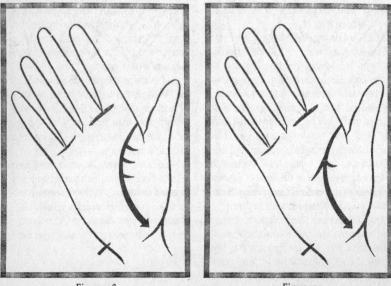

Figure 228   Figure 229

Confirming the branches as indicators of children also requires analytical deduction, but there are many clues which will support one's suppositions. The first, and most logical of these, is that the branches would occur during one's child-bearing years, spanning the teens to the forties.

Another feature which in many cases accompanies this marking is a movement branch. Very often, a couple expecting a child will move to a bigger house so a downswept branch will sweep out of the Life line towards the centre of the palm, a fraction before the inner branch breaks away from the inside of the main line (Figure 229).

Difficulties in pregnancy or complications with the labour may be marked by a trauma line cutting across the Life line just as the inner fork appears (Figure 230). These two markings occurring together lend weight to the interpretation of the branch denoting a possible addition to the family, and especially so if the trauma line has an island in it signifying problems with the mother's health.

Other accompanying features might include a rising branch either from the Life line or from the Head line. Both suggest the sense of achievement, of accomplishment, of an ambition fulfilled that many parents feel when they produce a baby (Figure 231).

And that same sense of achievement might also be reflected by the development of the Apollo line, emerging at the same time as the inner branch, and confirming the deep contentment and satisfaction that a child brings into a couple's life (Figure 231).

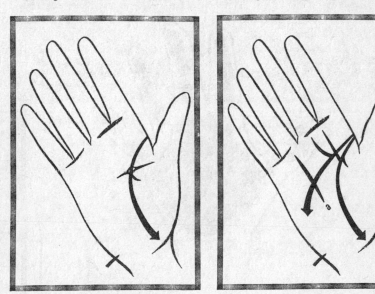

Figure 230   Figure 231

CHILD DEVELOPMENT

Once the children are born, taking regular imprints of their hands will show how they grow and change. These may be kept as a record of each child's development, illustrating the growth in awareness, the unfolding of their talents, the possible build-up of disease, the likely opportunities in store – in fact, their general progress, whether mental, physical or emotional.

Figure 232 comprises three imprints of a young girl's hand taken at regular intervals and showing the development of her hand between the ages of three and ten years. The progressive strengthening and consolidating of the main lines are evidence of the child's growing maturity.

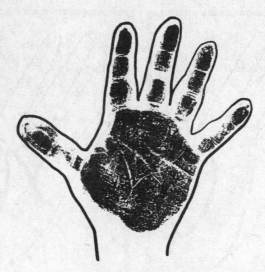

Figure 232A

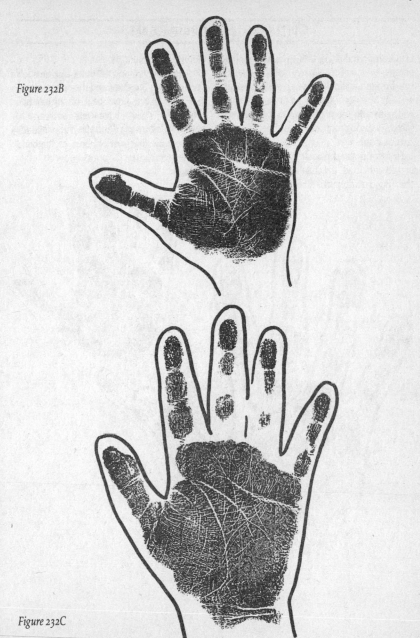

Figure 232B

Figure 232C

CHILDREN AND PARENTS

Children's hand shapes often take after their parents so many similarities will be seen to run through a family. The shape is already evident at birth although palms and fingers will grow and the digits may adopt different spacings throughout life, according to one's circumstances.

Fingerprints and palmar patterns, too, are usually inherited, the child's hand sometimes showing characteristics similar to those of the mother, sometimes similar to the father or, most intriguing of all, resulting in a blend of the two. Both the shape and the dermal markings will give a great deal of information about the child's character, ability and potential. Figure 233 illustrates the prints of a man and his four-year-old boy, highlighting the remarkable resemblances between father and son.

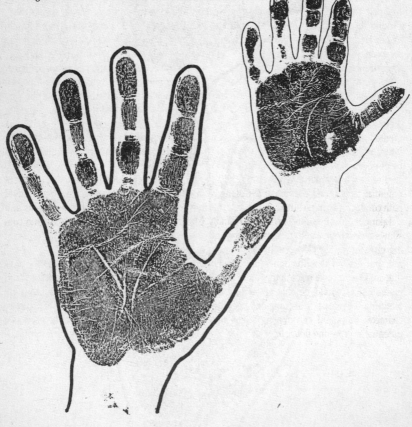

Figures 233A–B

THE LINES

The lines in many young children's hands may take several of those early years to strengthen and clarify. Each line may be interpreted in just the same way as the lines in an adult hand, with the anomalous markings pointing out possible opportunities or potential pitfalls to come.

Islands and chaining in the lines, for example, might suggest physical weaknesses which, if left unchecked, might seriously hamper the child's educational progress. Picking up the fact that a child has an island in her Heart line beneath the second finger, for example, might lead to early indication of a hearing problem.

Or perhaps a heavily chained Head line might alert one to the fact that the child's lack of concentration in class could be related to dietary or mineral imbalances. And a fragmented start to the Fate line would explain why a child is unable to settle. Here it would be of enormous value to analyse the hand in greater depth in order to discover the child's potential talents and encourage her along a path conducive to her nature.

Taking regular imprints of children's hands allows a parent not only to keep a record of the growth and development of those children, but also to monitor trends and events that are likely to take place in the future. Wise parents thus would be able to guide their offspring, perhaps discouraging negative character traits and encouraging talent and potential to grow and flourish.

However, it is vitally important for parents to 'monitor from a distance', as it were; to resist the temptation to force their children into a mould simply from the information they may glean in their offsprings' hands.

When analysing an individual's hand, great care must be taken not to colour one's interpretation with one's own prejudices. But when it comes to analysing the hand of a child, one must be even more circumspect. Children are impressionable and easily influenced; their minds are fertile beds in which ideas, like seeds, may be planted and which then grow unabated.

To state that a child should take a particular direction in life may condition or predispose her to a course of action from which she may never be able to free herself. On the other hand, undue pressure may dissuade her altogether from following a path which might otherwise have given her a great deal of satisfaction in her life.

Children grow and develop at different rates so their talents and abilities will unfold in their own time, their attitudes, ideas and preferences changing as they come into contact with different environments, different people and different situations.

Indications in the hand are just that – indications. They are possibilities of attitudes and events which might come about. But they are not certainties, for patterns in the hand are in constant flux. They are there to be used as a guideline but never as a straitjacket.

CHAPTER FIFTEEN

HEREDITY AND ENVIRONMENT

HEREDITY

It seems clear that an interplay exists between genetic determinants and environmental influences but the degree of influence and the manner in which each affects human behaviour remains the subject of controversy.

The interaction between genetically inherited factors and the uniqueness of an individual may be clearly illustrated in the hand. Each hand is made up of easily recognized and universally shared components. Fingers may be long, short, fat or thin, but they will always be fingers. Head lines may be straight or curved, forked or zig-zagged, but they will always be recognized as Head lines.

And each component, whatever its shape or construction, will be found to be inherited, handed down from one generation to another. Shapes of hands and of nails particularly recur in families, and the papillary ridge patterns, especially, may be traced back to identical markings in the hands of the father, mother, aunts or grandparents.

Yet, despite the fact that each and every component in a child's hand may hark back to her antecedents, the way those components are put together here in her own hand is completely unique. No other person, not even an identical twin, would have the same hand. Fingerprints, particularly, testify to each individual's uniqueness for these are personal signatures that no other human being can share. Indeed, better than personal signatures, for those may be forged by skilled hands, but no hand alive can pass off his own for another's fingerprints.

Figure 233 shows a father and his four-year-old son. Despite the infant's tender age, striking similarities are already evident between his hand and that of the father. The structure of the hands are similar even to the setting of the fingers into the palm. The Head and Heart lines follow identical courses and many of the papillary ridge patterns, too, are alike. Even the tell-tale gap between the two middle fingers is beginning to develop in the tiny youngster's hand to match that of his father.

Such similarities are already stamped in at birth and therefore must reflect genetically inherited factors. But despite the similarities, it has to be pointed out that there are marked differences between their hands – they are not exact carbon copies of each other and indeed many more discrepancies between one and the other exist in their right hands. Moreover, given that lines do change over time, it is expected that each will grow and develop further line markings irrespective of the other.

Figures 234-8 form part of an interesting study of a family group comprising Ellen and Robert, the mother and father, and their three sons. This case study is unusual principally because the three boys are each stepbrother to one another. The oldest, Peter, is the product of the father's first marriage; the middle son, Oliver, is the issue from the mother's previous marriage; and Theo, the youngest, is from their union together. A family tree of the group would appear thus:

? .... ROBERT m ELLEN .... ?

| | |
Peter   Theo   Oliver

Robert and Ellen's hands are markedly different: his, with its square palm and short, blunt fingers, belongs to the Earth category;

whilst her longer palm characterizes Ellen as a Fire type.

Peter, the son from Robert's first marriage, is the most unusual of the group. The long palm with equally long, elegant fingers firmly establish him as a Water type. Because it is so very different in construction to that of Robert's hand, it would appear that Peter has

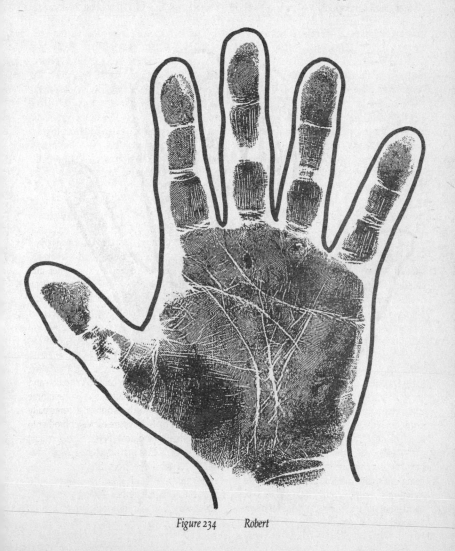

Figure 234   Robert

inherited many of his characteristics either from his mother, or, jumping a generation, from his grandparents. But because Peter's mother is a fine artist it would seem highly likely that his hand shape resembles hers.

However, on closer inspection, it emerges that, shape apart, Peter has many chirological characteristics in common with his father. Water hands notoriously sport a cobweb of lines, reflecting the highly-strung nature and emotional instability of this type. Peter's hand, however, is free from the plethora of such extraneous markings, his major lines closely resembling those of Robert.

The Heart lines, in particular, follow the same route in both hands and to a large extent so, too, do the Head lines. In fact, not only do both Head lines end almost on the same spot

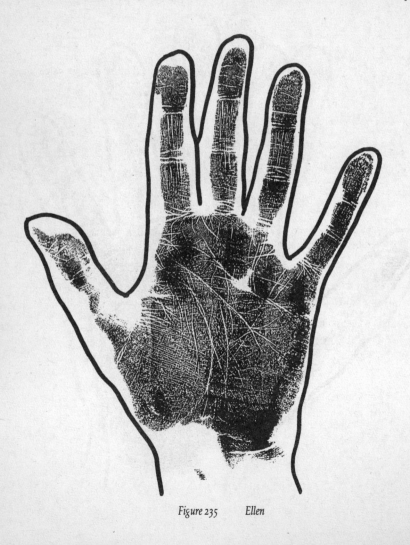

Figure 235   *Ellen*

in the palm, but disturbances can be seen on the lines roughly spanning the very same period in their lives. Like father, like son.

The stance of the digits appears to be alike in both prints, with the first two fingers leaning away from the third, which stands straight and independent, and the little finger leaning outwards. The fingers, too, are set into the palm on a fairly straight line. Even the angle at which the thumbs are carried are at a similar degree.

Peter's Water-type hand, then, reflects his musical accomplishments and artistic skills which he has no doubt inherited from his mother. His solid emotional stability and more scientific interests in, and approach to

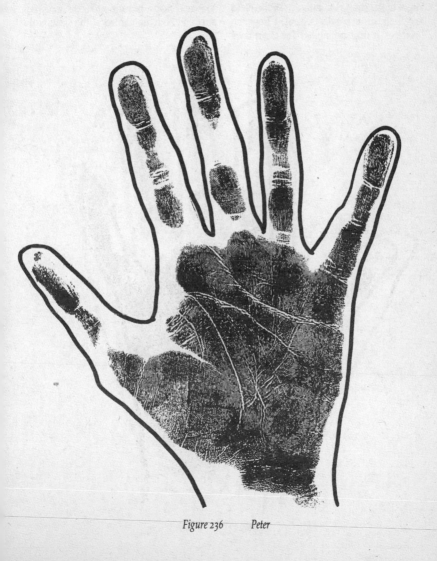

Figure 236   Peter

life, however, may be directly attributed to his father.

Like Robert and Peter, Ellen too has many chirological characteristics in common with her son, Oliver, from her first marriage. Unlike Robert, both have oblong palms with tapered fingers which are set into their palms in an arched formation. Both Head lines follow a much straighter path across the hand and both are markedly separated from the Life lines at their beginning. The Heart lines also follow similar routes, ending in a triple fork on the index mount. And curiously, even the Life line with its many branches and the section of Fate line bending in towards it, seems to have its echo in each other's hands.

Of the digits, the index, though leaning slightly away from true, has its tip bent back towards the second finger. The thumbs are the same shape, bearing a long second phalanx, and both are carried at the same acute angle.

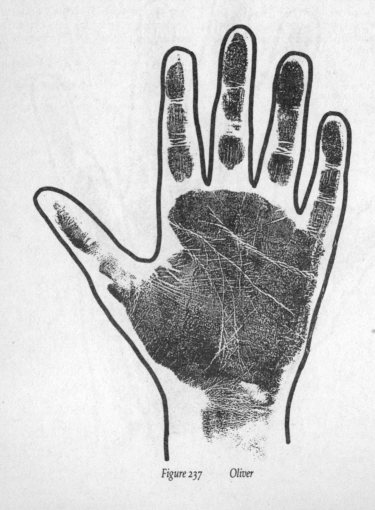

Figure 237   *Oliver*

Even so, there are glaring differences. The fingerprints, for a start, are not alike. Ellen has mainly whorls whilst Oliver has loops. And his little finger is markedly bent – very often an inherited trait which may be seen to run consistently through a family but this time not handed down by his mother.

Temperamentally, then, Ellen and Oliver are very much alike.

Theo, the youngest, shares both Ellen and Robert as parents and his hand, as would be expected, shows characteristics that can be found in both of theirs.

The construction of his hand is similar to Ellen's with its long palm and arched setting of the fingers. The digits, too, leaner and tapered, resemble those of the mother. The major lines of Head and Heart, like those in Ellen's hand, tend to be straight (Robert's are much more curved), with the Heart line also ending on the index mount, though without the triple fork. The Head line, too, is separated from the Life line, just like his mother's.

His fingerprints are mixed, with a preponderance of whorls and composites. Robert possesses loops without exception but Ellen's fingerprints, like Theo's, are also a mixture of loops and composites. However, the skin pattern across the top of the palm appears to match very closely that of his father, with its

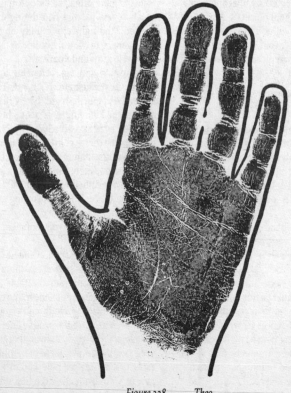

Figure 238   *Theo*

central interdigital loop (vocational loop) and the ridging sweeping in a collar from index to little finger. Interestingly, though, the loop on his percussion echoes a similar loop on his mother's hand.

In many ways, then, Theo is more like Ellen than Robert, and has more in common with Oliver than with Peter.

ENVIRONMENT

So much for biologically inherited characteristics, but what of environmental factors that influence an individual?

The answer to this question may be found in three fundamental principles that chirology teaches. Firstly, that left and right hands reflect different facets of our characters and lives and that discrepancies may exist between the two. Secondly, that lines can and do change throughout our lives. And thirdly, that we have free will and thus in many cases have the ability to avoid potentially negative indications that are represented in our hands.

THE DOMINANT VERSUS THE PASSIVE HAND

As far as 'handedness' is concerned, the passive hand deals with our **anima**, our inner selves – how we behave instinctively and in private. Here are represented our latent talents, our potential; what we *might be* and *might become*. This hand, too, reflects our childhood years.

The dominant hand represents our **persona**; the image we present to the outside world, how we behave in public. The dominant hand, in a sense, 'takes over' from the passive in that it reflects how we develop and put to use those inner talents.

Any discrepancies that exist between the two highlight differences between our innate potential and how we have developed or realized those latent resources that we possess. The Head line is particularly illuminating in this respect.

Should the Head line in the passive hand be longer, deeper, stronger or better constructed than that in the dominant hand, it suggests that the individual has more intellectual reserves than she has as yet developed, or than she uses in her everyday life. Intellectually, then, she has a vast reserve that is lying, for whatever reason, untapped. Perhaps she is mentally lazy or perhaps, which is more often the case in this type of situation, she has not had the right encouragement, the right opportunity or the right environment in which her talents would be allowed to grow and flourish.

Figures 239 and 240, belonging to a right-handed lady, illustrate this point. The Head line in the dominant hand, barely reaching to beneath the little finger, is noticeably shorter than that in her passive hand which reaches well past the centre point of the little finger.

Cases of this nature are seen frequently by hand analysts. Early family responsibilities or financial difficulties very often will have prevented individuals from following an educational course, career or particular way of life conducive to the full development of their talents and abilities.

With the right encouragement, perhaps attending evening classes, taking a degree, joining societies and organizations or taking up a different career, the line in the dominant hand can grow in strength and vigour, eventually even to match the passive line.

Biological determinists would argue, however, that the development of her intellectual capacities, no matter how late in life, is all part of an individual's biological inheritance pattern that is unfolding itself with matura-

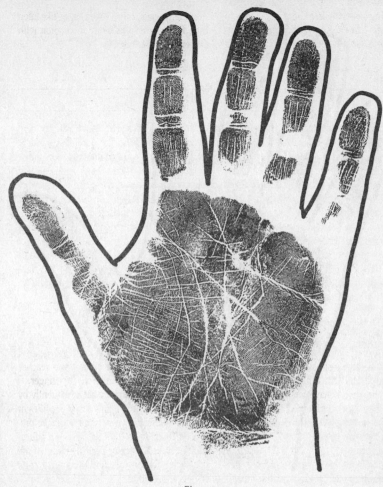

Figure 239

tion. And it is indeed a forceful argument that is difficult to counter. If the subject were to remain intellectually unstimulated, who is to say whether her present mental output is the limit of her abilities or whether she does, in fact, have the untapped mental reserves that are believed reflected in her hand? Once mentally stimulated into intellectual growth we are back to the argument that that is all part of her biological programme anyway!

I have seen far too many hands of potentially gifted and highly intelligent people who, whether for social, financial, or political reasons, have been unable to develop their talents to believe absolutely in biological determinism.

Cases may be cited of people whose hands reveal musical ability but whose uncultured

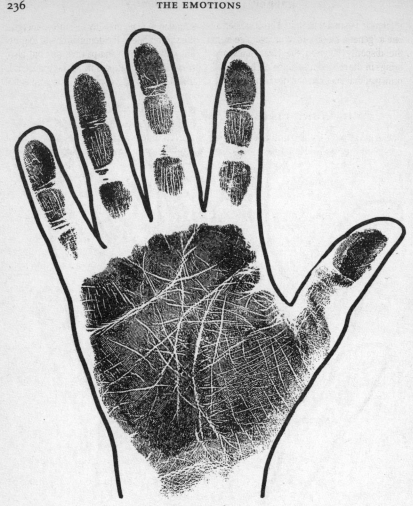

Figure 240

background deprived them of the means to play an instrument. Only by breaking away from that environment and finding their own independence later on in life did they get the opportunity to take up music and found that they were 'natural' musicians. Or of the lady from a strict Victorian background, unfortunate to marry an even stricter, repressive husband, who discovered her gift for healing only after the death of her spouse gave her the freedom to explore and develop her talents.

Culture, race, religion, sexual stereotyping, social and financial circumstances, may all be cited in cases where individuals have been prevented from developing further than their so-called 'biological lot'. The ability to grow beyond one's background and family influence, beyond what might be described as one's 'genetic ration', may be again seen in the disparity between the Head lines and brings in the second fundamental chirological principal that lines can and do change.

CHANGING LINES

In the cases with the disparity between the dominant and passive Head lines, intellectual stimulation may, in many instances, energize the shorter line in the dominant hand to grow not only to match the passive one but also, surprisingly, to surpass it. And, because it is the passive hand which represents potential and the dominant hand the unfolding or realization of that potential, a longer, stronger or better constructed dominant Head line than its counterpart in the passive hand must surely suggest that its owner has evolved

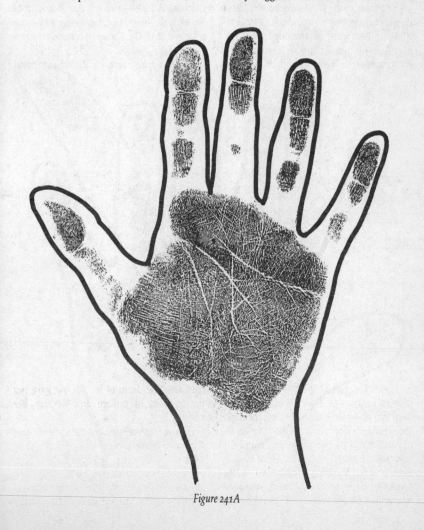

Figure 241A

intellectually beyond her 'biological allowance'.

This sort of intellectual growth is clearly illustrated by the series of handprints in Figure 241 which were taken periodically over a ten-year span. Here the lengthening of the Head line is evident, deepening and stretching its way towards the Luna area, as the subject encouraged her imagination to develop and her creativity to expand.

The prints belong to a lady who, ever since she was young, had a compulsion to write but who was hampered by a strong lack of confidence in her own abilities. With support and encouragement from her husband and family, however, her confidence was gradually bolstered to the point where she was eventually able to launch herself as an author and, by her early forties, was able to make her living from her writing.

FREE WILL

The growth of the Head line in this case also brings in the third principle that is at the fundamental core of chirology. That is, that we all have free will; that, as far as we are able, we have the ability to choose our own destiny for ourselves.

The fact that our lines can change, and

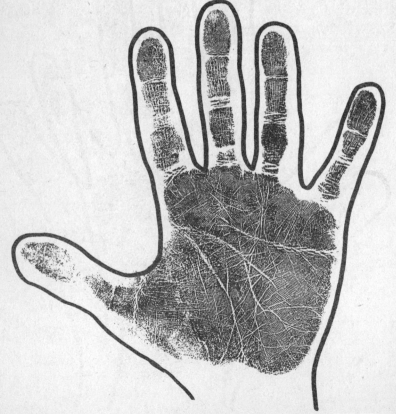

Figure 241B

sometimes quite frequently and dramatically so, testifies that we can each modify our behaviour, our expectations, our philosophical point of view, our attitudes to life. Our human nature is infinitely versatile, infinitely malleable, infinitely inventive, and as such is coloured and shaped by situations, experiences and interactions with other people.

But not only does the environment influence the individual, the individual, too, can influence her environment. Free will suggests that she does not have to slavishly follow her innate nature. If a mirror is held up to one of her negative traits, for example, she can condition herself to recognize and put a stop to that unfavourable behaviour. Similarly, an incipient talent may be encouraged to flourish, rather than be neglected or allowed to lie dormant.

And future trends that are so clearly marked in the hand may equally be influenced, their course and outcome changed. Supposing, for example, that an emotional upheaval were marked in an individual's

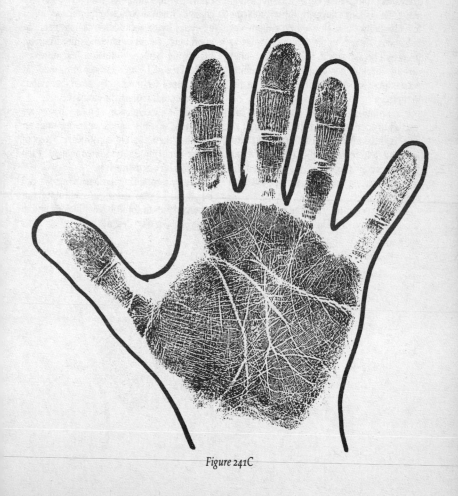

Figure 241C

hand to occur, say, eighteen months hence. By becoming aware of this possibility, the subject may (i) change her behaviour so as not to cause the rift, (ii) prepare herself psychologically for the fray and thus be armed at the point of challenge, or (iii) skirt around the whole problem and thus avoid it altogether.

An example might be cited of a woman whose marriage has hit a rocky patch. Knowing beforehand that serious marital problems could lie ahead means that she could take more notice of her own and her partner's grievances, be alerted to the friction points, insist on talking through their problems together. By changing the pattern of behaviour, then, it might well be possible to prevent a breakdown in her marriage, either directly through her own efforts or, jointly preventing the situation from arising in the first place.

If the problem, however, is already so serious as to appear irremediable, she might be able to shore up her reserves, take legal and financial advice, find a job to secure an income, recruit support or whatever, in order to be in a strong position when the eventual crunch occurred.

Health trends, too, may be influenced in the same way. Markings in the hand will highlight a build-up of stress/acid/toxins, which could develop into disease. But, with preventative action – rest/early medication/ change of diet – the progress of the disease may well be arrested.

As these strategies are put into practice so the markings in the hand will be adapted accordingly, changing direction, fading or disappearing as the emphasis on the problem is shifted.

Though perhaps in the vast microcosm of life it can be said that there will be aspects human beings may not have the power to change, when it comes to the microcosm of everyday living each individual may exert an enormous amount of influence directly upon his or her personal situation and environment. Free will allows choices to be made at every turn, decisions to be taken, behaviour to be adapted, action to be employed.

And the consequences of these choices are registered in our hands, marking and re-marking them, as we construct and reconstruct our daily life and environment, each one of us for our own selves.

And by recognizing those markings we can be ahead of the game, in control of our environment, in control of our biology and in control of our own destiny.

PART SIX

IN BUSINESS

CHAPTER SIXTEEN

CHOOSING A CAREER

One of the most valuable aspects of hand analysis is its ability to give direct information concerning career guidance. Whether it is the youngster, launching himself tentatively onto the job market, the married lady returning to work after her children have grown up, or the individual in mid-career who finds himself at a crossroads, hand analysis can give some critical insights to help in their decision-making.

Although every hand is unique, each with its own built-in clues indicating potential and talent specific to the individual, it is possible, nevertheless, to make statements across the board about suitable career areas based on generalized features that may be shared by a wider number of people.

This is because an analysis of the hand works on many levels, taking the general and working through to the particular, categorizing, confirming, sifting and refining all the features until a pure, unique portrait of the individual is arrived at. But along the way, the different levels will each yield a wealth of information, amongst which vital clues on occupational matters will emerge.

The first level deals with the general shape of the hand. This not only lays down the fundamental character but, in so doing, fits the temperament into specific occupational areas. The shape and construction of the fingers further refines the picture.

On the next level dermatoglyphics, or skin ridge patterns, provide information on inherent talents, often genetically handed down from one generation to the next.

The interpretation of the lines follows on from here, refining still further and adding one's intellectual abilities, range of interests, extent of knowledge and understanding and showing how these might be applied in the work context.

Finally, the last level deals with markings that point to specific skills which could be brought to the job market.

HAND SHAPES

THE EARTH HAND

The Earth hand is easily recognized by its square palm and short fingers.

Work-wise, the adjective that most applies to this type is **industrious**. People with the Earth hand are not afraid of hard work and are likely to be found across all types of occupations where persistence and dedication are required.

They are also practical, tackling any job that comes to hand with a great deal of honest-to-goodness common sense. They like to work steadily and to a routine and they function well in any capacity that carries responsibility. The more academically-minded members of this group gravitate towards any occupation that requiries logical, analytical deduction. Artistic originality is not their forte, but what they lack in imagination they more than make up for in practical application and expertise.

Because they are so down-to-earth many work especially well out of doors, enjoying the physical pleasures of tilling the soil or simply getting out and communing with Nature. Many farmers have this sort of hand and so do those with interests in agriculture, horticulture and gardening. And apart from the land, occupations involving animals come equally within their sphere of interests so that the vocationally minded Earth types may feel the call to become veterinary surgeons, breeders, trainers or gamekeepers.

Another facet of their character is a strong belief in law and order and thus square hands figure prominently amongst the judiciary and legal profession. The police force and the military forces, especially the army, often attract those with the Earth type of hand.

THE AIR HAND

Like the Earth hand this type, too, has a square palm, but its main distinction is that the Air hand possesses characteristically long fingers.

Communications are what these people are mainly about.

Air-handed people are notoriously inquisitive, with minds that are razor-sharp and quick as lightning. They have a prodigious capacity for picking up and storing facts and bits of information and, as such, they make excellent students and academics.

Unlike the Earth types, these people cannot abide the monotony of routine but are at their best working in a lively, buzzing, informal atmosphere where news and views are freely exchanged. In particular, they need variety in their work for they possess a low boredom threshold. For all these reasons, Air-handed folk find the media a particularly attractive and congenial vehicle for their talents.

It is in the field of communications that their Mercurial mentalities are at their best so they are often drawn towards language and literature. In terms of language, both the spoken word, as in oratory and debate would apply, as well as mastering foreign languages. On the literature side, many make fine writers and journalists.

Another facet of communications is travelling, and the Air-handed types do well in the travel industry, courier service and in the hotel business. Add to this their compulsive curiosity when it comes to modern developments in computer technology, and it is not altogether surprising to find them beating a path to occupations involving satellite communications and space technology.

Finally, politics and the diplomatic corps are particularly Air-type domains, both requiring as they do a good deal of rhetoric and Mercurial fleetness.

THE FIRE HAND

The Fire hand has a characteristically oblong palm with short fingers.

Energy and enthusiasm are the qualities that best typify those with the Fire hand.

These types are immensely active, throwing themselves heart and soul into whatever project they have in front of them. Of the four types, these are the creators, the inventors, the explorers, the pioneers, the daredevils at the forefront of the action. Not surprisingly, then, where there are new inventions to be tried out, new territory to be struck (whether literally or metaphorically) or new inroads to be made it will be the Fire-handed folk who rush to be at the very cutting edge.

Because they like the feel of the adrenalin coursing through their veins, they are well able to work under pressure. Consequently, they will not shy away from any occupation that carries heavy responsibility. In fact, they make excellent organizers and brilliant leaders, with their charismatic ability to motivate others and to inspire all those around.

In industry, then, their enthusiasm, their ability to withstand stressful situations and their readiness to take charge of any situation, quickly takes them to the top, into managerial and executive positions.

Another side of the Fire character is that they are very much people-oriented. Wherever there is a crowd of people, there will be a Fire hand in the very centre of the group. Fire-handed types seem not only to gravitate towards people but are magnetically attracted to them. Thus, any career that is people-oriented will be attractive to this type. Entertaining is one of their best attributes so any aspect of the performing arts will suit them well. In fact, they positively bask in the warmth of the spotlight. From clown in the big top to Oscar-winning actor, the Fire hand will be in her element.

For the more academically inclined, lecturing and the teaching professions make excellent outlets for their talents. Here they can combine their performing skills with their zeal to help others. But the academics amongst them will also be endowed with far-reaching, probing minds and will be in the vanguard of pioneering scientific research or space studies – two territories with vast tracts of land still to be explored. On the social side, they make fine counsellors, too, supportive yet able to fire others with their own enthusiasm for life.

In business, they enjoy meeting people on all levels and are at their best in any advisory capacity or entrepreneurial role. 'Rep' work, PR, sales and reception work suit them well, as do design and advertising.

The immense energy of this type is often channelled into sports and the best sportsmen and women perhaps belong to the Fire group. It is the danger and the sense of risk that especially appeal to their supercharged adventurous spirits. And that is why, too, those who narrowly fail to become sportsmen, or who eventually retire from the track and field, find their way into the leisure industry, still enthusiastically pitching in and giving it their best shot from the sidelines.

THE WATER HAND

The Water hand is unmistakable for its long palm, long fingers and a spider's-web of lines in the palm.

Gentleness and sensitivity characterizes the water-handed person.

People whose hands belong to the Water category are often found in the artistic fields for they are highly creative and imaginative individuals. The world of Fine Arts is filled with people possessing the Water hand, from artists to collectors. And so too are all areas of creativity such as fashion and interior design, millinery, floristry and all manner of fine craftsmanship.

Many make talented musicians, gravitating towards all aspects of the music business, both modern and classical. Their sensitivity to rhythm also draws them to dance. The theatre has a special fascination for them and many are to be found treading the boards, making the stage their profession.

Or else they turn their hand to writing, and to poetry in particular, sensitively portraying human emotion and delicately crafting their stories with an imaginative eye for intricate detail.

Just as the art world is peopled with Water-handed folk, so too is the glamour industry. The long, lean hand so characteristic of this group is invariably found to be possessed by models and the majority of people in the beauty business from hairdressers through beauty therapists to anyone in the *haute couture* line.

Academically, they make fine philosophers, psychiatrists or psychologists, carefully balancing conceptual theories or patiently listening to their client's problems. And, because they are sensitive and empathetic, they also make excellent healers, whether in the medical or counselling side, both in the orthodox or unorthodox traditions.

And it is in the latter field that many Water-handed individuals are to be found. Spiritual healers, dowsers and psychics often share this shape of hand.

The one area in which the Water hand does not usually thrive is in business because this type cannot function well under stress. What's more, Water-handed people are the most impressionable and least materialistic of the four groups, and so unsuited to the high pressure, cut-throat conditions of business life.

THE DIGITS

Next to the shape, the actual digits themselves give valuable information which in turn will provide useful pointers when it comes to choosing a career. Not only is the length of the digits relevant but, because each finger governs a particular aspect of the individual's life, its construction and formation can hint at certain inherent qualities which might be more suited to one type of occupation than to another.

LENGTH

In general, long fingers, (determined by the fact that the middle finger is either roughly three-quarters, or more, the length of the palm), denote a patient, thorough and meticulous attitude to work. Those with long digits, then, are best suited to any occupation requiring a keen eye for detail and a methodical approach to the job. Cartography, for example, would require just such skills but so too would accounting and fine craftwork.

But the punctilious nature of the long fingers does mean that their owners are necessarily slow, so jobs where speed is of the essence would not be especially recommended for these types.

The shorter-fingered people, however, are more suited to jobs where the pace is fast and furious. Pedantic detail irritates those with short fingers but their assets lie in a quick Mercurial grasp of a situation; in their ability to see the overall picture and in their inspirational approach to their work.

Occupations which require quick-wittedness and inspirational flair are best suited to people with short fingers.

Individual fingers, too, whose length is disproportionate to that of the rest, or whose construction is unusual, can highlight specific qualities. For instance, literary talent may be seen by a markedly long Mercury finger. And if its tip is particularly long and pointed, it shows that articulacy and sharp wit are especially marked in the personality.

A feeling for the land is represented by a very long bottom section on the middle finger (Figure 242). Agriculturalists, farmers, gardeners, smallholders and horticulturalists all come into this category.

Long top phalanges show an intellectual appreciation and turn of mind. Researchers and those in academic posts often possess this feature.

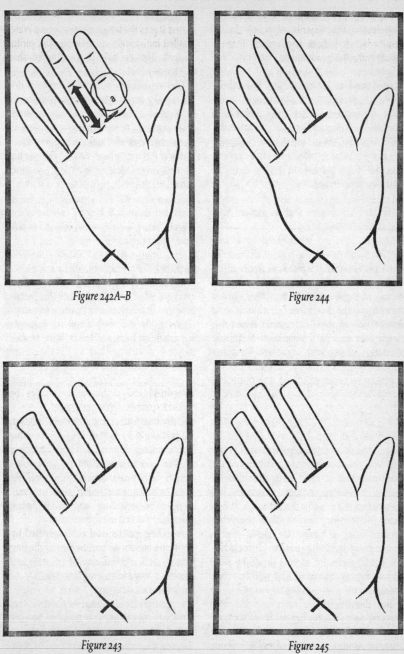

Figure 242A–B

Figure 244

Figure 243

Figure 245

When all the middle phalanges of the fingers are longer than the top and bottom ones, it is an indication of excellent managerial and executive abilities.

In the case where there is a long but well-padded basal section to the index finger it is a sign of culinary instincts. Good cooks, caterers and restaurateurs are often found with this formation (Figure 242a).

On the ring finger a full basal phalange denotes the collector. Dealers in fine arts and antiques invariably have a thick padding to the base of this finger.

Doctors and physicians are said to possess good Mercury fingers with especially long middle phalanges.

Manual skills are represented by a very angular formation at the base of the thumb, known as the **angle of manual dexterity**. Whether this implies a labourer, at one end, or the fine craftsman, at the other, would depend on the length of the thumbs and fingers. The longer and more elegant the thumb, the greater the sense of aesthetics. Painters, decorators, cabinet makers, watchsmiths, machinists, dressmakers and typists would all belong to this category.

The creative arts may be marked in several ways. A tell-tale hint of dramatic talent is highlighted by a spatulate tip to the ring finger (Figure 243).

General creative talent may be represented by long tapering fingers and supported by other markings in the hand, such as a curved percussion edge, for example (Figure 244).

When the majority of fingers are squared off it tells of practical ability. These people are good with their hands whether in a skilled or unskilled capacity. But practicality need not infer that there is a lack of creative spark. Indeed, many sculptors and musicians have solid, blunt-tipped fingers (Figure 245).

Spatulate-tipped tells of an inventive mentality. Such people would be at their best in any occupation where innovation and new ideas are called for. But spatulate tips can also be a sign of the craftsman, particularly so if it occurs on the thumbtip where the formation has classically been referred to as the 'potter's thumb'.

DERMATOGLYPHICS

Skin patterns in the palm have long been associated with special, inherent gifts and talents. Musical appreciation and ability, for example, have been linked to markings on the mount of Venus. Here a circular pattern, known as 'bee strings', suggests a special feel for stringed instruments (Figure 246a). A loop entering the mount from the wrist suggests a love of brass or percussion music (Figure 246b). These markings may be supported by an angular formation at the base of the palm where it joins the wrist and which, when present, invariably denotes a general love of music (Figure 246c).

A rare pattern in the normal hand is a loop, approximately two centimetres long, that enters from the percussion edge a little above the wrist and lies across the palm (Figure 246d). Here the marking suggests an innate understanding of flora and fauna which may usefully be incorporated into one's work, perhaps on a botanical or zoological level, perhaps in farming or horticulture or simply working in some way with plants or with animals.

An interdigital loop which enters the palm from between the second and third fingers is not so rare but it does reveal a fundamental vocational urge to help others (Figure 246e). Such instincts often carry their owners into the caring professions and, even if they don't, those with this marking will always be found to possess a strong sense of community and they are always ready to help others in need.

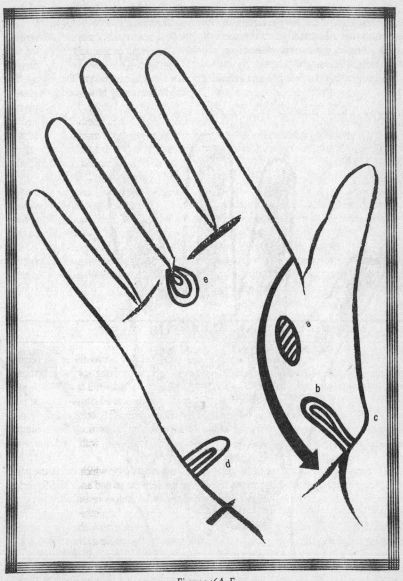

Figure 246A–E

THE LINES

When it comes to choosing a career, the lines which give the most relevant information are principally the Head line, revealing mental capacity and intellectual preference; the Fate line, directly representing the career and charting its course and progress; the Apollo line, supporting the Fate line and recording the sense of career satisfaction; and finally the Life line, reflecting the stamina and vitality affecting the day-to-day working life.

THE HEAD LINE

The Head line represents the way we think, and this line may be divided into two basic

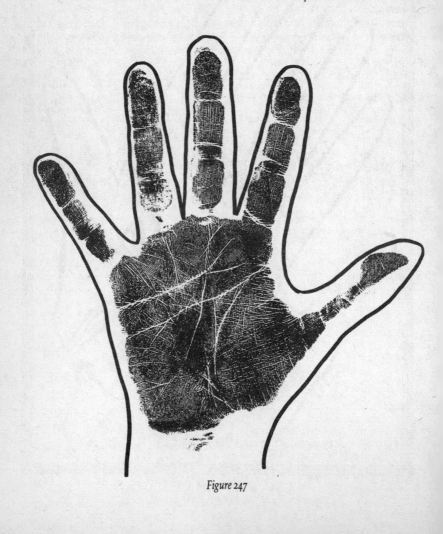

Figure 247

types. The first travels in a fairly straight course across the palm and the second is curved.

A Head line that lies straight across the palm denotes a logical, rational, practical and pragmatic mentality. People with this sort of mind enjoy scientific, mathematical, technological, business or, more generally, any of the practical subjects. A very long line would indicate strong academic powers of analysis so that scientists, engineers, accountants, dealers and bankers fit into this category (Figure 247). A short line describes someone who is more concrete and mundane.

When the Head line is curved it highlights artistic and creative flair. The steeper the curve, the more imaginative the individual (Figure 248). People with curved Head lines have the ability to think widely and laterally. They usually enjoy working in the arts or with people, are often good at languages and communications and are found in any creative occupation such as the media, advertising, PR, interior decor, design, hairdressing and floristry.

A Head line which is both straight and curved combines both the logical, rational mentality with creative flair. People with this

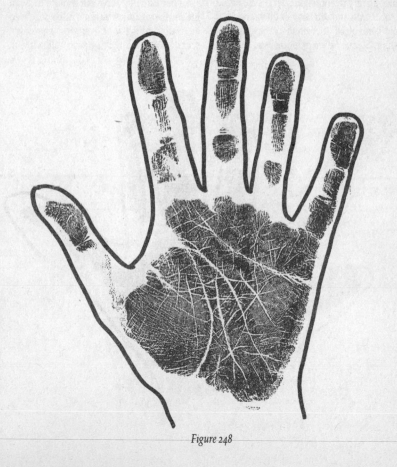

Figure 248

line may be torn between a career in the arts or one in the sciences (Figure 249). They need a job which requires both, such as a bilingual secretary, for example; or, if academically inclined, the social or environmental sciences might suit.

If the Head line forks at the end below the little finger it is a sign of business acumen (Figure 250). Those who possess this feature would probably do well to set up in business on their own and, if they have the necessary resources, should be encouraged to do so.

When the line splits into two below the ring finger it is known as the 'writer's fork' and it shows literary talent (Figure 251). Depending on the length and direction of the branches it could lend itself to factual or biographical writing, drama, fiction or journalism.

THE FATE LINE

The Fate line represents one's work, career and public life. This line charts the course and progress of the working life and any changes that might affect the occupational area are registered here. It is the starting position of the line which throws direct light on the choice and direction of career.

A Fate line that begins at the base of the hand and shoots its way straight up the middle of the palm shows a career path which its owner considers safe and conventional (Figure 252). Such people do not like taking risks but carefully carve out a route through life for themselves which might be described as fixed, traditional or even, in some cases, stuck in a rut. In times past, following in

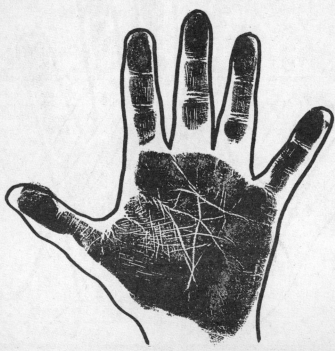

Figure 249

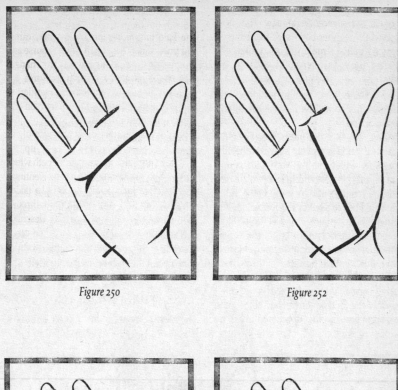

Figure 250

Figure 252

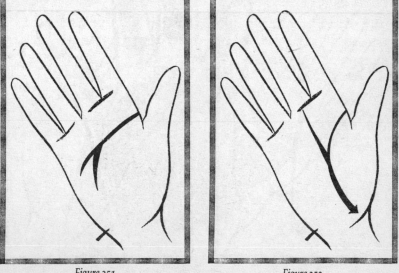

Figure 251

Figure 253

father's or mother's footsteps from cradle to grave would very likely produce this sort of Fate line.

Taking its beginning from the Life line, it tells of substantial family support in the choice and progress of one's career (Figure 253). Joining the family business, for example, might well be represented by this particular line.

When the Fate line takes root from the Mount of Luna it usually suggests that the individual will prefer to work with people (Figure 254). A job which involves dealing with the general public or being in the public eye would be reflected by this formation. Performers and entertainers, and all those whose careers take them into the eye of the camera or the glare of the spotlight, are more likely to show this starting position in their hands than any other.

The normal ending for the Fate line is beneath the middle finger but sometimes, instead of going in that direction, the line (as in Figure 255) suddenly swings over to end beneath the index finger. This, too, shows a turn in the individual's career which takes him very much into the public eye. Celebrities, politicians or even owners of country clubs, for example, whose job it is to deal with the general public in the course of their work, might well display this line.

When the Fate line is broken or fragmented at its beginning, as illustrated in Figure 256, it shows a lack of direction in early life. There may be difficulty in finding a job, or in settling into a particular career. These people may, for one reason or another, find themselves in and out of work and it may not be until the line consolidates that they settle and find stability in their working lives. Applying the timing gauge to the line will establish at which point the career consolidates itself.

THE APOLLO LINE

The development of the Apollo line as it

Figure 254

Figure 255

Figure 256

Figure 257

grows upwards, parallel to the Fate line, is said to denote creative talent. Moreover, there is usually a good deal of creative satisfaction in the working life of those who possess a long Apollo line.

More generally, though, it is perhaps one of the most favourable markings to possess, regardless of the nature of the employment, as it denotes contentment and self-fulfilment in one's job or way of life.

In the majority of hands, as in Figure 257, it is seen only in the top half of the palm, but occasionally it may be found occurring lower down nearer the wrist. In this event it would denote a rare talent, an actor or pop singer, perhaps, who makes it, whilst still very young, to superstar fame.

THE LIFE LINE

When it comes to considering career matters, although the Life line may not shed a great

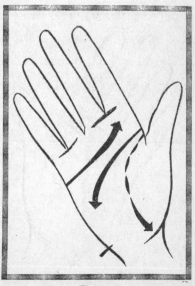

Figure 258

deal of light on the actual type of job that is selected, its strength and quality will, nevertheless, have a direct bearing on the success or otherwise of that choice.

The stronger and more robust the line, the more energy and spunk the individual will have in the pursuit of his chosen career. A strong Life line denotes a strong constitution with plenty of physical strength. Thus, this sort of line shows that the constitution will support a job that is high powered or physi-cally demanding without buckling at the seams.

If the line is weak, islanded or fragmented, however, it suggests that the individual lacks vitality and staying power (Figure 258). Here, stamina and physical reserves are low, consequently jobs that work on high octane should be avoided by those with this sort of Life line. Occupations of a more sedentary nature that do not tax the system unduly are perhaps more suitable for these people.

SPECIFIC CAREER-ORIENTED MARKINGS

Apart from the major lines, there are a few lesser line formations or markings which give significant clues to particular talents.

For example, a square formation beneath the index finger is known as the 'teacher's square' (Figure 259). When present the marking reflects a natural and sympathetic ability to impart information. Possessing this feature, then, might point to a career in teaching, lecturing or demonstrating.

Another specific marking is known as the 'medical stigmata', a formation of three little vertical lines crossed by a fourth one, the whole pattern lying between the base of the

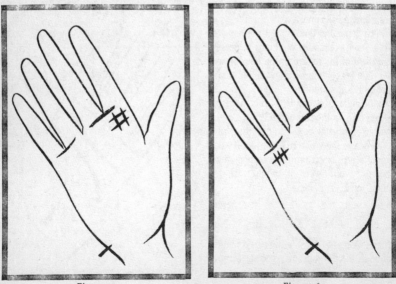

Figure 259   Figure 260

little finger and the Heart line (Figure 260). People with this feature are often drawn to the medical profession. Such natural healing talents, as represented by this marking, may be put to good use both in the orthodox medical profession – surgery, nursing or veterinary practice – as well as in the complementary fields – osteopathy, acupuncture or spiritual healing. Alternatively, the medical stigmata may just as readily imply counselling skills so that those with this marking could well turn their hands to the vast range of advisory or consultative occupations that might include, for example, social or welfare work.

CHAPTER SEVENTEEN

PROBLEMS ON THE SHOP FLOOR

It would be unrealistic to expect a career to run smoothly from first job to retirement. Inevitably there will be hitches. At some stage or other working life is bound to produce problems and obstacles that have to be surmounted. Frustration, opposition, missed opportunities, redundancy and bad publicity are all too often common experiences in the office, factory or shop floor.

Just as with emotional upsets, occupationally related problems are registered in the hand in a variety of ways and, of more value, trends which may lead to adversity at work may be detected well before they occur and, consequently, may be fended off or avoided altogether.

Although the shape of the hand in general, and the markings in particular, will highlight specific gifts and talents which suggest broad areas of suitable employment, it is not always possible to earn one's bread and butter working in a field in which one has just the right talents, or indeed, finds especial enjoyment. Lack of necessary training or experience, the wrong academic qualifications, missed opportunities, late intellectual development, emotional confusion, taking a 'wrong turning' on the career path – all these hiccups, and more, can limit the choice of career and seriously jeopardize one's chances in the employment market.

One of the greatest sources of occupational frustration amongst the clients who seek out the professional help of a hand analyst is simply due to the fact that they are unable to use their inherent skills and talents directly in their everyday working life.

But human nature is notoriously adaptable and resourceful and forever coming up with strategies to relieve the dissatisfaction and frustration that accompanies the feeling of being a square peg in a round hole. If changing to a more conducive job is out of the question one may, for instance, channel those talents into hobbies. Unfortunately, though, there will always be the inevitable few who feel so disaffected and overwhelmed by their work that they turn to drink or to drugs in an attempt to escape the drudgery of it all.

Strategies of a more positive nature, however, can be adopted. Remedial steps can, with encouragement and the right advice, be taken at any stage in one's career. But perhaps better by far would be to choose a career area that accommodates one's fundamental nature in the first place and thus avoid this sort of unnecessary frustration from the outset.

The difficulty, of course, lies in the ability to initially recognize one's innate talents and then to have the courage and self-confidence to match them to a suitable occupation. Then, having found the right direction, an added bonus would be the ability to pinpoint the specific factors that adversely affect each individual in the course of his work. And this is where an analysis of the hand can lay down valuable guidelines.

The shape and construction of the hand generally indicate what type of career will best suit. More specifically, a close analysis of the lines will give detailed personal information and warning about the problems that may lie ahead, specifically for each individual.

THE LIFE LINE

Health and vitality registered in the Life line will undoubtedly reflect upon the individual's working life. Islands, for example, may be looked at in two ways. Firstly, as a warning of a possible period of ill health ahead or secondly, as a potential weak link in the individual's make-up which might be aggravated under certain conditions.

An island low down in the Life line (Figure 261) might be an example of the former which, if accompanied by other signs, could suggest a serious debility necessitating considerable time off and perhaps even early retirement. In this case, taking care of one's health – good diet, exercise, avoiding stress – may all contribute to warding off the situation.

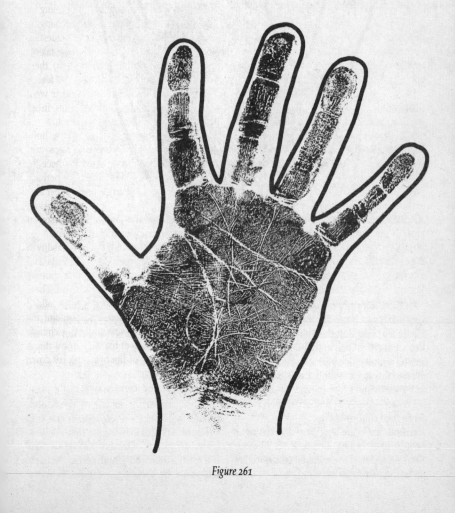

Figure 261

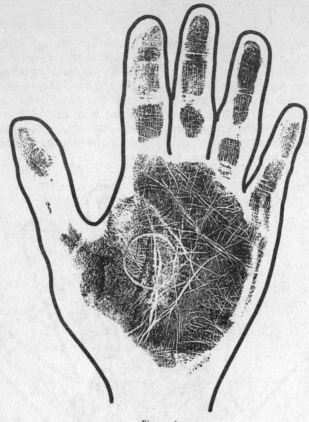

Figure 262

An Island centrally placed, which tells of a susceptibility to backache and spinal trouble (Figure 262) may alert the individual to avoid occupations that put a strain on the back. Serious consideration perhaps should then be given to this factor if the nursing profession, with its notorious heavy lifting, is mooted as a career, and equally to any occupation involving a good deal of standing.

Trauma lines, the long bars that cut right through the Life line, denote times of emotional upheaval. If these are accompanied by adverse markings on the Head and Fate lines then the emotional turmoil will have repercussions on the working life. The individual's mind will not be on her work and, in an industrial occupation, let's say, this lack of concentration could potentially lead to serious accidents.

In some cases a strong horizontal line may be seen lying across the mount of Venus and striking the Life line without actually crossing it (Figure 263). This marking is a sign of a time of decision, a time when the individual may feel torn between duty and desire. Perhaps this might be showing a conflict between

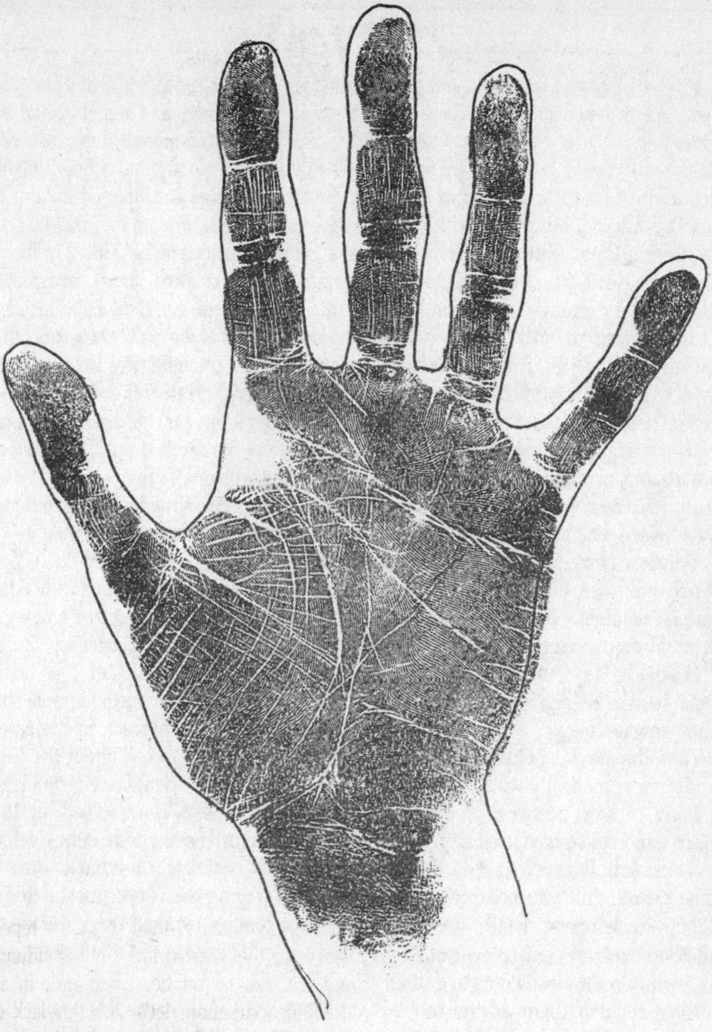

Figure 263

one's domestic and occupational life, or between a difficult choice of careers, or perhaps it might be purely an emotional decision concerning personal relationships. Whatever, it is likely to influence the individual's work in much the same way as a trauma line and thus allowances should be made for possible erratic behaviour during that time.

THE HEAD LINE

Confirmation that one is mentally suited to his or her career will be seen by the formation of the Head line.

Individuals with straight Head lines are better at analytical, mathematical, rational or practical subjects. Science, business, technology or practical occupations would suit. Someone with a straight Head line, then, would not have the necessary creative inspiration, nor indeed the interest, to hold down an artistically imaginative job such as fashion design, for example. But if there is a creative bent in the personality, that analytical and practical talent might well be channelled into furniture-making, or pottery, or architecture.

Similarly, the owner of a steeply curved Head line would not do at all well in the world of nuclear physics, perhaps, where a strictly scientific mentality, with its logical precision is required. But indeed opportunities for the more divergent thinking of the curved Head line do occur in the scientific fields and would be highly valued in the softer, human sciences.

In practice, though, it would seem unlikely that the divergent mentality would find itself in the world of hard sciences, or that the convergent mind would land itself slap in the middle of Fine Arts. But even so, it does occur that some people drift into occupations for which they are temperamentally unsuited. Late development of innate talents, for example, which in the adult may go contrary to her early childhood grounding, can be responsible for a good deal of frustration later on in life if the choice of career is not flexible enough to encompass the new mental needs. A simple comparison of the right and left Head lines will always throw valuable light on this very type of situation.

Any discrepancies between the two will highlight intellectual events and developments which take place from youngster to adult. If the left hand (with right dominance) shows a strong, long and straight Head line, the child would undoubtedly have followed a scientific course throughout school, possibly even taken sciences at further education. The more curved Head line on the right discloses that, with maturity, the individual is likely to become more creative, more imaginative, more divergent in her thinking. Embarking on a career that is too rigidly scientific, then, may not allow enough space later on for the newly emergent creative thinking, and there would be no scope for channelling the imagination. Thus the result is frustration and dissatisfaction with one's career.

With the reverse situation – if the left Head line is curved and the right is straight – the youngster might be persuaded to follow a more Arts-oriented route through the educational system, little realizing that a new convergent way of thinking later on in life, represented by the straighter line on the right, will demand more method, more structure, a more linear approach in the type of work that is carried out. Without the necessary mathematical, scientific or technological qualifications or experience to back up those new intellectual needs, that individual will find herself completely precluded from the very type of profession or occupation that she will later come to require. Again, the result is likely to be frustration and disaffection in her work.

Figure 264A-B illustrates this point. Notice the more curved Head line on the left in comparison to the one of the right, which is so straight it might have been drawn with a ruler.

On a more specific level, islands in the Head line point to periods of worry and anxiety which will inevitably affect one's performance at work. Figure 264B clearly shows an island in the right Head line spanning

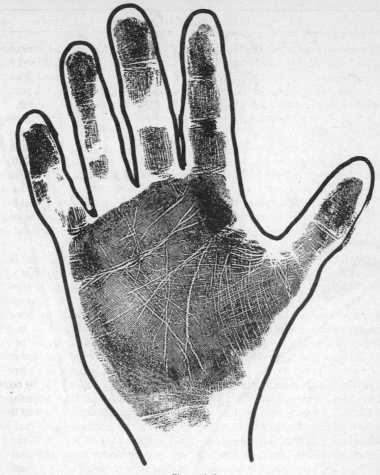

Figure 264A

roughly from the late-twenties until the mid thirties.

In some hands, islands are seen close to the beginning of the Head line directly beneath the index finger. In this position, stretching through the later teens, the island may well be showing a time of confusion, of doubt and indecision. There may be a dissatisfaction with school, college or with one's early occupation resulting in a lack of direction, an inability to chart clearly a course for one's future. Whatever the circumstances, the marking implies an unsettled phase which lasts for as long as the island is present.

One island in the Head line is of particular interest in this respect, and that is the island which occurs in the line directly beneath the middle finger. In the majority of cases, this feature would denote an inability to work under high pressure so those possessing the

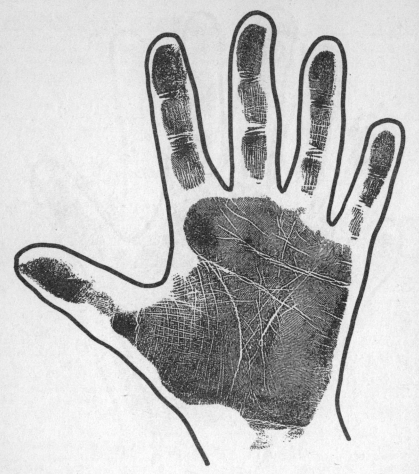

Figure 264B

marking would be wise to devise strategies for dealing with stressful situations and conditions, or, better still, should attempt to avoid them altogether.

A patch of line with a fluffy or fuzzy appearance to it denotes a period when concentration is lacking; memory may also be impaired throughout this time, and decisions become difficult to make (Figure 265).

Bars crossing the Head line are signs of opposition and obstruction which have to be surmounted. Corroborating information on the other lines will reveal the source of the conflict, whether it originates from work colleagues, from occupational matters or whether it is financially oriented. If the Head line is unimpaired after the crossbar, the problem, though frustrating, is of a temporary nature and thus soon resolved. If, however, the Head line develops any adverse

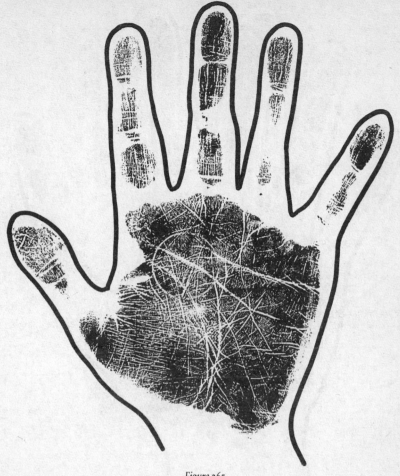

Figure 265

markings, such as an island after the crossbar, it is a sign that the problem will not only have a negative influence, but also a longer-term effect on the individual and her career.

THE FATE LINE

Changes of direction, islands, crossbars and breaks in the Fate line may each be considered as warning signs of possible difficulties, changes or adversity that will affect the career. Unlike the other major lines, not only the markings in this line, but also its

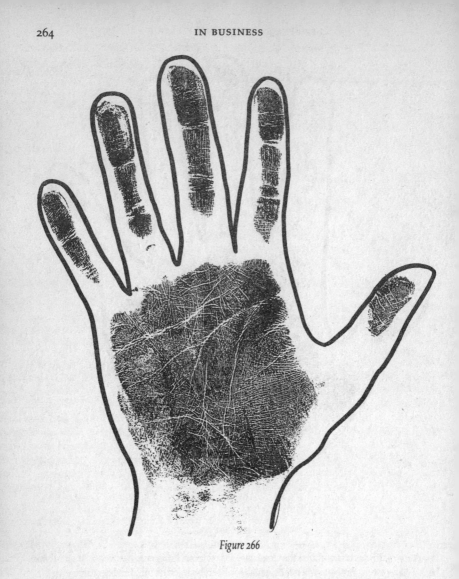

Figure 266

starting and ending points can give important clues.

A fragmented beginning shows vacillation, a lack of control or direction in one's career, an inability to settle into a job or solid course. Drifting from place to place, from one job to another, may well be described by this sort of line. Not until the Fate line solidifies does the subject find his or her niche in life (Figure 266).

Even the slightest bend, curve or deviation of the line will reflect a change of circumstances in the individual's public life or career. Another step up the rung, a promotion, side-step, greater responsibility, change of direction or new job may produce

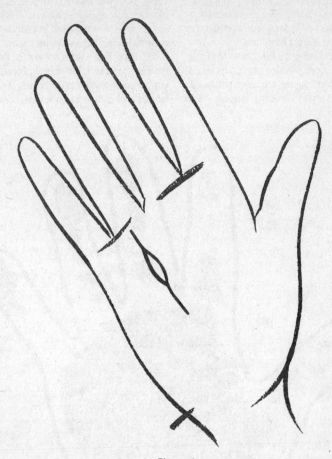

Figure 267

this sort of effect on the line. But it will be the markings directly following the change of direction that will show whether the changes have had a positive or negative effect on the person's working life.

Should the line thin out, weaken, fragment, chain, island or break after such a change in the line, it reveals that the change will have an adverse impact. They indicate a loss of control over one's life and destiny. Only with the return of strength in the line will the individual feel that she has once more taken the reins into her own hands.

Islands and chaining show distinct periods of difficulties and disillusionment in one's career. But an island in this line may also carry another message for here it may suggest possible financial difficulties. Timed in advance, the island allows the individual to make contingency plans (such as making investments, taking out insurances, for example) well in advance so as to cushion or avoid the occurrence altogether.

Crossbars cutting the Fate line warn of frustrations at work. Perhaps coming to loggerheads with colleagues, a clash of personality with workmates, crossing swords with superiors, a blocking of one's advancement or progress or any such general dissatisfaction with the job can be represented in this way. These crossbars show a temporary, albeit irksome, state of affairs, problems which have somehow to be surmounted but which, however, do happily improve in due course.

Both stars and crosses are rare to find on the Fate line but, when they do occur, they imply a sudden shock to the system. A devastating event such as a nervous breakdown or

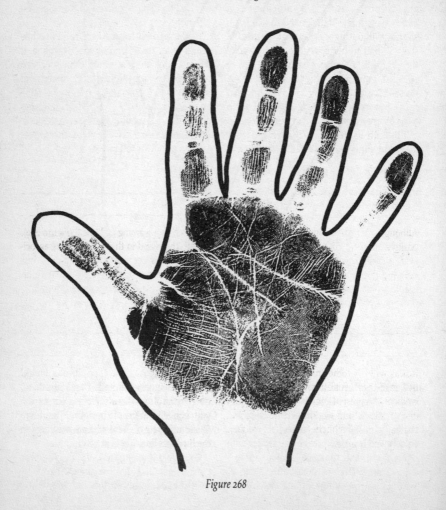

Figure 268

a sudden financial crisis might be registered on the line in this way.

There is a particularly interesting marking that occurs in some hands, which is an arrangement of tiny lines that form themselves into a square, attached to the main Fate line by one of its walls (Figure 267). Such a marking will denote a period of hard work, a time of extreme effort when work simply feels like an uphill struggle. Although during this period, it might appear that there is no light at the end of the tunnel it is, nevertheless, a time when, if the individual just plods on steadily without fighting against the trends, she will find to her satisfaction that despite the effort it is a time of great learning and of personal growth. By the time the square marking has come to an end she will find that in that period of intense hard work she has, in fact, laid down the foundations for her future.

If the Fate line at any point seems to come to an end but is overlapped by a new section it is a sign of a change of job (Figure 268). The wider the gap, the bigger the change implied. Such an event may be timed so as to plan one's course of action well in advance. Similar to the crossbar or change of direction, it is the condition of the line, after the break, that will reveal whether the change of job has been a positive or negative move.

In contrast to the overlapped line, one that comes to a complete stop shows the sudden ending of that particular job or career. This can be a warning of sudden and unexpected redundancy!

In the unusual case where the Fate line comes to an abrupt end on the Head line, it indicates that an unwise intellectual decision or move has jeopardized the career and brought it to a premature end. In the same way, ending abruptly on the Heart line suggests that an unwise liason or emotional decision has similarly brought the career under a cloud and to a premature stop.

THE APOLLO LINE

Although the Apollo line is a wonderfully positive marking to possess there is, however, one negative feature which is best if it does not appear in the line at all. This is an island which traditionally chirologists have described as a warning of scandal (Figure 269). Today, the island in the Apollo line is associated with adverse publicity – getting a bad press or developing a notorious reputation might be represented in this way.

THE BUSINESS LINE

Just as with the other major lines, the negative markings of islands, chains, breaks or crossbars represent adverse conditions in one's business and working life. Islands and chains would highlight times of worries, anxiety and business pressures together with possible financial difficulties. Breaks would suggest changes of direction and crossbars, interference, opposition or obstacles in the path of one's progress in business. Figure 270 illustrates some of these adverse markings in the Business line.

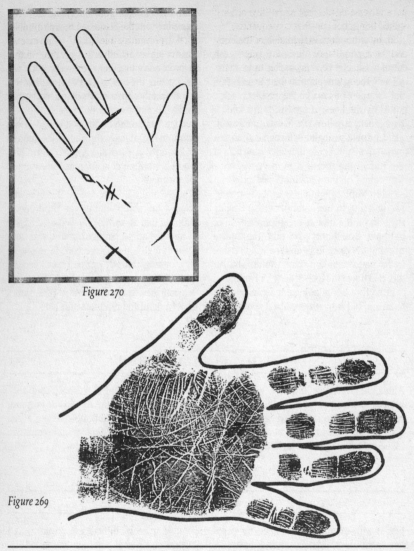

Figure 270

Figure 269

TIMING EVENTS

Because many of the line formations that have been described reflect a trend that is likely to occur in the future but which is based on the actions and decisions of the present, it is logical to expect that the markings will form themselves a considerable time before the events they represent actually take place.

Decisions, therefore, that are taken today will shape tomorrow's destiny so that negative actions and decisions are likely to produce adverse results just as positive actions should bring about positive consequences.

So, by a thorough examination of the lines and the application of the timing gauge, described in Chapter 10, it is possible to ascertain not only the nature but also the time of onset and duration of any of the problems suggested by the lines. Armed with this knowledge, then, it is feasible that an individual might be able to abandon a course of action which, she judges from the markings, will have adverse repercussions. She may be able to take preventive measures, to reverse a negative situation, either to stave off or avoid the problems altogether. And if the situation is not within her control she may, at the very least, be able to prepare herself materially and psychologically for any potentially negative situation so marked. Forewarned is forearmed, so the saying goes.

CHAPTER EIGHTEEN

POWER

Some people seem naturally to exude a charismatic personality. They bring with them a certain bearing that carries respect and that magnetically attracts others to follow. Throughout history they have been known as born leaders, men and women with power of will and strength of character that have carried people and nations to their destiny.

Such powerful personalities naturally gravitate to the very top of their professions. They become heads of state, politicians, military leaders, captains of industry and notable personalities in the media. When it all boils down, they will be found to share those common denominators which, though not at all common, mark them out as special; as leaders who, whatever their stature, rise head and shoulders above all the rest.

And it is those same common denominators, those special character traits which, chirologically, are so interesting because they are qualities that stand out in the hand, that can be picked out and counted. Some people may possess one, perhaps two or maybe even three of these qualities. But to possess them in abundance is the mark of one who is truly great.

The first quality that must surely be required is the *desire* to become powerful, whether that means the accumulation of wealth, prestige, gaining authority over others, or whatever else may be associated with climbing to the top of one's chosen career. That desire is usually known as ambition.

But ambition alone, no matter how great or how burning, will not achieve one's objectives. Other qualities must surely come into play, characteristics such as determination, strength of character, the ability to concentrate, self-discipline and a readiness to work hard in order to reach one's target. Good powers of intellect, too, are a must as well as a strong sense of independence and self-confidence in order to make decisions and carry them through to the ultimate goal.

And last but not least, there has also to be a certain element of luck although here a huge philosophical controversy might rage. Some would categorically say that luck does not exist; or that powerful people don't need it; or, if they do, that they make it for themselves anyway. Others have it that charismatics attract luck to themselves as naturally as honey attracts bees. Whatever it is, whether intentional, self-generated or conferred by the gods, there is no doubt that a little luck – being in the right place at the right time – smooths the progress to the top.

THE DIGITS

Ambition – that desire, that spur which drives an individual to gain power and success – may be measured against the index finger. A long digit here virtually guarantees a desire to succeed. If it is straight, success will be achieved through honourable means and power will be used for the betterment and furtherance of the lot of mankind. Bent or

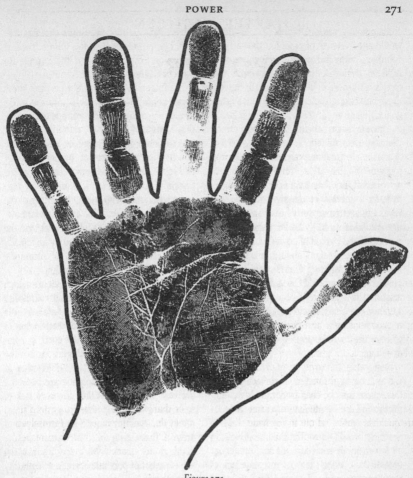

Figure 271

crooked, though, might suggest that the motives are more selfish.

When the index leans towards the thumb (Figure 271), it is not only a sign of ambition but, because of the wide space the stance creates between the first two fingers, it reveals mental independence, a preference to think things out for oneself, to formulate one's own opinions and arrive at one's own conclusions. Leaders of men usually have strong beliefs and original ideas, a factor which is reflected in the stance of the fingers

in this way. Those who prefer to be led are dependent on others for their cue and such people will be found invariably to hold their fingers much closer together.

But it is the thumb that registers the degree of will-power, the determination, the driving force that pushes the individual to achieve his objectives. The stronger and longer the thumb, the more self-discipline there will be and the more effort channelled into bringing to fruition the thoughts and plans that are reflected elsewhere in the hand. Without an accompanying strong thumb, a long index would show plenty of ambition, but alas no spunk, no bottle, no motivation with which to fulfil that desire. A thin, weak-looking thumb carries no power or authority at all; indeed, those possessing such a digit are usually easy to manipulate and just as easy to dominate.

A powerful personality possesses a strong thumb. Determination and strength of character are qualities registered in the top phalanx of this digit. Long and elegant reveals that its owner will achieve her objectives in a subtle yet decisive manner. But when this section is overly heavy and bulbous the individual is likely to be aggressive and ruthless in the pursuit of power.

The second phalanx should be as long as the first thus assuring that the will-power is guided and tempered by intelligence and reason. The ability to deal with people and situations in a tactful and diplomatic manner is expressed by a 'waisted' second phalanx, giving the whole thumb an hour-glass appearance.

Being able to carry through one's plans without being distracted or deflected along the course may be seen in both a fairly rigid thumb and one which does not form too great an angle to the hand. If the thumb is too flexible it would show that the individual can all too easily be swayed. One that opens out greater than ninety degrees reveals a lack of concentration and too great a dissemination of effort – all characteristics that would detract from the pursuit of personal success and power.

So a long, strong thumb that is not over-supple nor opens out too far from the hand is an excellent sign of the right degree of concentration, determination and strength of mind that will support an ambitious index finger. Add to this the other qualities that might be represented in the thumb, such as reason and diplomacy, and the formula for power and success begins to write itself.

The fingers can throw light on three more components that need to go into the mix – confidence, a responsible attitude and a spot of good luck.

Confidence in one's beliefs and abilities, which is crucial to the attainment of power and success, may be seen in the setting of the fingers. Self-assertion or assurance is normally associated with a straight setting of the fingers into the palm. The little fingers, however, are very often set slightly lower than the rest but these may be balanced by an equally placed index thus forming a pleasantly rounded arch to the top of the palm.

But a serious lack of self-confidence which would undermine the individual's authority is highlighted by a very low-placed little finger so that the digit, being half-buried in the palm, appears extremely short in comparison to the rest of the fingers. And if the Head and Life lines are joined together at their beginning for too long it exacerbates the problem, showing not only a severe lack of self-confidence, but also a fearful, timid nature, mistrustful of itself and of the world around. Possessing these two features in the hand rather stacks the odds against the achievement of personal power and authority over others.

And finally, 'good luck', that component which oils the wheels, however it might be described, may be expressed by a full mount of Apollo beneath a strong and well-formed ring finger. The addition of a long, clear and unhampered line of Apollo, too, confirms that fortune smiles upon its owner.

THE MOUNTS

Energy and vitality are essential components in leadership. Both physical and mental stamina are prerequisites to the sort of indomitable spirit that is required, not only to become powerful and influential, but also to sustain that impetus. A factor that distinguishes the leader from the led is that the former seems to find, and be able to muster, just that little extra reserve even, it would appear, after all energy has been spent.

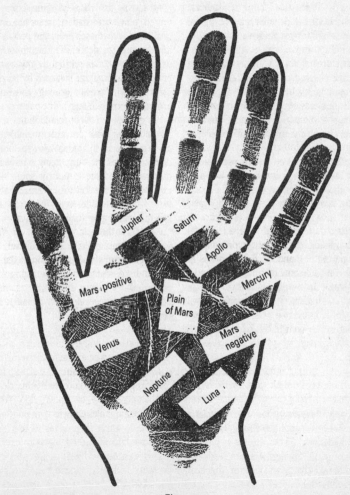

Figure 272

Weak and flabby mounts show none of the spark of vitality that full and fleshy mounts do. Well padded and springy, they reveal a constitution brimming with health. There's masses of resilience here, plenty of energy and staying power – essential qualities to support the strength of purpose and ambitious drive that leads to power.

A good leader would have all well-developed mounts across the top of the hand (Figure 272). When the Mount of Jupiter is high and padded it denotes honour, justice and a sense of fair play. Saturn adds stability, understanding and wisdom. Apollo shows charisma, acceptance by others and, of course, the element of luck too. A full Mercury mount highlights the necessary charm that will influence people. And Mars shows the courage and tenacity required if one is to believe in oneself and to push one's objectives through.

Particular emphasis on certain areas, either because the mount appears extra full or even broader than the rest, would highlight particular fields of expertise of the individual and the direction in which the power is used.

Politicians or spiritual leaders would usually possess an especially pronounced Jupiter mount, topped by a long, straight index finger. Charismatic figures in the media would show an emphasis in their Apollo mounts. Mercury, particularly well developed, is associated with business magnates but is also seen in the hands of politicians as well. This development, coupled with a long, straight Mercury finger, is of enormous benefit to anyone who needs to use rhetoric in order to persuade and influence others. And, of course, when the area of Mars stands out, taking its name as it does from the god of war, it is a principal sign of military generals and leaders. Curiously, though, industrialists too may possess this well-developed formation as well.

As far as the basal phalanges are concerned, power and leadership are not usually associated with these. True, the bottom sectors describe physical energy and robustness, which are vitally important in this respect, but the actual qualities that each of these two areas deal with are not generally those at the heart of empire-building.

For example, a well-formed Luna mount might indeed pick out the visionary, and many a powerful individual requires a certain degree of foresight with which to implement his dreams and ideas. But too large would exclude them as powerful leaders because they would be interested in other, more spiritual rather than material, concerns.

And then there is the Mount of Venus which is associated with love and sexual athleticism and prowess. But there are those who would argue that perhaps the accumulation of sexual conquests does bring a certain power. That, however, must remain a moot point.

THE LINES

Strong, powerful personalities who command authority and respect have strong, clear and well-formed lines. These ensure a positive attitude of mind, an alertness and readiness to act or to take charge and control whenever the situation requires.

Vibrant energy and vitality is reflected in a strong Life line. Few people with poor health are able to apply themselves to the rigours that a position of power demands.

Decisiveness – that ability to make decisions without demurring; to think clearly and rationally; to plan one's strategies and campaigns logically – all require a good intellect, and a good intellect is reflected in a clear Head line with no adverse markings to obstruct the mental processes.

It is best, too, if the Head and Life lines are either separate or break free from each other very early on as this formation confirms a readiness to take risks and chances and an ability to cope with personal responsibility. The early independence represented by the separate lines shows that the individual has learned to stand on her own two feet from a very early age. The longer the lines are attached together, the more dependent and timid the individual, and the less likely she will want to take personal responsibility in life.

The Fate line is a particularly important indicator because it is the deep, long, unimpeded line that is the sign of an innate sense of destiny. Powerful individuals possess just such a line.

Moreover, the stronger the Fate line, the more able the individual will be to shoulder responsibility. And the more powerful one is, the greater the burden of that responsibility. So the stronger the Fate line, the more equipped will be its owner to carry the can, to have the confidence to say that 'the buck stops here' and the courage to give the ultimate command that may seal the fate of nations and the destiny of men.

CHAPTER NINETEEN

MONEY

Wealth is a matter of opinion. Some might consider themselves wealthy if they had a few hundred in the bank. Others might not be contented unless they had a pile to their name to match the collective national debt of Latin America – and that's just for pocket money!

Attitudes to money vary enormously. There are those who are contemptuous of it and treat it frivolously, squandering every penny as soon as it comes in. Some hoard it covetously, whilst some believe in sharing it all out. For others, money is simply a status symbol; and then there are those for whom money is the be-all and end-all of existence – Mammon, the golden calf, the sacred cow.

From a chirological point of view, it is more the attitude to wealth rather than the possession of it that will determine how money is actually marked in the hand. For one who doesn't consider himself wealthy, although to all intents and purposes he may be sitting on a small fortune, the markings in the hand will be quite different to the next individual who has had to work long and hard for every penny and has an enormous sense of satisfaction watching the pounds growing in the bank.

So the question of money can be looked at from several different aspects and especially so whether wealth has been inherited, accumulated over time or suddenly acquired. From being born with a silver spoon in one's mouth, through scooping the jackpot, to working a whole lifetime in order to make one's pile, the markings that represent money in the hand are many and varied.

INHERITED WEALTH

A line originating either from the Life line or from the mount of Venus, which then shoots its way up towards the Mercury and/or the Apollo mount, is usually the sign of strong family links. A helping hand, a 'leg-up' from the family, or setting up in the family business is marked in this way. So, too, is wealth that is inherited from one's family, and especially so if the marking is accompanied by a star on the Mount of Apollo (Figure 273a).

Alternatively, the line from the Venus mount might travel out across the hand to meet with and merge into the line of Apollo (Figure 273b). This, too, is an excellent sign of inherited wealth and especially favourable if the line from Venus bears a star formation at

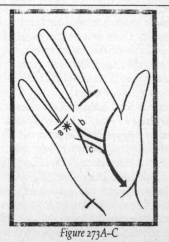

Figure 273A–C

its beginning.

If, however, the Venus line meets the line of Apollo but, instead of merging with it, cuts right through and crosses the main line, it suggests that there will be severe financial losses connected with inheritance or family bequests or that the individual has made some unwise or reckless investments with her money (Figure 273c).

Another feature which may denote an inheritance is a pair of parallel lines running from the centre of the palm up towards the ring finger and ending on the mount of Apollo. Here, because the line does not originate from the Venus or family area, the inheritance is likely to come from outside the family, left by a friend or employer perhaps.

ACCUMULATED WEALTH

Although very generalized, the actual feel and shape of the hand will give some broad clues as to how people handle their earnings and treat their savings.

A hard hand is the sign of a ferociously hard worker with a prodigious output. People with this type of hand often don't know when to stop. They drive themselves hard and everyone else in their charge as well. Those with firm but springy hands tend to work hard too, and enthusiastically so, but perhaps they are more sensible and don't tend to push themselves, or their employees, over their limits. These two types tend to accumulate their earnings steadily.

Soft doughy hands reveal the indolent workers, too lazy to work hard enough for their money. The cleverer ones get others to earn it for them! These doughy hands, flabby but with no spring to them, can also be a sign of extravagance, so money tends to go out just as quickly as it comes in.

Earth-handed individuals are characteristically hard-working. Security is important to them so they are likely to put money away carefully and methodically in order to feather their nests. But because they're not the sort to take risks and chances in life, they are unlikely to make vast gains, unless they inherit their wealth. More typically, they will work systematically to provide a comfortable and secure home for themselves and their

families and to ensure that their lives are financially sound.

Air-handed folk are likely to make money in life. With their love of technology and communications, they are likely to be in the forefront of new techniques and inventions that will make them a packet. They also make clever businessmen and women so tend to have their fingers in many pies. Perhaps they will juggle several jobs at the same time and, although not steady plodders like the Earth hands, they will make their money through their cleverness and their intellect.

People wth the Fire type are also likely to make a good del of money through their work but because of their lifestyles, they may not accumulate quite as much as they would like. Because many of them make their careers in the entertainment world, their success, and therefore their earnings, very often depend on people's acceptance and approbation of them. Those who are loved, then, are likely to make a lot of money whilst the fortunes of others will be sporadic.

The Water-handed type is the least materialistic of the lot. If they do make money, which many of them do, it will be through their creative and artistic talents. However, they are not wordly wise and many lose their fortunes through their trust in unscrupulous advisers. With good financial advice, they can pile up quite a tidy little fortune – much of which will be used as a vehicle for investing into works of arts and into the beautification of their surroundings.

The development of individual mounts, too, can shed a good deal of light on the habits and attitudes people have about money.

Someone with a well-developed mount beneath the middle finger is known as a Saturnian type. Saturnians are notoriously characterized as careful and cautious with their money; even parisimonious, some would say. Any money they make is likely to be saved, and though their bank accounts grow fat they continue their frugal lifestyle, for all intents and purposes as if they were poor as church mice – which is indeed how they believe themselves to be. No wonder, then, that the very well-developed Saturn mount is so often associated with the miser!

People who possess a well-padded Mercury mount are brilliant at dealing with money – especially other people's. They are particularly good in the City, and in business, making excellent bankers or investment brokers. In general, then, when all the other markings are sound, it may safely be said that Mercurians, with their excellent entrepreneurial skills, are never short of a bob or two.

Those with a well-developed Jupiter mount have a magnanimous spirit when it comes to money. Whether their wealth is inherited, acquired or accumulated by the sweat of the brows, they, more than any other type, have a strong social conscience and will want to share at least part of their good fortune with others. Philanthropy, therefore, is very much associated with the Jupiterian.

Still in this area of the hand, a line, having originated from inside the Life line and shooting up to end on the Jupiter mount, is a pleasing augury of success which is very likely to be accompanied by substantial financial rewards. If a star appears on the line as well, the odds on making a lot of money from a

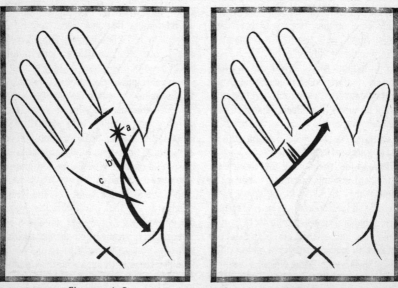

Figure 274A–C   Figure 275

position of power and authority are greatly increased (Figure 274a).

Success is similarly associated with the line from Venus which, instead of sweeping up to Jupiter, swerves up to end on the mount of Saturn. Here the wealth is accrued from one's work but helped along by friends and family (Figure 274b).

A Venus line to the Mercury mount suggests wealth from business dealings and commercial affairs (Figure 274c).

In the majority of hands the Apollo line is seen either to begin above the Heart line or to show considerable strengthening of the line from this point on. Such an Apollo line, when it is also clear and deeply etched, promises warmth and contentment in one's later years.

Traditionally, three such Apollo lines taking root above the Heart line are said to be a sign of luck with money (Figure 275). Although the subject may never actually become stinking rich, there will always be just enough money to keep the wolf from the door. Even when one's purse is empty and the bills are piling up, those with this formation find that the money somehow turns up to cover their needs – it might be a tax repayment or repayment of an old debt, or perhaps the individual is given a raise or a new contract is offered out of the blue. In later life, the formation shows that money worries ease away and one can comfortably enjoy the financial security that has been built up through the long years of work.

ACQUIRED WEALTH

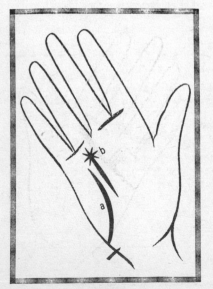

Figure 276A–B

Figure 277

A well-developed mount beneath the ring finger categorizes an individual as an Apollonian type. People with this formation have the reputation of possessing the Midas touch. Whatever they lay their hands on or put their minds to seems to turn into gold. New ideas bring in handsome returns; businesses flourish in their hands; even their talents are lauded and applauded and turned into revenue. Apollonians just seem to attract money – not necessarily steadily, but when it does come in, it arrives in great big lumps.

A line sweeping in from the top of the Luna mount and paralleling the Sun line as it shoots up towards the ring finger can be a sign of a windfall (Figure 276a).

Stars which occur either on or just touching the Apollo line are particularly associated with windfalls and sudden prosperity (Figure 276b). A stroke of good luck, an unexpected bequest or winning the pools might all be represented in the hand in this way.

Marrying into money, too, may be indicated by the Apollo line. In this case the Apollo line would rise at the same point as a relationship line feeds into the Fate line. A star, possibly on the Jupiter or Apollo mounts or just touching the Apollo line itself, would confirm the new-found wealth (Figure 277).

But the other side of the sudden acquisition of wealth is the sudden loss of money. Taking risks and gambling are quick ways of losing a great deal of money in a very short time. A gambling instinct is revealed by a long ring finger, as long or sometimes even longer than the middle finger. Twisted or badly formed Mercury fingers, when not an inherited characteristic, are signs of a cunning, scheming nature, someone who is underhanded and tends to get involved in crooked deals. Both these unusual features bode ill when it comes to financial management.

Yet another bad sign which shows financial problems or strictures is an island in the Fate line, often coupled with another island in the Business line. Although this formation in the Fate line may have alternative meanings, indicative of anxieties and frustration at work, such problems are often also linked to money worries. When both lines form into islands at the same time it is highly likely that a period of belt-tightening is on the cards.

CHAPTER TWENTY

LEISURE AND TRAVEL

Although hands show quite clearly inborn characteristics which befit particular types of career and fields of expertise, there are many reasons why an individual may not slot neatly into an occupation that encompasses all of her talents and skills. Lack of training, experience and opportunity may preclude many from entering professions to which they would be admirably suited. Equally, some people are unsure of, or lack confidence in, their talents. Or perhaps those talents develop only later on in life.

For whatever reason, then, many people simply drift into occupations which are totally unsuited to their natures, and, before they realize it, it is too late or too difficult to change course. For these, their only recourse is to channel those gifts and talents into their spare-time activities.

But whether it is that hobbies and pastimes are avenues along which we channel our unused talents, or that we now have more time and money to pursue our interests or even that we now realize the benefits to health and well-being of relaxing away from our work, leisure has become big business. And the hand, as with all other aspects of life, can give some general guidelines as to the sort of activities the different types will lend themselves.

THE EARTH HAND

Earth-handed people are characteristically practical, logical and down-to-earth. Robust, sturdy types, they are hard workers with masses of common sense. Systematic, solid, stolid types with feet firmly planted on the ground, they need routine in their lives and work and generally like to play it by the rule book. Conservative in their views, they are great upholders of law and order. Their pet hate is being cooped up indoors for any length of time for they long for the open air and the great outdoors. True children of the earth, they are close to nature with a strong rapport for all manner of flora and fauna.

For the majority of those belonging to this type, gardening is a favourite pursuit – even if it is only caring for a few potted plants or a window-box. Of all the types they are the most greenfingered. Many will be found spending their evenings and weekends on their allotments, growing superb flowers and vegetables in neat, weeded rows along traditional methods that have been tried and tested for generations past. Their great fund of knowledge seems to be instinctive – at one with Nature, with the rhythms and cycles of Mother Earth.

The Earth-handed individual is much more at home in the country than in the city. Those, however, who do live in town should try to get out and about into the countryside for long walks, perhaps taking the dog with them – an excellent way of keeping the notorious Earth-hand pear-shaped figure in trim! There's something invigorating for them in filling their lungs with the heady scents of wood, of grass crushed underfoot, of damp soil.

Women in this category might collect pretty twigs with autumnal coloured leaves to arrange in earthenware vases when they get home, a little reminder of their roots and their affinity to the earth. Or better still, they might pick blackberries, beechnuts or sloes. Mother Nature's food for free will appeal to their serendipitous natures and their industriousness will soon turn these into delicious pies that grace their tables or into sloe gin, perhaps, to keep out the cold winter night.

THE AIR HAND

Those belonging to this category are lively and adaptable people who hate routine but need plenty of variety to keep their enthusiasm alive. Communication is their great love in life, whether that involves satellite telecommunications, travelling, speaking in a foreign language or simply reading a good book. They gravitate towards any environment which is buzzing with news and views and activity. So in their leisure pursuits, too, they will look for variety and probably have dozens of interests to keep them busy and stimulated. Air-handed individuals are known for their curiosity and their love of learning. As eternal students, then, they will go through their lives picking up new information, adding to their fund of knowledge and repertoire of skills. Their need to pick up new skills would send them hotfoot to evening classes in ikebana, interior decorating or jewellery making. And they're a dab hand in the kitchen, too, forever experimenting with new dishes, especially if the recipe is foreign or exotic.

Women in this category have an extraordinary flair with clothes, an ability to transform even a humble sack into a stunning outfit that will turn heads in the street. Saturday mornings might be spent rummaging through jumble sales, emerging triumphantly with 'treasures' which they then work on for the rest of the weekend, turning them into personal masterpieces ready to wear to the office on Monday morning.

The other side of their nature is that love of communications: travel, reading, writing, learning a new language. Foreign countries with their different cultures fascinate them, so travel will figure largely in their holidays and spare time. And at weekends they will probably tour around, seeing the sights, jump in the car and just go.

But if for some reason they can't get out there's still masses they can do at home. They could always watch that travelogue they recorded on their high-tech video last week, or the Open University programme about the rise of philosophical thought through the Renaissance. They might strip down the car engine, programme their personal computers, catch up with their letter writing to old friends or, whilst they have their pen and paper out, they could make a start on that book they keep meaning to write. But if it's a cold and rainy afternoon, there's nothing they would rather do than put their feet up and read the Sunday papers from cover to cover.

THE FIRE HAND

Fire-handed people are energetic types, full of enthusiasm and excitement in life. Indeed, activity characterizes people in this group, for they have a terrific amount of physical stamina and a huge appetite for adventure.

There are several facets to the nature of the Fire type. Some, because of their love of activity, are sporty. Others are inventive with a far-reaching mentality and the ability to come up with original ideas. But most, with their inborn gift for spreading cheer and enthusiasm, have a love of people.

Sport and leisure are synonomous to many who possess the Fire hand. They enjoy all forms of exercise, aerobics or any sort of hard emergetic work out. Many join their local gym or sports centre and spend a happy Sunday morning playing a game of tennis or swimming a few lengths of the pool before meeting friends for lunch. The young and vigorous might spend an hour pumping iron and then sweating it out in a sauna.

Because these also thrill to the *frisson* of danger, any of the more adventurous sports would suit them: skiing, flying, wind-surfing, hang-gliding; anything that satisfies the dare-devil in them.

For those who are more intellectually adventurous rather than physically active, there are dozens of outlets for their energetic and inventive minds. Some become tutors in their spare time, offering their skills to the local adult education service. Learning any scientific or technological subjects, too, would grab their attention – anything from meteorology to motor mechanics. The more seriously academically minded might consider taking a degree. Psychology, perhaps, would suit. If they can't physically hack their way through jungles or canoe the Amazon, they can always explore the hidden pathways of the human mind.

But their naturally gregarious instinct and love of the limelight will make them gravitate towards people. Joining the local amateur dramatics group would be a good outlet for their talents. And so too would any local charity work. The bubbly personality of the Fire type would make a wonderful prison visitor or hospital friend. Alternatively, helping out at a playgroup or volunteering with the Samaritans would also satisfy the sense of missionary zeal that most in this group possess.

With all energy spent and the good works done, the Fire types might like to indulge that tiny hint of sensuality in their make-up. There is little they would enjoy better, on a rainy Sunday afternoon, than putting their feet up and watching a classic movie on TV. A glass of champagne and a box of chocolates at their sides, if they have a sweet tooth, or else a round, mature port with a wedge of stilton would just add that touch of luxury that Fire hands adore!

THE WATER HAND

People with Water-type hands are gentle, artistic and imaginative folk. Of all the categories these are the most sensitive – the dreamers, the poets and the visionaries of our times. Cultured and urbane, their interests encompass all forms of the Arts, *belles-lettres* and music. And they are usually accomplished themselves, creative and artistic in their own right. But another facet of the sensitivity that is so much part and parcel of the Water-handed group is a visionary, almost psychic nature which gives them a deep understanding and an ability to sympathize and empathize with others.

The beautiful long fingers of the Water type reveal their extraordinary patience. Couple that with their artistic eye and it becomes evident that any fine, intricate work like watchmaking, embroidery or tapestry would be of interest to them.

They have a passion for Art in all its forms, so as a pastime they might like to paint, sketch, make beautiful pottery or take stunning photographs. Undoubtedly, they would derive great pleasure in visiting art galleries or exhibitions, or popping into the local museum whenever possible. For their holidays they would probably travel to places of historical interest and culture: Egypt, Athens, Rome, Florence, Venice. Closer to home, they might take advantage of one of those creative breaks; painting in the Lake District, for example, or lapidary in the Cotswolds. The younger, more energetic ones might even offer their assistance at the local archaeological digs.

Music, too, is immensely important to them. Going to concerts, music recitals or poetry readings would especially please or some would learn to play an instrument themselves. And, because peace and tranquility are so essential to these people, just lying back and listening to their favourite records can bring the solace they so require.

As might be expected from the name, people in this group have a special affinity to water, so a walk along a riverbank or by the seashore would provide inspiration or revive their spirits, especially if they're down. Swimming would also appeal, and so too would classical ballet.

As far as intellectual pastimes are concerned, many enjoy taking up home study courses, such as the history of art, for example. Or that sensitive side of their nature might enjoy studying any of the complementary subjects such as astrology, graphology or homeopathy. And for those who feel they have had a stressful time at work, unwinding at the weekend with a massage and a facial, or with yoga, aromatherapy, reflexology – anything that is gentle and relaxing – will be greatly beneficial and soothing for both their bodies and their minds.

TRAVEL

Whether it is to visit El Alambra or Disneyland, the carvings on Easter Island or the Sydney Opera House, or simply to make frequent trips to visit granny in Bolton, travel plays a large part in today's leisure pursuits.

Journeys, trips, movement, comings and goings and all manner of travel are represented in the hand in different ways.

The most common is by movement branches which peel out of the Life line and shoot their way towards the Luna area (Figure 278a). The importance of the event and its impact on the individual largely depends on the length and strength of these branches. Cutting deep and reaching right into the Mount of Luna suggests an important trip which probably takes the individual far overseas.

Smaller and finer branches denote movement too, but perhaps with not quite so much impact on the owner. Very often these markings represent a removal or change of address, particularly so if a fine branch is seen to emerge from the same spot and shoots up towards the Saturn finger. This marking invariably highlights the buying and selling of property (Figure 278b).

If either the branch to Saturn or the one to

Figure 278 (A-D)

Luna should be marked adversely with, say, an island in it, this will suggest problems and frustrations connected with the move, journey or property deal (Figure 278c). Any effects from such an event, whether positive or negative, may be reflected on the Head, Fate or Life lines.

Indeed, any adverse markings at all on the travel branches could spell trouble. Islands here, as in all lines, are particularly worrisome because they do suggest problems. Bars, too, are a nuisance because they show impediments to one's progress. Breaks in the travel lines have similar meanings: hindrances and obstructions. But stars in this context are perhaps the most troublesome as they show sudden, unexpected difficulties or crises *en route*.

In the case where the Life line itself swings out towards the Luna mount, it may be suggesting that the subject will not only travel overseas, but could well end up emigrating altogether.

Interestingly, Life lines that decidedly tuck themselves firmly around and underneath the ball of the thumb show no love of travelling whatsoever. Owners of this marking seem to have an aversion to all the inconvenience of moving and travelling around. Consequently, these people are quite happy to stay put at home.

But a much travelled individual will be given away by other markings in the hand. Seasoned travellers, those people who aren't happy unless they're on the road, will have a series of transverse lines originating from the percussion and cutting across the Mount of Luna on their way to the Life line (Figure 278d) – always a tell-tale sign of people with itchy feet.

HEALTH IN OUR HANDS

CHAPTER TWENTY ONE

THE HANDY HEALTH GUIDE

Although it is not as yet fully understood why, years of careful observation have led chirologists to recognize that illness and disease make characteristic markings in the hand.

Links between irregularities in the skin ridges and diseases due to chromosomal abnormalities have already been scientifically established. And so, too, has the discolouration of skin and nails as a symptom of a variety of physiological disorders.

At the same time that the skin ridges are being formed, so too are the major lines. And if any trauma that affects the foetus during those critical early months also affects the skin ridges, why shouldn't similar foetal trauma affect the lines as well?

In addition to congenital markings in the hand, long before a disorder is even detectable through a stethoscope or by a blood test, minute changes in the body chemistry work subtly on the palmar surface, changing the construction of the lines, fading some away or adding new ones where no lines previously existed.

Though we may not as yet know how, or indeed why, observation tells us nevertheless that it is so; that our psychological, emotional and physical states of health imprint their own patterns, their own signatures, into our palms.

But, when signs of health in the hand are being considered, it must be constantly borne in mind that they are merely showing **predisposition** to disease and not necessarily stating the development of clinical illness. The hand must be viewed simply as a good diagnostic tool which can pinpoint potential psychological and physiological imbalances. Sometimes such imbalances develop, in time, into serious disorders, and sometimes they don't.

Because the lines in the hand change and respond quite sensitively, and sometimes rapidly, to changes of attitude, lifestyle, nutrition and diet, specific indications which point to disease in the hand one day may quite undramatically start to fade on the next and eventually disappear altogether. An awareness of our susceptibilities or any detectable early warnings may help us to take preventative action, or indeed to avoid any possibility of their development in the first place.

No one sign in the hand stands alone, or is

enough by itself categorically to make a statement about an individual's health. Each indication is simply a clue which must be corroborated by other factors, refining, confirming and building up to give a total picture. And, when several factors seemingly point to a certain disorder, even then, diagnoses *should not* be made. The proper course of action, should any doubt arise over a person's health, is for the individual to be encouraged to seek medical clarification from a physician.

THE SHAPE OF HANDS

It is well known that endocrinal disturbances affect the actual shape of the hand. Doctors have long recognized the broad palm and short, blunt-tipped digits so characteristic of the underactive thyroid, or the ultra-flexible, short, tapering fingers that are associated with the underactive pituitary.

So, from a chirological point of view, when considering health aspects the first line of attack is to establish the actual shape of the hand; for it is the shape that lays down the fundamental character, the disposition and constitution of the individual. It is the shape, again, which describes the first level of the basic psychological and emotional needs of that person.

Once that has been understood it is possible to see how going against that fundamental nature, living a life which is alien to one's constitution or for which one is not psychologically or emotionally suited, can cause stress and eventual ill health.

Thus, to obtain a picture of one's susceptibility or predisposition to disease, it is important to recognize one's basic hand shape and relate that to the underlying implications for one's health.

THE EARTH HAND

The Earth hand belongs to the broad category, and broad hands denote a strong constitution.

This hand reveals a solid, sensible, down-to-earth individual. These people like to work methodically, to a routine, at their own pace. They are perhaps at their happiest out of doors. Health-wise they are robust, both physically and mentally, enjoying what used to be known as 'rude' health. They have strong recuperative powers so when they are ill, which is rare for this type, they are usually able to pick themselves up pretty quickly.

Stress-producing situations for this type would include being forced to rush their work so that they have to cut corners, or having their routine upset. And being cooped up either indoors or in an office for too long would make them feel physically sick. For best health these need plenty of exercise and fresh air.

THE AIR HAND

The Air hand also belongs to the broad category, so the constitution here too is good.

The fundamental character of the Air hand is lively and inquisitive. Unlike the Earth type, these people loathe routine and a steady, plodding life.

Air types need variety and change in their lives. Stick them in a dull routine where they cannot exchange news and views with other people and these will simply pine away – they will become disinterested and unmotivated. They will lose their vibrancy, their vivacity, and their spirit will be totally crushed.

Physically, they are not quite as robust as the Earth types, but they may be described as possessing a wiry constitution. Nervous anxiety is one of their weaker links.

THE FIRE HAND

Like the Air-handed people, the Fire types also need excitement in their lives. They are at their happiest centre-stage with the spotlight fully on them. Take the people and the fun out of their lives, and the stuffing will be knocked out of the Fire-handed individual.

These people like to live life to the full, very often in the fast lane. Passionate individuals, they have strong appetites with a special penchant for rich food and good wine. As their category name implies, Fire-handed folk can have fiery tempers and this, together with the sort of fast lifestyles they like to lead, suggests that their particular Achilles' heel is their cardiovascular system.

THE WATER HAND

People with Water-type hands are gentle and sensitive. They tend to be highly strung and prone to nervous tension. A spiritual, creative and sensitive environment suits them best, whilst coming bump against harsh reality will make them suffer. They need a great deal of support and understanding in which to flower. Without these elements the Water types can become anxious and neurotic.

Apart from their delicate nervous systems, Water types have a tendency, in general, to suffer from the sorts of conditions that might be described as of a 'phlegmatic' nature, with a particular emphasis on the reproductive system.

THE MOUNTS

After having established one's fundamental character and susceptibilities according to the basic shape of the hand, the next line of attack is to superimpose any information that may be gleaned from the formation of the mounts (Figure 279).

The mounts act like energy stores; they are the centres for vitality and health. When these appear weak and underdeveloped they reveal a lack of vitality and strength. Well padded, these areas show plenty of vigour and life.

The two basal mounts of Luna and Venus in particular denote physical energy and, for best effect, both should be equally well padded. When the Luna area overshadows the Venus mount it is a sign that the inner, imaginative and nervous side of the nature outweighs the physical robustness of the individual. Such a formation could well lead to nervous tension.

Venus overdeveloped in comparison to the Luna mount, though, would suggest an overabundance of physical energy – a jittery,

fidgety type who can't keep still for long.

A strong, well-padded Venus mount will always indicate a strong constitution and a healthy, robust individual. But a weak mount here, pale and underdeveloped, will denote a lack of strength and poor physical resources. These people will succumb to all sorts of illnesses and find it more difficult to recover than those with full and fleshy Venus mounts.

When the Luna mount appears to be the most dominant, the individual is known as a Lunarian type and there are certain physiological problems to which these people are susceptible. Depending on the markings, the weak links associated with Lunarians are intestinal and rheumatic problems, gynaecological and urological conditions. Signs and symptoms of a predisposition to these disorders are described below.

When the central part of the palm is dominant with the two mounts at each side of the palm – one above Venus and the other above Luna – pronounced, the individual is known

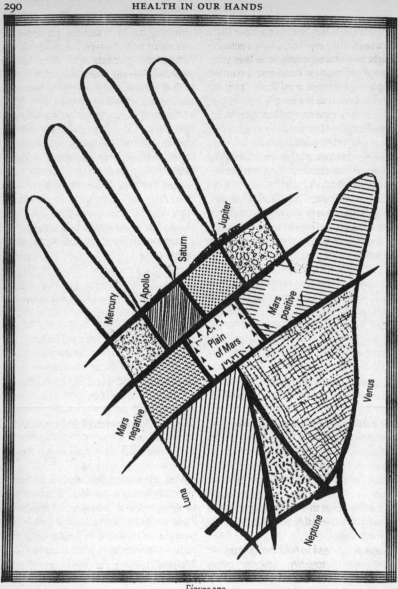

Figure 279

as a Martian type. Martians are often easily recognized by their physique; strong, solid and muscular. These people are known for their strong constitutions but their main weakness is that they are prone to feverishness. Circulatory problems may also affect them.

Jupiterians are recognized by a predominant Mount of Jupiter beneath the index finger. For a start, many Jupiterians have a notorious weight problem, especially so in later years. Much of the problem stems from a pure and simple enjoyment of good food – they are, after all, known as the *bon viveurs*! So if they can curb their appetites and keep their weight in check, they will be less likely to suffer from any of the weight-related problems to which these types are susceptible. Such conditions can range from intestinal, liver and stomach problems to respiratory and blood circulatory disorders. Having said that though, Jupiterians are tough and their systems can tolerate a good deal before feeling the strain.

For the Saturnian, whose mount beneath the second finger predominates, the problem may lie with nerves, bones and joints. In some, liver dysfunction may also be a problem as well as a lack of calcium in the system. Saturnians can be fretful, inner worriers and it is their anxiety that affects the nerves. Dis-

orders of the bony skeleton are sometimes associated with this type too; rheumatic conditions and problems with their feet are especially marked. The tendency towards a lack of calcium, which affects the bones, can also result in orthodontic problems.

The tip of the ring finger and the area at the root of the digit are associated with the cardiac and circulatory system. These are the health aspects which are mainly connected with the Apollonian type, the individual whose Apollo mount predominates above all the others. Being of a fairly strong constitution, though, they generally enjoy good health just like their fellow Jupiterians.

An overdeveloped mount beneath the ring finger is the sign of the Mercurian. Nervous anxiety and hyperactivity are the health problems more often than not associated with this type. In fact, any condition that stems from nervousness or overanxiety, such as indigestion, may also be applied to them.

FINGER POSITIONS AND SETTINGS

One's attitude to life often determines one's mental health, and it is how we feel psychologically about ourselves and our lives that influences the general tenor of our health. Both the way we hold our fingers and the way our digits are set into our palms give valuable information about those attitudes and expectations which inevitably reflect back on our very well-being.

Some people tend to hold their fingers and thumb tightly together, whereas others noticeably hold their digits widely apart, one from the other.

Fingers held close together often signify a 'closed' nature, someone who is dependent but who tends to bottle up their feelings, who cannot open out to others. There is a certain negativity and lack of spontaneity about these

people, which in psychological terms can lead to repression.

People whose fingers seem naturally to open widely are better balanced and have a better mental attitude for they take a healthier, more positive view of life.

When looked at palm-side up, some hands have the fingers set into the palm on a fairly straight and even line, whilst others are attached unevenly, in what is known as the **Perpendicular arch** formation.

The straight setting is the more healthy pattern to possess as it usually denotes plenty of self-confidence. Such folk are not the anxious, fretful types; indeed, worries seem to bounce off them like water off a duck's back.

Those with the Perpendicular setting, however, tend to be more timid, lacking in self-confidence and self-assurance, especially marked by a low-set little finger. A low setting of the index, though, is psychologically more serious as it denotes an inferiority complex.

THE FINGERS

Through years of observation hand analysts have established a link between the fingers and various parts of the anatomy, including the endocrine system (Figure 280). The thumb is said to be linked with the general nervous system. The index is related to the stomach, respiratory system and the pituitary. The middle finger deals with the intestines and the pineal gland. The ring finger is connected with the renal and circulatory systems and also with the thymus. And the little finger deals with the intestines, the reproductive system and the thyroid gland.

In cases where the endocrine system is upset or where there is a general hormonal imbalance, vertical lines may appear on the tips of the fingers (Figure 281). The area of greatest disturbance may be deduced by the greater concentration of these vertical lines on any one particular finger. When all the finger tips are so marked, including the thumb, it is a sign that the whole system is run down and that the individual may be suffering from nervous exhaustion. These markings of physiological debility also suggest that the autoimmune system is being weakened, leaving the individual vulnerable to ill health and disease.

Stress, that other big factor at the root cause of so many ills, has its own way of making its presence known on the hand. At the earliest sign of tension and frustration tiny horizontal dashes, either known as 'stress lines' or as 'white lines', may be seen to form across the fingertips. When signs of ill health or of psychological trauma are detected elsewhere in the hand, these horizontal lines on the tips of the fingers act as corroborative evidence that all is not well.

Because, chirologically, each finger governs a certain aspect of the individual's life, it is often possible to gauge not only the amount of tension that is occurring, but also the area in the individual's life that is causing the strain.

For example, if a concentration of the stress lines should occur on the middle and ring fingers, it denotes that the problem centres around the individual's emotional contentment and sense of security. Basically, because the middle finger governs the property and home while the ring finger deals with one's happiness, the stress lines here show some sort of relationship conflict that is threatening that individual's home life.

Stress lines across the index would show tension in connection with one's career and standing in life, and an all-time low in personal morale. On the little finger, they indicate a blockage in communications with a resulting lack of self-confidence and self-esteem. On the thumb, the stress lines denote general strain and fatigue in all areas of the individual's life.

It is interesting to note that these markings can appear and disappear fairly rapidly, but when they are spotted they do indicate that excessive stress and strain are settling in. At this point the owner should take steps to slow down and relax, work out the problems and try to find a solution or at least come to terms with them. Like the hormonal imbalances and weakening of the immune system, chronic stress, over a long period of time, can lead to a breakdown in the body's defences thus lowering its resistance to disease.

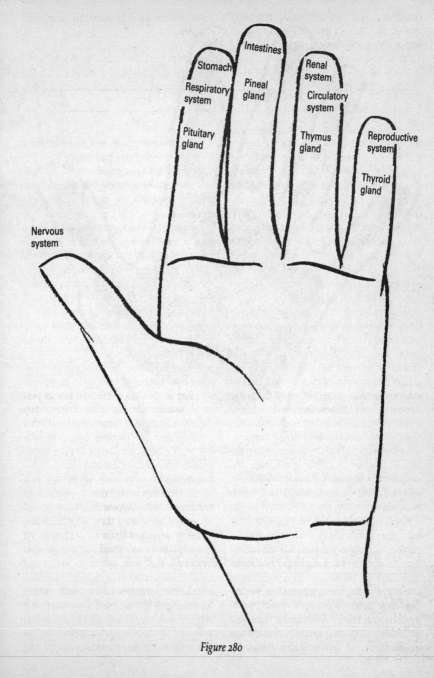

Figure 280

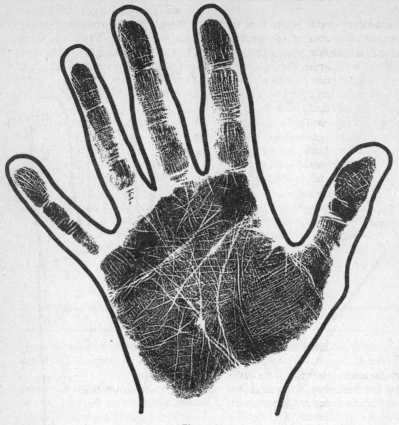

Figure 281

The stress lines may be accompanied by tiredness lines, which are vertical creases running down the two lower phalanges of the fingers. Again, when these are seen, it is a sign to slow down and give the body a little time to recuperate its forces.

FULL HANDS AND EMPTY HANDS

The shape of the hand, mounts and fingers gives very general indications of our predisposition to disease, but it is in the lines that we can pinpoint specific tendencies. Irregularities and defects in the lines may either have developed in the womb during the growth and formation of the lines or they may be part of an ongoing process which automatically reflects and responds to the way we live, the way we experience life and the way we use or abuse our own bodies and minds.

In considering health aspects it is the quality and construction of the line that, when analysed minutely, yields a great deal of information. However, even before the microscopic investigation of the lines, the first feature that gives a very big clue to the overall picture of the individual's health lies in the quantity of lines that exist in the hand, and it is this quantity that is referred to in the terms 'full hand' and 'empty hand' (see p.109).

A hand that is covered in a rich cobweb of lines is known as a 'full hand'. This hand, with its myriad superfluous creases, is unmistakable in its appearance and is always a sign of ultrasensitivity. It is a complex hand to analyse, mirroring as it does the emotional complexity of a highly strung type of individual. Nervous anxiety is the label most usually attached to this hand. People possessing it would be well advised to find some form of relaxation – deep-breathing exercises or yoga, perhaps – to help calm them down and give them peace of mind. With a more relaxed attitude, the extraneous lines can and do eventually disappear, leaving a much clearer pattern to represent the easier attitude to life.

As opposed to the 'full hand', the 'empty hand' appears much more economical containing, as it does, just the bare essential lines. Whereas the 'full hand' describes complexity, this hand suggests a certain simplicity, an economy in the use of nervous activity. Though the lack of secondary lines might imply a narrower psychological view of life, owners of this type of hand are strong, resilient types who seem hardly aware that they even possess a nervous system at all!

THE LINES

Potential health indicators may be stamped into the main lines in one of two ways. Firstly, the actual construction, or the quality of the line itself, may be impaired; and secondly, marks cutting into or across a line may represent actual influences or events that affect the health and well-being of the individual.

Careful observation of each line in turn will throw up valuable clues each of which (although none should be taken on its own as categorically representing disease or ill health), may contribute towards all the other clues in the hand to build up a complete picture of the individual's psychological and physiological state of health.

CONDITION OF THE LINE

Ideally, lines should be well chiselled into the palm, not too deep and not too shallow, not too broad and not too narrow. In fact, using the analogy of a river helps to describe the condition of a line.

The energy and power that is represented by a particular line in the hand may be likened to the water that is carried in a river. Too deep, the water becomes torrential; too shallow and it will soon dry up. Too broad results in torpidity, and too narrow restricts the flow.

In some hands, the Head line may have sections which appear fuzzy or fluffy-looking. When this occurs it suggests that the individual is undergoing a period of indecision or of confusion, a time when there is a lack of clarity in the thinking and a general inability to cope with the demands that life is imposing.

In certain cases, lines have been known to fade and disappear. When this happens to the many extraneous lines in the 'full hand' it is a positive indication that the owner is reducing her high anxiety state and stress levels.

When it happens, however, to the major lines it is a more serious matter. This phenomenon, though, is most unusual. It has been known to occur in certain very rare conditions of a type of nervous disorder. And equally rare, it has also been observed to occur in certain cases of mineral imbalances and deficiencies, notably where there is a lack of copper in the system.

COLOUR IN THE LINE

Whatever the race of the individual, healthy lines should be of a deeper tone to the background pigmentation of the palm itself. If, when the hand is stretched out, the lines seem to drain of colour, turning pale or even white, it could be a sign of iron deficiency anaemia.

Conversely, lines – and especially so the Health line – which turn red and angry-looking may be pointing to heart or circulatory disorders. Here, other symptoms which would give corroborating evidence might be the shape and colouring of the nail: shell-shaped nails with accompanying cyanosis, or a bluish tinge to the nail bed.

Lines that run with a very dark colour suggest an emotional block which can result in repressive behaviour.

UNUSUAL LINES

The Simian line is instantly recognized in the hand in that it appears as a thick transverse crease which incorporates both the Head and Heart lines in one and which lies across the entire palm from edge to edge.

Although the Simian line is usually associated with Down's Syndrome, or Mongolism, it does, nevertheless, also occur in other conditions caused by chromosomal disturbances, and it can equally be found in a small percentage of the normal population.

With Down's Syndrome subjects the Simian line is only one of the features highlighting the condition. Other contributing factors include abnormalities of the thumb and little finger and unusual configurations in the dermal patterns.

Other than reflecting chromosomal disorders, though, when the line is seen in a normal hand it usually denotes specific psychological characteristics and behaviour. Such individuals may be described as extreme, emotionally intense and may display tendencies towards egocentric behaviour.

The degree to which the Simian displays these characteristics very much depends on the type of Simian line the individual possesses. The pure type would describe someone with the single transverse crease on both hands. Simian lines, either occurring on one hand only or with the tail ends of the Head and Heart lines sweeping out from the crease line, would show a moderation or a mellowing down of the more extreme Simian tendencies.

Another form of Head line with similar characteristics to the Simian line, but also with some distinct differences, was first investigated by a team of medical researchers in Australia who christened it **the Sydney line**.

Like the Simian line, the Sydney line stretches across the entire palm from the thumb side of the hand right over to the percussion. It may easily be distinguished from the Simian line in that it is not amalgamated with the Heart line but sits quite independently, with a separate Heart line standing on its own.

Also similar to the Simian line, the Sydney line may be found in normal hands as well as in the hands of those suffering from diseases linked to chromosomal abnormalities. On the physiological side, recent tests have discovered that children with either a Sydney or

Simian line run a 20 per cent greater risk of contracting childhood leukaemia than those with a normal Head line. Congenital heart problems, too, have been associated with this marking.

Research has also shown that, psychologi- cally, children with the Sydney line are more likely to display behavioural difficulties, due to the late development of emotional matur- ity, and to experience more learning problems than children with a normal Head line.

SPECIFIC MARKINGS ON THE MAJOR LINES

ISLANDS AND CHAINS

An island in a line occurs when a section of the line is split into two and then comes back together again. In appearance, the island looks like an elongated bubble. A chain is simply a sequence of islands, giving the line the appearance of a beaded necklace (Figure 282).

Wherever islands occur, they are not a good sign. In the Life line, especially, the division they cause in the line splits the cur- rent that is being carried along, weakening the energy and rendering the body vulnerable to illness and disease. In this main line in particular, the island denotes a period of general constitutional weakness, when the physical resources are low and the subject is especially prone to aches and pains and other aspects of ill health.

Islands at various locations in the Life line have specific meanings. Occurring high up towards the beginning of the line, they denote a predisposition to bronchial and res- piratory problems. In some cases, they also suggest actual illnesses, perhaps of a more severe or unusual nature than one might expect in young children.

Occurring lower down, as the Life line passes beneath the middle finger, an island here would point towards a susceptibility to back or spinal problems. Often when an island is seen in this position it tells that the subject suffers with backache, possibly on and off throughout her life, but particularly so

Figure 282

for the period of time the island represents.

Lower down still, an island would denote problems connected with ageing or with diseases associated with old age. In women, gynaecological problems linked with the menopause might be marked in this way here; whilst for men urological conditions or problems connected with the lower intestines or with the reproductive organs might be implied.

As the line sweeps its way down and around it occasionally forms itself into a small island close to the wrist and towards its end.

Some hand analysts have suggested that an island in this position may be showing a predisposition to cancer. However, further research is required in order to substantiate this claim, and in any case many more corroborative signs elsewhere in the hand would have to exist before it was possible to make any categorical statement about the disease.

A chained effect in the Life line would denote that the constitution was generally weak and the overall health poor.

Islands in the Head line refer to nervous tension caused through worry and anxiety. Occurring at any point in the line, an island would suggest a period of stress lasting throughout the length of time the island is present.

Typically, through its duration on the line, the subject would experience a period of indecision, of doubt and uncertainty. There would be a lack of clarity in the thinking and decision processes and the whole period might be characterized by strain, by woolly-mindedness and nervous tension.

An island occurring in the Head line directly beneath the middle finger has a particular meaning. In this position it is a sign that in general stressful situations should be avoided as much as possible for there is an inability to function properly under such circumstances. In short, people with this feature do not cope well under stress.

It is considered that an island formation within the Head line denotes a mineral imbalance, a deficiency of potassium has especially been thought to contribute to this formation.

Islands in, or chaining of, the Heart line may have either of two interpretations. They may refer either to emotional problems or to organic disorders. Markings elsewhere in the hand would support which of the two alternatives was implied.

On the psychological level, an island or a chain of islands might suggest emotional upheavals which result in nervous upsets.

With other corroborating markings, a Heart line that is chained throughout its length may point to cardiovascular deficiencies, such as poor circulation, hypertension, or weaknesses of the heart itself.

In some circumstances the chained Heart line may be denoting a mineral imbalance and, like the Head line, it could be deficiency of potassium that is at fault. The imbalance is more likely to be the culprit if both the lines are chained.

Another sign of a mineral deficiency is the fragmentation of the Heart line directly beneath the ring finger. Here, the line does not break as such but slits to form what is termed as a 'step ladder' effect. When this feature occurs it may well be pointing to a basic lack of calcium in the system.

Traditionally, an island in the Heart line beneath the second finger suggests hearing problems.

And traditionally again, an island in this line occurring beneath the ring finger suggests ophthalmic weaknesses.

In the Fate line, islands usually signify frustration and dissatisfaction with particular aspects in life connected with career, working colleagues and finances. The consequent anxiety caused by the stressful situations described by an island here pervades the individual's whole life and contributes to a general malaise thus lowering one's resistance to disease.

Found in the Health line, an island or chained effect points to possible problems of the respiratory tract.

BREAKS

Sudden breaks in the lines should always be considered as serious and requiring further investigation and clarification.

In the Life line a sharp break might imply an accident or the sudden onslaught of disease, sometimes grave enough to be life-threatening. With this formation, both hands need to be checked for similar indicators as well as for corroborating clues elsewhere. A formation of tiny lines, however, shaped into a square over the break does mitigate the seriousness of the situation implying protection and intervention of some sort that eases the problem.

Psychologically, a break in the Head line suggests a dramatic volte-face, a reorientation, a change in the thinking processes that lead to a new approach and a new direction in life. Supporting factors contributing to this conclusion might lie in a change of direction in the Fate line, or the Life line sweeping out further towards the centre of the palm. Physiologically, a break in this line can denote an injury to the head. Confirmation of this finding might come from a break, a cross or a star in the Life line.

In the Heart line, breaks have been associated with cardiovascular problems, with circulatory disorders and possibly even with a weak action of the heart.

CROSSING LINES

Bars that cut across the main lines usually denote obstacles and upheavals that affect the well-being of the individual.

The most obvious crossbars are seen cutting through the Life line and here they denote emotional upheavals or traumatic events. The longer and stronger the bar, the more serious the consequences of the situation. And if an island is formed into the crossbar itself it may allude to ill health – whether that of the subject or of a loved one – being at the centre of the trauma.

A series of fine crossbars cutting through the Life line in a sensitive or 'full hand' merely confirms a highly-strung individual and does not refer to specific events or emotional upheavals. With relaxation and easing of tension, the lines can fade and disappear.

Crossbars cutting through the Head line suggest obstacles that affect one psychologically, adding pressure and strain during the time indicated in the individual's life.

BRANCHES

Depending on its direction, a branch may be either a positive or negative sign. Positive branches usually shoot out in an upwards direction whereas negative branches, other than travel lines off the Life line, sweep out and down.

Tiny downswept branches off the Head line are invariably a sign of extreme emotional upset leading to depression at the time the branch occurs.

Similar downswept branches shooting out of the Heart line suggest a susceptibility to circulatory and cardiac problems. Some hand analysts consider that an association might exist between this formation and stroke or paralysis, but more work has yet to be carried out before such a link can be positively identified.

A series of fine hair-like branches sweeping out of the Life line often warn of a dissipation of energy. The formation looks as if the very fibres that make up the line are fraying and the body's natural resources draining away through them. Rest and relaxation usually restores the situation and strengthens the constitution.

STARS AND CROSSES

Very often stars can be wonderful indicators of glory and success but occasionally, in a few positions in the hand, the star can be a serious warning sign.

Star formations are formed by the intersection of several lines rather like an asterisk in appearance. They may free stand on the mounts where, in the main, they are considered welcome and positive features or, conversely, they may occur on the major lines where, perhaps 90 per cent of the time, they act as warning signals.

Similar to star formations, crosses too may be both positive and negative. In general, a cross straddling a major line may be considered as the latter.

Either formation, but especially so the star, occurring on a major line (other than on the line of Apollo), suggest a sudden impact, whether physical or emotional. A blow to the head, for example, or the shock of a sudden death in the family might be represented in this way by a star on the Head line. A fall from a ladder, a car accident or surgery could be denoted by a star on the Life line. Whilst on the Heart line, either or both might indicate the possibility of a stroke or of sudden cardiac trouble. On the psychological level, an emotional trauma may be represented in this way as might occur, for example, when one's partner decides, seemingly out of the blue, to terminate a longstanding relationship.

SPECIFIC MARKINGS

Other specific lines and markings that are directly associated with health matters may be found in the hand either attached to the main lines or standing independently.

A susceptibility to a variety of conditions affecting the alimentary canal, or associated with an unhealthy diet (such as intestinal acidity, dyspepsia or indigestion, for example) is denoted by a set of oblique dashes rising through the centre of the palm.

A build-up of uric acid, considered to be implicated in diseases of a rheumatic nature (such as gout, for example) is seen by a formation of tiny dashes that cut across the percussion edge of the hand.

Orthodontic problems and general weaknesses of the gums and teeth may be represented by a set of tiny oblique lines that sit just over the Heart line beneath the little finger. Confirmation of a problem with the teeth may be found in a wavy Health line. Incidentally, as problems with the teeth are also very often linked to gastric conditions, the twisted Health line will also corroborate any evidence for stomach or intestinal activity that is found elsewhere in the hand.

A series of tiny indentations along the Head line, almost as if the line had been punctured with a blunt needle, is often a reliable sign of a susceptibility to headaches, particularly to migraines.

Tendencies towards urological, gynaecological, or more general problems with the reproductive system in both men and women are often marked in the hand by a triangular or diamond-shaped formation attached to the outside of the Life line about a quarter of the way up the palm. It is, however, important to stress that the marking merely reflects a susceptibility to such complications. Not everyone with this formation develops any serious clinical symptoms at all.

Another marking which reflects problems of the reproductive system is a cross-hatching formation of lines at the base of the Luna mount.

CHIROLOGICAL COMPARISONS

CHAPTER TWENTY TWO

HAND ANALYSIS AND ASTROLOGY

There is no doubt that strong parallels exist between hand analysis and astrology.

Both are tools of psychological self-discovery and self-knowledge.

Both have been practised by civilizations for centuries throughout the world.

Both adhere to the same principles of plotting trends and potential occurrences that may affect an individual's life.

Both share a common shorthand language which incorporates similar symbolism.

Both are based on a set of scientific rules that require deductive reasoning as well as intuitive interpretation.

And because of that, the accuracy and reputation of each stand or fall according to its practitioners.

But equally there are vital differences, strengths and weaknesses occurring in both disciplines.

Hand analysis works on tangible markings that are caused by one's own body chemistry, whilst astrology bases its findings on the planetary positions at the time of an individual's birth.

Given that the exact birth time and place data are known, astrology can outline the timing of trends and events with astounding accuracy, sometimes to the very day of likelihood. Because no two hands are completely alike, but all differ in shape and size, it is impossible for hand analysis to establish a timing gauge that will fit all hands uniformly. The timing gauge, therefore, has to be necessarily adjusted for each individual, thereby laying itself open to individual inaccuracies. But even if a perfect fit of the gauge to a hand were achieved, exact timing – to the day – would still be impossible to establish due to the infinitesimally small area representing one whole year that an analyst has to work on.

Hand analysis is instantly visible and infinitely accessible. Astrology requires complicated mathematical conversion tables and ephemerides in order to erect a birth chart before analysis can begin.

SAME SYMBOLISM, SAME SHORTHAND

Every field of expertise evolves its own shorthand of technical terms; its own symbolism or concepts in code form which are easily understood and recognized by its members.

In just this way, chirology and astrology have each, over the centuries, developed their own jargon, their own symbolical language as a short cut to technical concepts. The particular terms they employ in common are derived from classical mythology and from the ancient philosophy on the nature and composition of matter.

This latter traditional philosophy taught that all living things were governed by one of the four elements: Earth, Air, Fire and Water, and it was the fundamental characteristics of each element which coloured and influenced its subject. Thus, in brief, the element Earth imparts solidity and practicality. Air is breezy and intellectual. Fire is vibrant and enthusiastic. And Water is sensitive and emotional.

Modern hand analysis has adopted these principles and attributed them to the four types of hand, so that an individual who possesses a hand that belongs to the Air category, for example, will predominantly reflect those qualities associated with the element Air.

Similarly, the four elements are used in astrology to divide up the twelve signs into four groups of three:

EARTH	AIR	FIRE	WATER
Taurus	Gemini	Aries	Cancer
Virgo	Libra	Leo	Scorpio
Capricorn	Aquarius	Sagittarius	Pisces

So, subjects born under the Water signs of Cancer, Scorpio and Pisces may be described as adaptable, impressionable, sensitive, easily influenced, emotional and receptive, together with all the other characteristics that are associated with this element.

By far the most obvious links between the two are the concepts that have been named after Roman gods, each describing a particular set of characteristics.

The Venus mount in chirology corresponds to the planet in astrology and deals with love and aesthetic tastes. The Mars area in the hand stretches horizontally across the centre and corresponds with the astrological planetary influence concerning staying power, physical and moral strength and persistence.

With the exception of Apollo, the fingers and other three mounts across the top of the palm, Jupiter, Saturn and Mercury, are analogous to the planetary characteristics of sociability, responsibility and the power of communications. Some see a similarity between the Apollo mount and the Sun. Others argue the case that the astrological principles behind the Sun characteristics are more aligned with the thenar eminence in the hand, that mount which, in chirology, is said to be governed by Venus. Whichever, one of the salient characteristics associated with both Apollo in chirology and the sun in astrology is creativity, so in this respect they find a parallel in each other.

Astrologically the Moon and chirologically the Mount of Luna directly echo each other. Both deal with the emotions, with imagination and the passive, subconscious facet of the individual.

Of the three slow-moving planets only Neptune finds its correlation in the hand, although this area, situated at the base of the palm between the mounts of Venus and Luna, is not a mount that is recognized by all modern hand analysts.

The other two, Uranus and Pluto, have no direct correspondence with specific areas in the hand but their action, one of unpredictability, and the other of a tendency to put obstacles in a person's way, might well be reflected in the subsidiary lines or markings.

The major lines in the hand, too, find their analogies in astrology. The Life line, with its idea of vitality and quality of life corresponds to the Sun. The Head line, representing the intellect, may be paralleled to both Mercury and Jupiter. The Heart line to Venus and the Fate Line, or perhaps aspects of it, to Saturn.

As far as the astrological houses, or zodiacal signs, are concerned, several attempts have been made to correlate them to particular areas on the hand, but the different systems tend to conflict and so this particular exercise, it would seem, loses its credibility.

HANDS AND HOROSCOPES

Perhaps, though, rather than striking comparisons between the two, combining them to arrive at a fuller psychological profile of an individual would be of greater value. In this way it would be possible not only to confirm each other's findings but at the same time to capitalize on the strengths of each and minimize their failings.

Figure 283 is the handprint belonging to the internationally renowned astrologer Julia Parker. Beside it, Figure 283b is Julia's birth chart, somewhat simplified for the sake of clarity and erected according to the Equal House System.

Julia was born in late July so her Sun is in Leo and her ascendant is Sagittarius – both belong to the element Fire. Yet her hand, with its long fingers, could not be said to belong to the Fire category, whose members notably have short fingers and whorled fingerprints. It might just fit into the Air group but would seem to have more in common with the Water category – except for the fact that the lines are clear and uncomplicated. And its elegance could not, by any stretch of the imagination, be said to meet the criteria for the Earth category.

And yet, adding up the planets in their houses it can be seen that there are four in the Fire triplicity (Sun, Jupiter and Mercury in Leo, Uranus in Aries), two in Earth, (Moon in Taurus, Neptune in Virgo), three in Air (Mars and Venus in Gemini, Saturn in Aquarius) and one in Water (Pluto in Cancer).

The emphasis on the elements of Fire and Earth as portrayed in the astrological birth chart, then, does not seem to be borne out at first glance by the shape of Julia's hand.

However, the liveliness of the fingers, with their wide spacing, does bring to mind the extroversion and enthusiasm and go with a fiery nature. This is the sign of a sunny disposition with a generally outgoing, trusting and happy-go-lucky character. Very much a description that fits the Sagittarius rising. It shows, too, animation and liveliness coupled with a quick intelligence and an agile mind.

From the chirological point of view, Julia's hand indicates that she's bright, active, alert and intelligent. This is essentially an instinctive, intuitive and feminine hand and the fine, long palm and fingers denote an elegant and sophisticated individual. This type of hand essentially belongs to someone who is urbane, cultured and who possesses refined tastes. Indeed, everything here speaks of refinement, of a love of aesthetics and of the arts. Here we see balance, symmetry and a delicate, discriminative eye; a preference for quality rather than quantity – pleasure is found being surrounded by beauty, elegance and good taste.

This description corroborates astrologically with the Moon in Taurus in the sixth house, and Libra on the MC. The latter especially highlights a need for balance and harmony in Julia's life, but it also underlines her strong sense of justice and fair play.

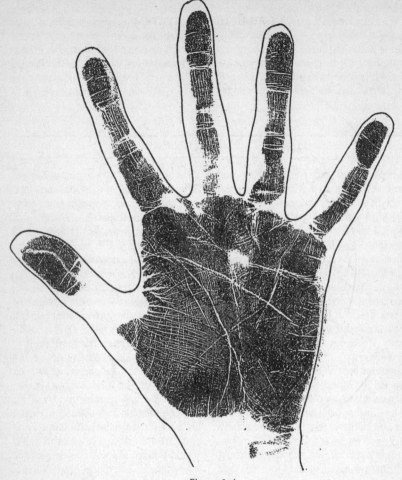

Figure 283A

The chart, too, places a good deal of emphasis on creativity not only because of the position and line-up of Leo but also in the fact that Uranus is in the fifth house in the fiery sign of Aries. The Moon in Taurus in the sixth house additionally brings in its own quantity of creativity too.

All this is reflected chirologically by the Venus mount which is well defined, thus confirming her enjoyment of life, art, love and fun whilst also stressing the creative and artistic side of her nature. The left percussion edge is especially rounded so her intuition is indeed supreme and probably one of her greatest assets. There is a considerable degree of insight and foresight outlined here which is matched astrologically by Neptune high in the sky and, more spectacularly, by Jupiter, the ruler of the chart which, at twenty-seven degrees Leo, is placed in one of the four

EQUAL HOUSE SYSTEM

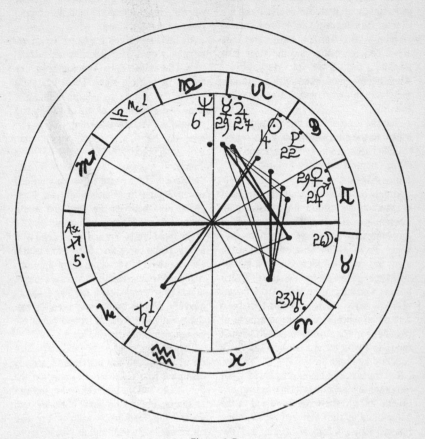

Figure 283B

'astrologer's degrees'. In the hand, the importance of Jupiter is revealed by the fact that it is full and well developed, noticeably standing out amongst the other mounts.

Julia's fingers are long and elegant and as such they denote a gentle and sensitive disposition, excellent for any job requiring meticulous detail and fine, elaborate and intricate work – again, Libra MC, Taurus in the sixth house. The index finger, otherwise

known as the finger of Jupiter, leans markedly outwards, giving her a strong sense of independence and a need for challenge and adventure. Very typical of the Sagittarius ascendant with its ruling planet Jupiter in Leo!

But, next door to the index, the finger of Saturn stands up straight as a die, giving the whole hand stability and purpose, keeping it upright and on an even keel. And, looking at the natal chart, it is not in the least bit surprising to find this confirmed by the planet Saturn, which opposes the Sun, a vitally important aspect that controls and disciplines all those fiery impulses, converting them into practicality and common sense. The trine aspect between Saturn and the Moon consolidates the sense of responsibility, stabilizing the emotions and giving a purpose and direction to her work on a day-to-day basis.

That she is careful and methodical is highlighted by the prominent joints of the fingers, so she needs order and a neat and tidy environment in which to live and work – Taurus in the sixth house.

Despite her evident urbanity, the long basal phalanx on her Saturn finger tells of an inherent love of horticulture and possibly of gardening too – again, Earth sign in the sixth house. Perhaps with her creative strengths, then, this could be interpreted as a gift for landscape gardening or designing garden layouts. Certainly the tip to the Apollo finger, which is fairly square, confirms a practical disposition when it comes to all manner of creative or artistic pursuits, especially when it comes to any of the arts which are tactile or entail working with her hands.

The thumbs, like the fingers, are long but with a sense of solidity to them which act as a driving force to the whole hand and to the nature, and as such they highlight a strong but well-adjusted, fairly self-assured and confident individual. The thumb too, shows that she has excellent powers of reason and logic. She seems to know exactly what she wants out of life and how to go about getting it. This

entails the ability to handle others with her refined awareness of the workings of the human mind, together with her perspicacity when it comes to analysis and deduction – Pluto in the eighth house.

All her fingerprints are loops, which are essentially the sign of flexibility and adaptability – the planets Mars, Venus and Neptune are all in mutable signs. These indicate a graceful mind, a desire to learn, to find new ideas and a need for plenty of variety and stimulation. A very interesting loop is also seen on her Luna mount, which often indicates a special affinity to water – Pluto in Cancer. In addition, the markings beneath the Apollo finger reveal a close rapport and understanding of animals whilst the interdigital loop between the third and fourth fingers tells of a dry sense of humour.

The Head line is long and well formed with a very gentle curve to it. Such a line as this shows a blend of a practical, logical approach combined with an artistic and creative turn of mind. This, coupled with the long finger of Mercury, denotes good literary talents; something that is astrologically represented by the conjunction of Mercury and Jupiter.

The Life line is long, strong and untroubled by islands or adverse markings of a really disruptive nature. She has the strength of the Sun in Leo and the Moon exalted in the sign of Taurus, in the sixth house of health. And finally, the Fate line, equally strong and untrammelled, would find its parallel in the position of Saturn, which, although opposing the Sun, stabilizes the career and gives her the sort of tenacity and dedication to her work that has assured her much deserved success.

PART NINE

APPENDICES

TAKING AN IMPRINT

Taking an imprint of the hand can be a little messy but it can also be fun – especially for the children. Or maddening, if the phone rings just when one's hands are inked up!

An inked imprint is both a good medium to work from when analysing the hand and excellent, too, for keeping as a record. The professionals use special inks and rollers, but a variety of household products can be substituted with good effect.

The ink used is Rowney's water-soluble Lino Printing Ink, or Block Printing Ink. It must be the water-soluble type so that the ink can be simply washed off the hands with soap and water. If the ink used is not water-soluble, special solvents will have to be used to clean the hands after the printing session. I am reliably informed that in the US Speedball Block Printing Ink is similar to the British Rowney ink.

A little of the ink is first squeezed out on to a sheet of glass and spread thinly with a printer's rubber roller. The ink is then applied, from the roller, onto the hand.

Listed here are the materials (with equivalent household products), and procedure for a do-it-yourself imprint of the hand.

MATERIALS

Ink/lipstick/boot polish
A sheet of glass/a formica board/silver foil/
   glossy magazine
Printer's roller/milk bottle/rolling pin
   (covered in foil or clingfilm)
Paper – large enough to take the whole
   hand

Sharp pencil
Table knife
Tissue/cotton wool
A soft towel/a square of foam rubber/a
   thin cushion

PROCEDURE

Place the paper on a table with the knife and pencil in readiness. Squeeze approximately one and a half centimetres of the ink onto the glass and roll out thinly with the roller.

Using the roller, spread the ink evenly over the entire palm, the fingers, and covering two centimetres of the wrist.

Place the hand in as comfortable a position as possible onto the paper and press down. With the sharp pencil, draw around the outline of the hand and wrist. Slip the table knife under the paper and press up into the hollow of the palm.

Repeat the process several times for each hand until a satisfactory imprint of each is obtained.

If the central hollow of the palm simply refuses to print then alternatively the paper may be placed on the soft towel so as to mould itself around the hand. If all else fails, the hand may be held palm-side up and the paper carefully laid on top of it and gently pressed down.

If lipstick or boot polish are used, these should be applied **sparingly**, straight onto the palm if lipstick, or with a tissue, if polish. Too much will simply produce a sticky mess and an unreadable print.

Next, the thumbprint should be dabbed separately onto the paper beside the print, and carefully traced around.

Finally, a record of the date and the individual's particulars must be included on each sheet: date; name; date of birth; sex; whether right- or left-handed; notes of any scars or injuries.

PHOTOCOPIES

Modern photocopiers are now able to take adequate copies of hands. Although these will give a true picture of the shape of the hand and fingers, and also highlight the major lines, the definition will not be clear enough for an in-depth analysis. However, photocopies can successfully be used as back- ups to the inked prints or, if inked imprints are out of the question, they will at least make passable alternatives.

When taking a photocopy, it is essential that the palm is rested lightly on the glass so as to avoid distortion of the hand.

BIBLIOGRAPHY

Benham, W. G. *The Laws of Scientific Hand Reading*, Hawthorn, 1974
Brandon-Jones, D. *Practical Palmistry*, Rider, 1981
Fitzherbert, A. *Hand Psychology*, Angus & Robertson, 1986
Gettings, F. *The Book of the Hand*, Paul Hamlyn, 1965
Jaquin, N. *Hand of Man*, Sagar Publications, 1967
– *Practical Palmistry*, ed. D. B. Taraporevala, 1964
Hutchinson, B. *Your Life in Your Hands*, Sphere, 1967
Masters, A. *Mind Map*, Eyre Methuen, 1980
Reid, L. *How to Read Hands*, Aquarian Press, 1985
The Female Hand, Aquarian Press, 1986

RELATED SUBJECTS

Morris, D. *Manwatching*, Jonathan Cape, 1977
Ornstein, R. E. *The Psychology of Consciousness*, Jonathan Cape, 1975
Howard, P. *What the Hand Reveals about the Brain*, MIT, 1987

SCIENTIFIC PAPERS

Annett, M. and Manning, M. (1989) The disadvantages of dextrality for intelligence. *British Journal of Psychology*, **80**, 213–26
Bishop, D. V. M. (1989) Does hand proficiency determine hand preference? *British Journal of Psychology*, **80**, 191–9
McManus, I. C., Sik, G., Cole, D. R., Mellon, A. F., Wong, J., Kloss, J. (1988) The development of handedness in children. *British Journal of Developmental Psychology*, *80*, 257–73
Newrick, P. G., Affie E. & Corrall, R. T. M. (1990) Relationship between longevity and lifeline: a manual study of 100 patients. *Journal of the Royal Society of Medicine*, **83**, 499–501

INDEX